INTRODUCTION TO COMPUTING AND PROBLEM SOLVING USING PYTHON

AF660132

About the Author

E Balagurusamy is presently the Chairman of EBG Foundation, Coimbatore. In the past he has also held the positions of member, Union Public Service Commission, New Delhi and Vice-Chancellor, Anna University, Chennai, Tamil Nadu. He is a teacher, trainer and consultant in the fields of Information Technology and Management. He holds an ME (Hons) in Electrical Engineering and PhD in Systems Engineering from the Indian Institute of Technology, Roorkee, Uttarakhand. His areas of interest include Object-Oriented Software Engineering, E-Governance: Technology Management, Business Process Re-engineering and Total Quality Management.

A prolific writer, he has authored a large number of research papers and several books. His best-selling books, among others include:

- *Programming in ANSIC, 7/e*
- *Fundamentals of Computers*
- *Computing Fundamentals and C Programming*
- *Programming in C#, 3/e*
- *Programming in Java, 5/e*
- *Object-Oriented Programming with C++, 5/e*
- *Programming in BASIC, 3/e*
- *Numerical Methods*
- *Reliability Engineering*

A recipient of numerous honors and awards, he has been listed in the Directory of Who's Who of Intellectuals and in the Directory of Distinguished Leaders in Education.

INTRODUCTION TO COMPUTING AND PROBLEM SOLVING USING PYTHON

E Balagurusamy
Chairman
EBG Foundation
Coimbatore

McGraw Hill Education (India) Private Limited

Published by McGraw Hill Education (India) Private Limited,
Registered Office: Anjana Complex No: 5/90 A, Butt Road, St. Thomas Mount, Chennai – 600016, Tamil Nadu, India.

Introduction to Computing & Problem Solving using Python, 1e

Copyright © 2016, by McGraw Hill Education (India) Private Limited. All Rights Reserved.

Sixteenth reprint 2026

This book is protected under copyright law. Any unauthorized copying, reproduction, distribution, adaptation, conversion, transmission, storage or use of this publication or any part or extract of it, through any means or any medium, including electronic, mechanical, photocopied, recorded, or otherwise, whether for any direct/indirect commercial gain or not, and without the prior written consent of the publisher, is explicitly prohibited and will result in severe legal consequences. Such restrictions apply to social media channels/groups, YouTube videos, audiobooks, AI applications, and any other means of copying, reproducing, distributing, adapting, converting, transmitting, storing the content of this book, using current or future technologies.

This edition can be exported from India only by the publisher,
McGraw Hill Education (India) Private Limited

ISBN-13: 978-93-5260-258-2
ISBN-10: 93-5260-258-7

17 18 19 20 21 APO 30 29 28 27 26

Information contained in this work has been obtained by McGraw Hill Education (India), from sources believed to be reliable. However, neither McGraw Hill Education (India) nor its authors guarantee the accuracy or completeness of any information published herein, and neither McGraw Hill Education (India) nor its authors shall be responsible for any errors, omissions, or damages arising out of use of this information. This work is published with the understanding that McGraw Hill Education (India) and its authors are supplying information but are not attempting to render professional services. If such services are required, the assistance of an appropriate professional should be sought.

Typeset at The Composers, 260, C.A. Apt., Paschim Vihar, New Delhi 110063, and
Printed and Bound in India at A.P Offset Pvt. Ltd., 25/487, Zulfe Bengal, Dilshad Garden, Delhi 110095

Visit us at: www.mheducation.co.in
Toll free in India: 1800 103 5875
Write to us at: support.india@mheducation.com
CIN: U80302TN2010PTC111532

CONTENTS

PREFACE

Developments in the field of digital electronics and the huge amount of data generated during the last few decades ushered in the second Industrial Revolution which is popularly referred to as the Information Revolution. Information technology played an ever-increasing role in this new revolution. A sound knowledge of how computers work, process and analyze data has, therefore, become indispensable for everyone who seeks employment not only in the area of IT, but also in any other fields. Rightly so, many institutions and universities in India have introduced a subject covering the fundamentals of computation and problem solving with *Python* for their undergraduate students. This book caters to those needs of the undergraduate students.

Why learn *Python*?

Python is a high-level, interpreted, reflective, dynamically typed, open-source, multi-paradigm, and general-purpose programming language. It is quite powerful and easy. It offers no special tools or features that let you do things that you cannot do with other languages, but its elegant design and combination of certain features make Python a pleasure to use.

What's Special in this Book?

The book ensures a smooth and successful transition to a skilled expert in *Python*. This book uses a simple-to-complex and easy-to-learn approach throughout the book. The concept of 'learning by-solving' has been stressed in all the chapters of the book. Each feature of *Python* is treated in-depth followed by a complete program example to illustrate its use. Wherever necessary, concepts are explained pictorially to facilitate better understanding. It presents a contemporary approach to programming, offering a combination of theory and practice.

Each of the 8 chapters follow a common structure with a range of learning and assessment tools for instructors and students.

SALIENT FEATURES of the Book

The salient features of the book include the following:

- Bottom-up approach of explaining concepts has been adopted in the book.

- Algorithms and flowcharts have been discussed extensively in an appendix.
- Codes with Comments have been provided throughout the book to illustrate the use of various features of *Python*.
- Supplementary Information and important notes that complement, but stand apart from the text, have been included in special boxes under the head *Notes*.
- *Always Remember* consists of important summary points at the end of every chapter to help the readers recollect the topics covered with ease.
- *Check Your Understanding* helps the readers evaluate their learning after every section within the chapters of the book.
- Important *Key Terms* within the chapter have been listed at the end.

Review Exercises comprising Multiple choice questions along with answer keys, short questions and programming exercises are provided at the chapter end to help readers test their conceptual understanding.

Organization of the Book

The book spans across eight chapters. The first two chapters introduces the learner to digital computers–the basic structure, programming languages, operating systems, problem solving strategies and conventional introduction to programming. The next six chapters present a more-or-less the conventional introduction to programming. The readers learn about variables, types, statements, conditionals, loops, functions, recursion, classes and inheritance. In all the chapters, first the basic ideas are explained, and then the reader is led through a process of experimentation that helps them find and test the limits of their understanding.

Web Supplements

The web supplements can be accessed at https://connect.mheducation.com (See the inside front cover for more details) which contains the following:

- Solution Manual
- Lecture PPTs covering
    1. Important standard library
        (a) argparse
        (b) csv
        (c) math
        (d) os
        (e) pickle
        (f) random
        (g) subprocess
    2. How to install third party libraries
        (a) Using pip
            (i) Installing pip under Windows and Linux
            (ii) Using pip to install a package
        (b) Installing packages from source.

3. Some important third party libraries
    (a) Requests
    (b) BeautifulSoup
4. Debugging the code
    (a) Understanding exception
        (i) List of exception and possible reasons
    (b) Python debugger-pdb.

Acknowledgements

A note of acknowledgement is due to the following reviewers of the book for their valuable suggestions:

Sujith Kumar
Sree Narayana Gurukulam College of Engineering, Kolenchery, Kerala

Jini Raju
Thangal Kunju Musaliar College of Engineering, Kollam, Kerala

Sanjiv Singh
Impetus Technologies, Noida, Uttar Pradesh

Aswathy Ravikumar
Mar Baselios College of Engineering and Technology, Thiruvananthapuram, Kerala

Pawan Kumar
Mphasis, Noida, Uttar Pradesh

A token of special appreciation to **Mr. Jayarajan J N** (Rajagiri School of Engineering and Technology, Cochin) for his valuable contribution in development of this book.

Publisher's Note

Remember to write to us. We look forward to receiving your feedback, comments, and ideas to enhance the quality of this book. You can reach us at *info.india@mheducation.com*. Please mention the title and authors' name as the subject. In case you spot piracy of this book, please do let us know.

1 Introduction to Digital Computer

1.1 INTRODUCTION

In earlier days, the term "digital computer" was used to refer a person who drew mathematical tables and solved complex calculations. In less than a human lifetime, computers have changed from massive, expensive and unreliable calculators to the dependable and versatile machines that are now omnipresent in society.

Computers were once the size of rooms and used to take a day to change the program and now, it is just a double click away. Computers help the impossible become possible. They have become a necessary tool in today's society. Without computers, it is hard to do pretty much anything. Computers process information in 1's and 0's (usually referred to as On and Off respectively). This operation identifies instructions in Binary Code. This is the language understood by the computer to complete a command. By 1953, it was estimated that there were almost 100 computers in the world.

It is believed that the first computer was invented in Berlin, Germany, in 1936.

- The Z1 was invented in 1936 by Konrad Zuse in Germany. This was a programmable machine that was able to remember numbers. This process is now referred to as memory.
- IBM followed suit and introduced the Harvard Mark 1 which was completed at Harvard University in 1944. It was a large calculator. This computer was able to calculate many different types of numbers.
- With the advancement of technology and research, major companies like IBM, Apple, and Intel have contributed to the explosion of the personal computers as we know today. For example, Apple 1 was released in 1976 which was having memory of 4 KB expandable to 8 KB. The Macintosh was released in 1984 which was having memory of 64 KB expandable to 256 KB.
- CSIRAC was the first computer to play digital music in 1949.
- UNIVAC 1 was used by CBS to predict the results of the 1952 presidential elections in USA.
- On December 2, 1954 IBM's NORC calculated PI 3089 digits.
- In 1958, Jack Kilby invented the Integrated Circuit.
- COBOL (Common Business Oriented Language), one of the oldest programming languages, was developed by Grace Murray Hopper in 1959,
- In 1962 Space War, the first computer game was written by MIT student Steve Russell.
- In 1975, the first personal computer Altair 8800 was invented.
- In 1976, Intel & Zilog introduced new microprocessors

- Single - board computer known as apple -1 was designed by Steve Wozniak some more important developments and was marketed by his friend Steve Jobs.
- In 1980 IBM introduced its Personal Computers (PC). The first IBM PC was known as IBM Model 5150, was based on a 4.77 MHz Intel 8088 microprocessor
- In 19993, Pentium microprocessor was released by Pentium followed by the release of Microsoft window's NT
- In 1994 Sony entred the home gaming market with release of play station console.
- In 2006, Amazon web services launched cloud-based services.

A Personal Computer (PC) is a digital computer designed for the usage by one person at a time. PCs can be classified into desktop computers, workstations and laptop computers. Today, PCs have five major applications which are as follows:

1. Internet Browser: Internet browser is a software application used to access the Internet. For example, *Internet Explorer*, *Firefox*, *Opera,* etc., are all Internet browsers.

2. Data Compression Software: Data compression software is used to reduce file size. *ZIP* is widely used as the data compression software on personal computers.

3. Windows Media Player: *Windows Media Player* is used to create music libraries for listening music.

4. Image Editing Software: Image editing software is used to develop good quality pictures. Examples of such software include *Photoshop*, *Microsoft Publisher* and *Picasa*.

5. Audio Editing Software: Audio editing software is used to edit audio files and also to add audio effects.

Check Your Understanding

1. What is a computer?

Ans. A computer is an electronic device capable of executing programs written in different languages.

2. What is the use of data compression software?

Ans. Data compression software is used to reduce file size.

Note *The first personal computer was Altair 8800. Later IBM introduced IBM PC.*

Computers have become an integral part of the society because of the following characteristics they possess:

- A computer can perform millions of calculations in a second.
- A computer works with precision every time.
- A computer can store billions of bytes of information. For example, the capacity of a terabyte = 2,00,000 songs.
- A computer can work continuously without getting tired.
- A computer can be used to perform various tasks simultaneously.
- A computer will remember the information stored for as long as required.

1.2 VON NEUMANN CONCEPT

In early computers, the data and instructions were not stored in the same memory. However, such storage became possible in the Von Neumann architecture, also known as "stored program" architecture because it could store the program and instruction data in the same memory. In the Von Neumann architecture, computers can perform complex operations within less time. Besides performing calculations, they can manage to do a sequence of calculations as well. The basic structure of Von Neumann architecture consists of the memory, processing unit and the control unit.

The characteristics of Von Neumann architecture are as follows:

1. The hardware system comprises the following:
    - **Memory:** In Von Neumann architecture, there is a main memory system – Random Access Memory (RAM) which holds the data or program.
    - **Arithmetic Logic Unit (ALU):** As the name suggests, this is useful in arithmetic and logical calculations such as addition, subtraction, division and comparisons.
    - **Control Unit:** In the central processing unit (CPU), there is a control unit (CU) managing the process of data or program. The execution of the program is done by the Control Unit. For example, the fetch-decode-execution.
    - **Input-Output System:** Using this system, an input is given and output is generated after execution. The information can be stored by using compact disk (CD), floppy, etc.
2. Data or programs are stored into the main memory.
3. Processing of instructions is sequential.

> ***Note*** *A process describes how the processor takes the data or program, decodes it and finally executes it. The fetch-decode-execute cycle is also known as the Von Neumann execution cycle.*

Check Your Understanding

1. Who developed the basic architecture of computers?
Ans. John Von Neumann

2. What do the following terms stand for?
CPU, ALU, CU, RAM
Ans. CPU: Control Processing Unit
ALU: Arithmetic Logic Unit
CU: Control Unit
RAM: Random Access Memory

1.2.1 A Simple Model of the Computer

A Computer system has three basic components which are as follows:

1. Processor: It is also known as the **Central Processing Unit (CPU)**. The processor is the brain of the computer. It takes data in the form of input and processes this input using arithmetic or logical operations in the ALU, thereby transforming it into the output.

2. Memory (Storage): Memory refers to the data storage, permanent or temporary. Computer memory understands only two bits, 0 and 1. The temporary memory is called RAM and the permanent memory is called Read Only Memory (ROM).

3. Input/Output: It refers to the communication mechanism. Input and output devices are significant portions of the computer accessories. Input devices provide data to the computer as input from the external source while output devices generate information for the user after processing the input.

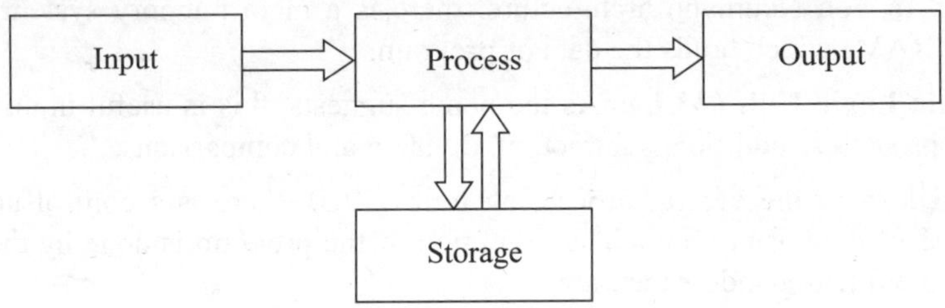

Figure 1.1 Model of Computer

TIP

Before buying a computer, one should check the processor speed. To determine the processing speed of the CPU, the clock speed is checked. The CPU can perform a certain number of clock cycles per second. The computer's clock speed is measured in gigahertz (GHz). One GHz equals to one billion cycles per second. A higher clock speed indicates that the CPU can execute more operations per second.

Note *The very first commercially produced and sold computer in 1951 was UNIVAC.*

1.2.2 Components of the Digital Computer

A digital computer performs calculations and solves complex problems. Thus, it must be equipped with the following components:

1. Input Devices: These are the devices through which the information is provided to the computer. There are different types of input devices, such as keyboard, mouse, scanner, touch pad, etc.

2. Output Devices: These are the devices through which the output is being provided to the user. There are different types of output devices, such as printer, speakers, screen, etc.

3. Processing Unit: CPU is the brain of the computer. It takes data in the form of input and processes it, thereby transforming the data into output. A CPU basically consists of the following:

- **Arithmetic Logic Unit (ALU):** The ALU performs both arithmetic and logical operations including addition, subtraction, division and bits manipulation.
- **Registers:** Registers hold values in the CPU. Each register has a unique name and is capable of holding a byte or word of data.
- **Control Unit:** The Control Unit controls the operation of the CPU, the Memory and the input-output components based on a sequence of instructions in the Memory.

4. External Memory: The External Memory is a physical device used to store programs (set of instructions) or data temporarily or permanently for use in a computer or some other digital electronic device. It is classified into two categories which are as follows:

- **Primary Memory:** The primary memory is also known as main memory. The program is loaded in the main memory before it can be executed. The information within the Primary Memory can be lost when power to the computer is turned off. Thus, the Primary Memory is volatile by nature.
- **Secondary Memory:** The secondary memory is a non-volatile, low-speed memory. The information within this memory will not be lost even if the computer is turned off due to power failure. Examples of secondary storage include hard disk, DVD, floppy drive, etc.

5. Bus: In a computer, all the components described above are connected by cables and each cable can only send one bit at a time. These cables are called bus and are responsible for the movement of data from input devices to output devices.

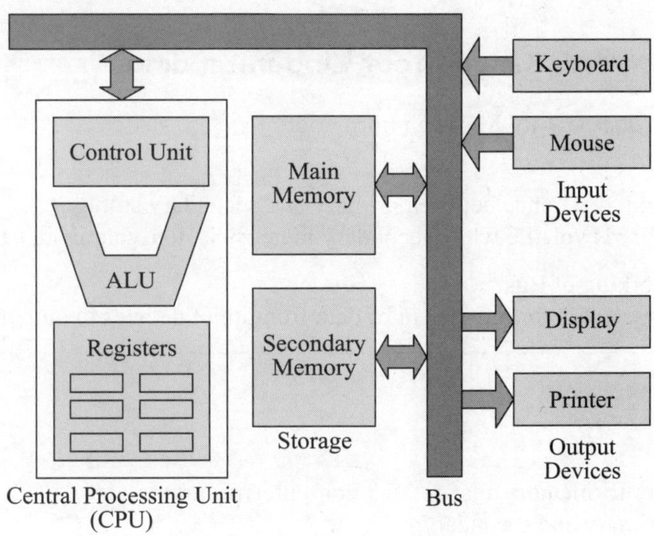

Figure 1.2 Components of Computer

Computers have become a huge part of our life nowadays. We use them every day to complete different tasks. They are basically composed of two main things-the software and the hardware. The software has all the instructions and information needed for the computer to run. This includes the operating system and the programs or applications. The hardware consists of all the physical elements that make the computer work. This includes the CPU, RAM, ROM, Cache etc.

Let us imagine a restaurant. Every day a keeper comes to open the restaurant and makes sure everything is ready and working well. Here, the keeper and the computer is called read-only memory or ROM which can be modified. To keep everything running properly in a restaurant we need an administrator, this is the central processing unit or CPU. It is called a microprocessor in cell phones and it contains the arithmetic logic unit or ALU and the control unit or CU. The ALU in a computer is the manager who takes care of the numbers and logical part. The control unit is the head chef who organises the incoming information and gets everyone task. Let us see a customer making an order. The order acts as the input data. The waiter or data bus then carries this information to the kitchen, and then goes to the head chef who decides where it should go further. The kitchen represents the mother board inside, where there is a fridge and you keep everything that is used frequently for easy access. This is called random access memory or RAM in a computer. Cache will be like a small recipe book in which the computer keeps the frequently used instructions. There is also a warehouse for rest of the information stored and this works as a hard disk. We can also get the things delivered through the back door which acts as an optical disc in the computer. These are called the secondary storage devices.

Let us imagine, we also have a timer in the kitchen. Every time the timer starts, everyone starts preparing a dish and has to get it done by the time gets over, so this keeps everything synchronised. In a computer, it is called the internal clock.

We get an order, the buses carry it and it goes through the control unit in the CPU which supervises that it reaches the right destination. If we need something that has been recently used, we can easily get it from RAM, and if not, then the computer has to look for it in the secondary storage devices. The data is processed now, and it is time for the chefs to turn into some delicious food that we can eat. This is the task of the video card converting data into images. This is how our computer works.

Check Your Understanding

1. In which form does CD-ROM store information?
Ans. Digital form

2. What is the main difference between primary and secondary storage?
Ans. Primary memory is volatile while secondary memory is non-volatile in nature.

3. What is the working of Bus?
Ans. The Bus is responsible for movement of data from input devices to output devices.

1.3 STORAGE

The term ***Storage*** refers to memory that retains computer programs and data. There are basically two categories of storage: primary and secondary.

1.3.1 Primary Storage

It is also known as the temporary storage since it is a short-term memory. There are three types of primary storage:

1. RAM (Random Access Memory): The RAM is a very important part of the computer. It stores the data accessed by the CPU. The RAM is the place where the programs or data in current use can be kept. This memory is volatile in nature as the information within it is lost when power to the computer is turned off. RAM is also known as working memory or main memory.

Figure 1.3 Random Access Memory

2. ROM (Read Only Memory): The Read Only Memory gets its name from the fact that the computer can only read information from it but cannot write any information on it. A part of the operating system is stored in ROM. When the computer system is turned on, the CPU executes instructions stored in ROM. The information stored in ROM cannot be changed and will not be lost even if the computer is turned off.

Figure 1.4 Read Only Memory

3. Cache Memory: Cache memory stores the data recently processed by the CPU. The size of cache is very small and execution is very fast. In order to process an application, processor first searches the cache memory and then, the RAM.

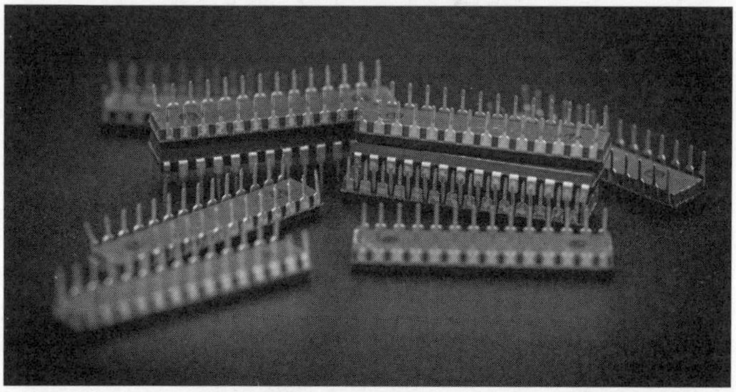

Figure 1.5 Cache Memory

1.3.2 Secondary Storage

Secondary storage is also known as the permanent storage. It is not constantly accessible to a computer system. When required, secondary storage devices and media can be accessed by plugging or inserting them into a computer. Examples of secondary storage include the hard drive, DVD, memory card etc. Secondary storage is like long-term memory since the data remains stored in the secondary storage device even after the computer is shut down.

The various types of secondary storage are:

1. Hard disks: Hard Disk or Hard Disk Drive (HDD) stores and provide relatively quick access to large amounts of data on an electromagnetically charged surface or set of surfaces.

2. Floppy Disc: A floppy disc consists of a plastic case inside which there is a very thin piece of plastic coated with microscopic iron particles. Floppy discs store very less data—a maximum of 1.44 MB.

Figure 1.6 Floppy Disc

3. Flash Drive: A flash drive can be inserted into a USB port for data retrieval and data storage. It is small in size and portable. Nowadays, flash drive comes in many shapes.

Figure 1.7 Flash Drive

4. Memory Card: A memory card is a very small data storage medium. It is portable and can be used in remote computing devices.

Figure 1.8 Memory Card

5. Compact Disc: A compact disc is a kind of optical disc used to store digital data. Data can be accessed faster here compared to the floppy discs, but it is still slower than the hard discs. A compact disc stores the same data as a floppy disc does.

Figure 1.9 Compact Disc

> ***Note*** *An early method used to store data or information in the computer was the Punch card. The machine Analytical Engine invented by Charles Babbage had a punched card system to store and retrieve information.*

1.3.3 Register

It contains the address of the memory location where data resides. Register is highly accessible by the CPU. Speed of the CPU is determined by the number of registers it has.

Memory hierarchy is the arrangement of the storage in a computer. Each level of memory hierarchy is distinguished by the response time. It is illustrated in Figure 1.10.

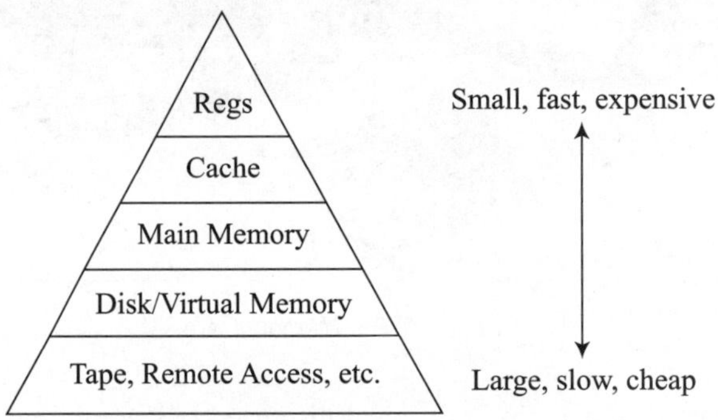

Figure 1.10 Memory Hierarchy

Check Your Understanding

1. How can memory be measured?

Ans. A byte is the unit of memory of a computer. The smallest unit of memory is bit.
1 byte = 8 bits
1 kilobyte = 1,024 bytes
1 megabyte = 1,024 kilobytes
1 gigabyte = 1,024 megabytes
1 terabyte = 1,024 gigabytes

1.4 PROGRAMMING LANGUAGES

A computer language is used to make a computer understand what the user wants to say. When a user writes a program, he/she uses the computer language.

A program, written in a programming language, is a set of instructions by which the computer comes to know what is to be done. It is a coding language used by programmers to write the instructions that a computer can understand.

There are three types of computer languages as illustrated in Figure 1.11.

- High-level Language
- Assembly Language
- Machine Language

1.4.1 High-level Language

Symbolic languages are very tedious to work with because each machine instruction needs to be coded individually. High-level languages on the other hand uses English-like languages allowing the programmer to focus on application problems instead of focusing on the intricacies of the particular computer. High-level languages are converted into machine level language using a converting software called compiler. It is a computer programming language that does not requires great efforts from the programmer. It is called high-level language because it is close to the user. The first high-level language used was FORTRAN, which was followed by COBOL.

1.4.2 Assembly Language

Assembly language is a low-level programming language. It is more machine friendly and requires more efforts from the programmer. Assembly (or symbolic) language closely resembles machine language. Symbols and mnemonics are used in this language to represent various machine language instructions. Assembly language is directly converted into binary language and is machine-dependent.

This language is known as symbolic language because of the symbols it employs. Since the computer does not understand symbolic language, a program called **assembler** is used to translate the symbolic code into machine language, and is the reason why it is called assembly language.

1.4.3 Machine Language

Machine language consisting of 0s and 1s, was the earliest mode of programming language. The computer understands only 0's and 1's because it is made of switches, transistors, and other electronic devices which can only be in the state of either *on* or *off*. The *off* state is represented by 0 and *on* state by 1. A machine language is a low-level computer programming language and is more machine friendly. This language is known as machine language because it is close to the machine.

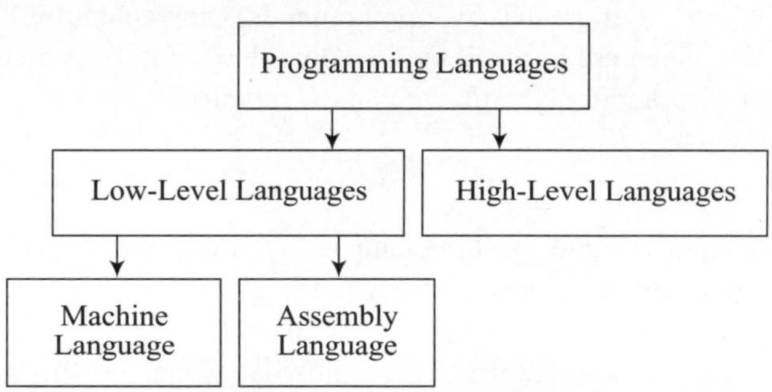

Figure 1.11 Programming Languages

Check Your Understanding

1. What do you mean by a programming language?

Ans. A programming language is a coding language used by the programmers to write instructions that a computer can understand and act on.

TIP

If you want to learn programming languages, first choose a language that you want to learn. After that, you need to learn the core concepts of that language. Install the software that is required to compile the program. Now, create your first program.

1.5 TRANSLATORS

A translator is a computer program that can instantly translate between any languages. It converts program language to machine level language for the debugging and execution of the programs. While the computer understands only binary code i.e. 1's and 0's, it is not easy for humans to read and write in such code. So, the translators are used to translate a computer program into binary code. There are three types of translator programs, namely Compiler, Assembler, and Interpreter.

1.5.1 Compiler

A compiler is very important in giving the application a performance boost. The compiler of a language is a computer program that converts the source code of an application written in the computer programming language to the target language with its binary form.

The compiler checks for syntax errors in a source code of a program. If no error is found, the program is declared to be successfully compiled. If the program does not contain any syntax error, the compiler translates the source code of the program into the machine language of the computer, so that the computer is able to understand the instructions given to it.

Source files are the program files created by a programmer. They contain information and instructions written by the programmer, which are checked by the compiler during the process of compilation. These source files are compiled by a compiler and run with an executable file.

1.5.2 Assembler

To translate the assembly language into machine language, a translator is needed. This translator is also called an assembler. Each assembly language is unique to the particular computer architecture. In assembly language, we use some mnemonic such as 'add', 'sub', 'mul' etc. for all the operations.

For example, if we want to add 4 and 3, then in assembly language, we will write `Add 4 3` where `Add` is a mnemonic and both `4` and `3` are the arguments of the operand. Now, the assembler will map this to the binary code.

1.5.3 Interpreter

Like a compiler, an interpreter also translates high-level language into low-level machine language. An interpreter reads the statement and first converts it into an intermediate code and executes it, before reading the next statement. It translates each instruction immediately one by one. This is a rather slow process because the interpreter has to wait while each instruction is being translated.

The interpreter stops execution at the time of error occurrence and reports it, whereas a compiler reads the whole program even if it encounters several errors.

Check Your Understanding

1. What is the difference between a compiler and an interpreter?

Ans: An interpreter translates each instruction one by one, while a compiler reads the whole program first and then translates it into the machine language.

1.6 HARDWARE AND SOFTWARE

Computer systems have become an essential part of our life. Most of our work is done with the help of computer system in a fast and efficient manner. Hardware refers to the tangible objects that can be run using software. Software refers to a set of instructions to the computer. Without hardware, software cannot work and vice versa. For example, a car without a driver is like hardware without software. Software tells hardware what to do and how to do it. To reiterate, the computer system is made up of two major components: Hardware and Software that are essential for functioning of the system.

1.6.1 Hardware

Hardware are the physical components of the computer system. The hardware components consist of several parts like input devices, Central Processing Unit (CPU), primary storage, output devices and auxiliary storage devices.

1. Input Devices: These are the devices such as keyboards that are used to enter the program and data. Mouse and audio input also fall in the category of input devices.

2. CPU: It processes all the instructions given to the computer and is also used for doing arithmetic calculations and comparisons, and for controlling the movement of data.

3. Primary Storage: It is the main memory of the computer system. In primary storage, programs and data are stored temporarily for processing. The data in the primary device is erased when the computer is turned off.

4. Output Devices: Devices such as monitor or printer are used to get the output.

5. Auxiliary Storage: Programs and data are stored permanently in auxiliary storage. It is also known as secondary storage and used for both input and output. This storage is very useful as the data remains stored even when the computer is turned off.

1.6.2 Software

Computer software is a collection of programs used to manage the entire file system of the computer. It is also necessary for the running of computer hardware. The working of the computer hardware depends on the computer software. Computer software is classified into two categories, namely, System software and Application software.

1. System Software: The system software provides interface between the user and the hardware (components of the computer). It also manages the system resources, enabling the working of all hardware components (hard disk, RAM, CD drive, etc.) of the computer. Computer hardware resources are managed through this system software with the help of programs.

These programs fall into following three types:

- **Operating System:** It provides the interface between the user and computer hardware, managing all files and folders, and providing ease of access to the database. The operating system makes the computer perform efficiently.
- **System Support Software:** It provides all the services of the operating system and system utilities. For example, disk format program is the system utility made to do the formatting of the storage. Other services include data encryption and bit lock for locking storage devices.
- **System Development Software:** It works as a language translator that converts program language to machine level language for debugging and execution of the programs.

2. Application Software: The application software runs under the system software. It helps the user to solve problems. It can be further classified into general-purpose software and application-specific software.

- **General-Purpose Software:** It refers to software meant to be used for more than one application. For example, Word Processor.
- **Application-Specific Software:** As the name suggests, it refers to software generally used for a specific, intended purpose. For example: a general account ledger used by the accountants for managing accounts.

The examples of application software are as follows:

a) Microsoft Internet Explorer
b) VLC Media Player
c) Adobe Reader X

> **Note** *Auxiliary storage is very useful since when the computer is turned off, the data remains in the secondary storage, ready for the next time we need it.*

Check Your Understanding

1. What is System Software?

Ans: System software is a part of software. It helps the computer function properly. It also controls the computer hardware operations.

2. What is Hardware?

Ans: Computer hardware is the collection of all the parts that can be physically touched. For example: motherboard, CPU, RAM, etc.

1.7 OPERATING SYSTEMS

An operating system is a software environment in which the program runs. Most of the operating systems are described as a combination of the software and the underlying hardware. The operating system works as an interface between hardware and user. It controls file and database access besides providing the interface to communication systems such as internet protocol. The working together of the various hardware and software can only be achieved by the operating system. It is the mother of the computer without which computer is nothing more than blank box. The functioning of every component of the computer depends on the operating system.

Some commonly used operating systems are *Windows 98*, *Windows server 2000*, *Windows XP*, *Windows Vista*, *Linux*, *Ubuntu*, *UNIX*, *Macintosh* (for apple computer), *Windows 7*, and *Windows 8*.

The main functions of an operating system includes:

1. The main objective of the operating system is to ensure the efficient working of the computer system and to stimulate various hardwares.
2. The operating system performs basic tasks, such as taking input from the keyboard, displaying output on the screen, managing files and operation on files on disk drives, and managing other devices including keyboard, mouse and printers.
3. The operating system can enable users to do multitasking. Multitasking refers to the situation where two or more than two programs can run simultaneously on a single operating system.
4. The operating system also allows users to do multithreading. Multithreading refers to the situation where two or more parts of the single program can run concurrently on single operating Systems.
5. The users can interact with the operating system with the help of commands.

Figure 1.4 shows the operating system and the range of tasks it performs. Without an operating system, the computer system becomes useless.

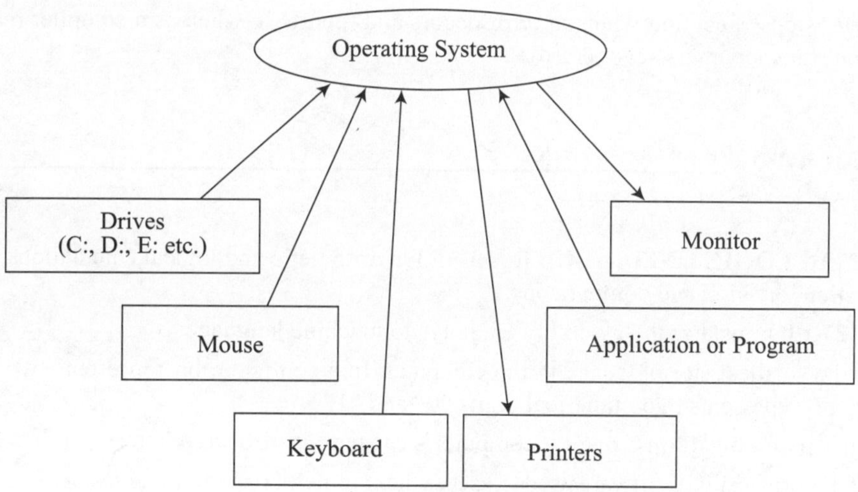

Figure 1.12 Operating Systems and Related Task

ALWAYS REMEMBER

- The Von Neumann architecture is also known as "stored-program" architecture because in this architecture, the program data and instruction data are stored in the same memory.
- The basic structure of Von Neumann architecture consists of the memory, the processing unit and the control unit.
- In the central processing unit (CPU) there is a control unit that manages the process of data or program.
- Input devices are used to give data to the computer as input from the external source.
- Output devices are used to convey the information after processing to the user.
- Primary storage is also known as temporary storage and is used for storing data and programs temporarily.
- Secondary storage is also known as permanent storage. Examples of secondary storage include the hard drive, DVD and memory card.
- The computer understands only machine language. All instructions are written in 1s and 0s form.
- When a high-level language is translated into machine language, there are two ways to translate it: compiled or interpreted.
- Hardware is the physical component of the computer system. It consists of several parts including input devices, CPU, primary storage, output devices and auxiliary storage devices.
- Computer software is used to manage the entire file system of the computer and is necessary for the running of computer hardware.
- The operating system can allow users to do multitasking, by allowing two or more than two programs to be run simultaneously on a single operating system.
- The compiler checks for syntax error in a source code of a program.
- The interpreter stops execution when an error occurs and reports it, whereas a compiler reads the whole program even if it encounters several errors.

KEY TERMS

✓ **ARITHMETIC LOGIC UNIT (ALU):** It is useful in arithmetic and logical calculations, such as addition, subtraction, division and comparisons.

✓ **ASSEMBLER:** It translates the assembly language to machine language.

✓ **BIT:** Bit is the smallest storing space in the computer. In a computer, bit represents two states: either "on" or "off". It represents two numerical digits "0" and "1".

✓ **BYTE:** A group of 8 bits form a byte. A computer's capacity is measured in terms of bytes.

✓ **BROWSER:** A browser is a software used to access the Internet. For example, *Internet Explorer*, *Mozilla*, *Opera,* etc.

✓ **CENTRAL PROCESSING UNIT (CPU):** It takes data in the form of input and processes the input by some arithmetic or logical operations using ALU, transforming the data into output.

✓ **COMPUTER:** A computer is an electronic device that is able to execute programs written in different languages.

- ✓ **COMPILER:** A compiler is a software program that converts high-level language into low-level language understood by the processor.
- ✓ **INTERPRETER:** Just like a compiler, an interpreter also translates high-level language into low-level machine language. It translates each instruction immediately one by one.
- ✓ **OPERATING SYSTEM:** Operating system works as an interface between the hardware and the user.
- ✓ **PROGRAM:** A program, written in programming language, is a set of instructions by which computer comes to know what is to be done.
- ✓ **STORAGE DEVICE:** Storage devices are used to store the digital data and programs which can be accessed by the computer system.
- ✓ **PRIMARY STORAGE:** Primary storage is also known as temporary storage. It is used for storing data and programs temporarily.
- ✓ **SECONDARY STORAGE:** Secondary storage is not constantly accessible by a computer system. When required, secondary storage devices and media can be accessed by plugged or inserting them into a computer.
- ✓ **SOFTWARE: A** software is a collection of programs. Computer software is used to manage the entire file system of the computer and is also necessary for the running of computer hardware.
- ✓ **HARDWARE:** Hardware is the physical component of the computer system.

REVIEW EXERCISES

Multiple Choice Questions

1. Which was the first microcomputer?

a. Altair 8800 **b.** Altair 8600
c. Altair 8400 **d.** Altair 8000

2. Which of the following comprises Von Neumann architecture?

a. Arithmetic logic unit, control unit **b.** Memory, processing unit, control unit
c. Integrated Circuits, Monitor, Mouse **d.** Processing unit, control unit

3. Which of the following are the components of the Central Processing Unit (CPU)?

a. Control Unit, Monitor **b.** Arithmetic logic unit, Memory
c. Control Unit, Memory **d.** Arithmetic logic unit, Control Unit

4. Which storage device is permanent?

a. Tertiary **b.** Primary
c. Secondary **d.** None of the above

5. Which of the following languages is Assembly language?

a. Machine language **b.** Medium-level programming language
c. Low-level programming language **d.** High-level programming language

6. Which of the following programs can be used to convert high-level language into machine-level language?

a. Assembler **b.** Compiler
c. Translator **d.** Interpreter

7. What works as an interface between the hardware and the user?
   a. Operating System b. Software
   c. Computer d. Memory
8. Where are the saved files stored in the computer?
   a. Cache b. RAM
   c. Hard disk d. ALU
9. Which component of computer is considered as its Brain?
   a. Microprocessor b. Monitor
   c. Keyboard d. CPU
10. Which type of software is system software?
   a. General purpose software b. Operating System
   c. Application software d. All of the above
11. If two or more parts of the single program can run concurrently on single operating systems, what will it be known as?
   a. Multithreading b. Multitasking
   c. Multiprocessing d. Multiprogramming
12. Which of the following types of software is application software?
   a. Compiler b. Assembler
   c. Word processor d. All of the above
13. RAM stands for?
   a. Read Access Memory b. Random Access Memory
   c. Read Arithmetic Memory d. Random Arithmetic Memory
14. What is a register?
   a. Set of paper tapes b. Set of capacitor
   c. Part of auxiliary memory d. Temporary storage unit within the CPU
15. An error in computer data is called?
   a. CPU b. Chip
   c. Bug d. Storage device
16. The secondary storage devices can only store data but they cannot perform?
   a. Logic operation b. Arithmetic operation
   c. Fetch operation d. Either of the above
17. Which of the following is not a computer language?
   a. Low level language b. Medium level language
   c. High level language d. Machine language
18. From where the term 'computer' is derived?
   a. English b. Greek
   c. Latin d. Sanskrit
19. Main storage is also known as?
   a. Memory b. Mother board
   c. CPU d. Register
20. Which American computer company is called Big Blue?
   a. Apple b. Microsoft
   c. Lenovo d. IBM

21. Memory is made up of?
   a. Set of registers   **b.** Large number of cells
   c. Set of circuits   **d.** None of the above

22. Which of the following is the most powerful computers?
   a. Mini computers   **b.** Micro computers
   c. Super computers   **d.** Mainframe computers

23. What is responsible for movement of data from input devices to output devices?
   a. Bus   **b.** Circuit
   c. Memory   **d.** Register

24. Which one of the following is the correct statement?
   a. 1KB = 1000GB   **b.** 1GB = 1,024KB
   c. 1MB = 1,024TB   **d.** 1GB = 1,024MB

25. A CD-ROM basically is used to store up to….. data?
   a. 680 bytes   **b.** 680 MB
   c. 680 KB   **d.** 680 GB

26. Which of the following storage devices can store the largest amount of data?
   a. Flash Disks   **b.** CD-ROM
   c. Hard Disks   **d.** Floppy Disks

27. A program which interprets each line of high level program at time of execution is called?
   a. Interpreter   **b.** Compiler
   c. Translator   **d.** Instructor

28. Process of reading data from permanent storage and writing it to computer's main storage is known as?
   a. Linking data   **b.** Reading data
   c. Relocate data   **d.** Loading data

29. Which one of the following is the most quickly accessible storage?
   a. RAM   **b.** Registers
   c. CD-ROM   **d.** ROM

30. What was the very first commercially produced and sold computer?
   a. ABC   **b.** ENIAC
   c. UNIVAC   **d.** Vacuum tubes

Short Questions

1. What is a digital computer? What are the components of digital computer?
2. What are the characteristics of Von Neumann architecture?
3. What is the difference between primary storage and secondary storage?
4. Explain the terms hardware and software.
5. What do you mean by programming languages? What is the difference between machine language, assembly language and high-level language?
6. What is compiler? How is compiler different from interpreter?
7. What is assembler? What are the differences between compiler and assembler?
8. What is the difference between RAM and ROM?
9. What is an operating system?

10. What do you mean by system software and application software?
11. What are memory card and hard disk?
12. What are peripheral devices? List different types of peripheral devices.

Answers to Multiple Choice Questions

1. a	**2.** b	**3.** d	**4.** c	**5.** c	**6.** b	**7.** a	**8.** c	**9.** d	**10.** b
11. a	**12.** c	**13.** b	**14.** d	**15.** c	**16.** d	**17.** b	**18.** c	**19.** a	**20.** d
21. b	**22.** c	**23.** a	**24.** d	**25.** b	**26.** c	**27.** a	**28.** d	**29.** b	**30.** c

2 PROBLEM SOLVING STRATEGIES

2.1 PROBLEM ANALYSIS

Before applying a particular method or technique to solve a problem, we need to analyse the problem first. There are few dimensions basis on which a problem is analysed before any particular method is applied to it. In case of complex problems, it is important to identify the best or most appropriate technique that can solve the problem.

Following are the key dimensions basis on which an appropriate method is applied.

1. **Decomposable/Non-decomposable:** Analyse whether a problem is decomposable, i.e., whether it can be broken down into sub-problems. Please note that if it cannot be decomposed, then such a problem is non-decomposable.
2. **Solution steps–Can/Cannot be Ignored:** It is important to determine if we can/cannot ignore a few steps while solving a problem. On the basis of this key dimension, a problem can be categorised into the following:
    - **Ignorable:** In case of ignorable problems, a few steps can be ignored since they are not extremely important to follow for solving the problem.
    - **Recoverable:** As the name suggests, recoverable problems are those in which previously executed steps can be easily backtracked.
    - **Irrecoverable:** In case of irrecoverable problems, we cannot backtrack previously executed steps; hence it is important to carefully solve the problem.
3. **Predictable/Unpredictable**: This dimension determines the certainty/uncertainty factor attached to a problem. It is important to know whether there will be an expected/unexpected output after applying a particular input.
4. **Good solution: Absolute/Relative:** It is important to determine whether we are trying to achieve an optimum solution or idea to identify the best solution. On the basis of this decision, appropriate techniques can be applied to achieve the best solution.

2.1.1 Formal Definition of Problem

A problem can be defined as a gap between the actual and desired conditions. It is an unfulfilled customer need. For example, there will be a problem when a standard is not achieved or customer's requirements are not fulfilled. If your goal was to achieve 100% growth but you end up attaining only 70%, this implies that you have not met the actual standard.

While solving a problem it is acceptable to skip a few steps if these steps are not really important. On the basis of this key dimension, a problem can be categorised as ignorable, recoverable and irrecoverable.

> **Note** *The very first step of writing a program is to understand the problem. In order to understand the problem, it must be thoroughly analysed.*

Check Your Understanding

1. What do you mean by a problem?

Ans. A problem can be defined as a gap between the actual and desired conditions.

2.1.2 Methodology of Problem Solving

After carefully understanding a problem, an appropriate solution is developed. The process of developing a solution consists of development of a structure chart, a pseudo code and a flow chart. A structure chart is used to develop the whole program and a flow chart or a pseudo code is used to develop individual parts of a program. These parts are also known as modules.

1. Structure chart A structure chart is a hierarchy that shows the functional flow of a program. Large programs are complex structures comprising interrelated parts. Hence, they must be very carefully laid out. A structure chart shows a logical breakdown of a program into different steps. Each step has separate modules that are related to different modules. Before writing any program, it is important to design a structure in line with the structure chart.

2. Pseudo code A pseudo code is used by almost all the professional programmers. Pseudo codes are easy to understand. These are used to depict the design of an algorithm.

For example: The pseudo code for a sum of two numbers can be written as:

a) Read a, b
b) Add two numbers
   Sum = a + b;
c) Result sum "the sum is";
d) End

3. Flow chart A flow chart is a graphical representation of the logical flow of data. It uses the standard graphical symbols to narrate the sequential process of a specific module. These steps must be followed while designing the whole program.

2.2 ALGORITHMS

In computer science and mathematics, an algorithm is a set of instructions used for solving problems in a step-by-step manner. This step-by-step explanation of doing something is known as an algorithm.

a) Algorithm is a finite and ordered sequence of steps.
b) It is a description of a process independent of any programming language.
c) It can be implemented in many different languages by using different methods and programs.

Following example illustrates a simple algorithm to put a book in the box.

1. Open the box.
2. Pick up the book.
3. Put the book inside the box.
4. Close the box.

For example: An algorithm for sum of two numbers can be written as:

1. Start
2. Read number n1 and n2;
3. Sum = n1 + n2;
4. Write sum "the sum is";
5. Stop;

Typically, algorithms are executed by computers. However, humans follow algorithms too. How would you count people in a room? You will probably point at each person, one at a time, and assign a number to it, starting from 0: 1, 2, 3, 4 and so forth. This is also an algorithm. In fact, algorithms can be formally described in pseudo codes that have English-like syntax and resemble programming language.

An algorithm can be written in following two ways:

1. Pseudo code
2. Flow chart

A pseudo code for counting people in a room:

1. Let P = 0	(A variable called P will initialise its value to zero.)
2. For each person in a room, set P = P + 1	(This is a sequence of steps that will repeat a few number of times.)

Step 2 will be repeated until every person in the room has been counted. If there is no person in the room, then only step 1 will be executed and there will no step 2.

Check Your Understanding

1. What is algorithm?

Ans. An algorithm is a set of instructions used for solving a problem in a step-by-step manner.

2. What is pseudo code?

Ans. A pseudo code is used to state an algorithm in an English-like syntax.

TIP

If an algorithm is correctly written, there are very low chances of generating a bad program.

2.3 FLOW CHARTS

A flow chart is a simple diagram that illustrates a sequence of operations to be performed for obtaining a solution. It allows you to identify the actual sequence of events in a process that any product or service follows. Flow charts are very effective in understanding how a process works. Even a quick glance at a flow chart can offer a clear idea of how a process or a series of processes works. In a flow chart, the flow of data is represented by arrows. It is a graphical representation of the algorithmic solution of a problem.

Flow charts are also known as process maps that can be used to identify:

a) Flow of information
b) Number of steps in a process
c) Branches in a process
d) Inter-dependent operations

2.3.1 Flow Charts Symbols

There are six basic symbols that are used to draw a simple flow chart which are as follows:

1. Start/Stop: Every flow chart has a starting point and a terminating point. The symbol that is used for both the starting and terminating points is a rounded rectangle, a rectangle with round corners. It is called a 'terminal' (Fig. 2.1).

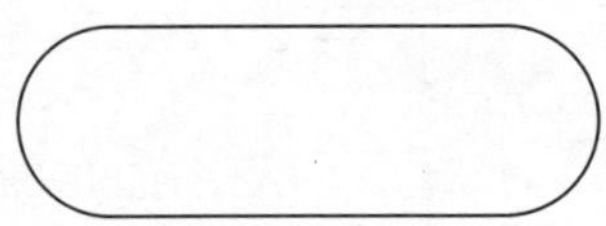

Figure 2.1

2. Input/Output: Every time you take an input from a user and return an output to the user, an input/output symbol is used in the flow chart. The symbol that is used for both input/output-related actions is a parallelogram as shown in Fig. 2.2.

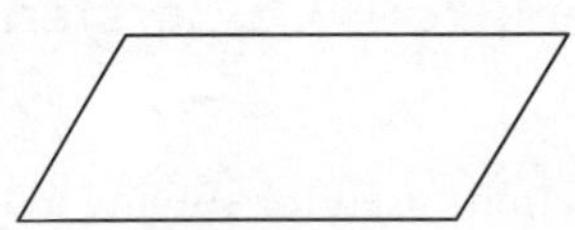

Figure 2.2

3. Process: If you are running a processing instruction, you need to use a rectangular box in the flow chart. This rectangular box, as shown in Fig. 2.3, is used for processing needs.

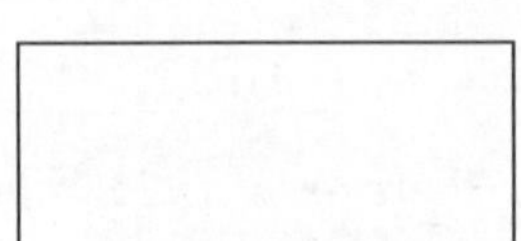

Figure 2.3

4. Decision Symbol: In a flow chart, a decision symbol, as shown in Fig. 2.4, is used for answering questions in the form of either true/false or yes/no. Please note that each answer can lead you to a different path in the flow chart. A 'yes' to a question can take you to one path and a 'No' to the same question can generate a completely new path.

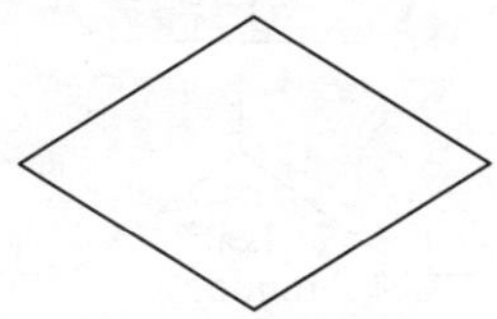

Figure 2.4

5. Flow Lines: Flow lines depict the direction of a flow in a flow chart. There are four types of flow lines. Flow lines, as shown in Fig. 2.5, can depict a left, right, top or bottom direction.

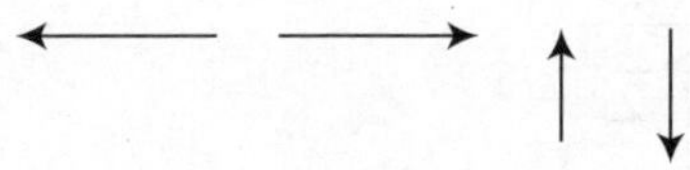

Figure 2.5

6. Connector: As the name suggests, a connector connects. It connects different steps in a flow chart that are on different pages and gives a sense of continuation. Generally, it is used in extremely complex flow charts and it is denoted by a small circle as shown in Fig. 2.6.

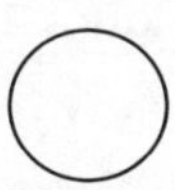

Figure 2.6

Check Your Understanding

1. What is flow chart?

Ans. A flow chart is a simple diagram that illustrates a sequence of operations to be performed for obtaining solution to a problem.

2. What is a terminal in a flow chart?

Ans. A rounded rectangle symbol that is used for both the starting and terminating points in a flow chart is a terminal.

TIP

To draw a correct flow chart, it is imperative to know the function of each flow chart symbol.

Flow Chart Convention

- **Selection Structure (Fig. 2.7)**

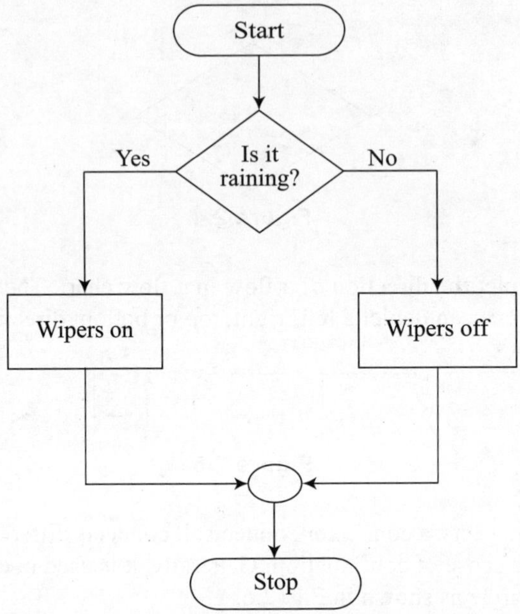

Figure 2.7

- **Repetition Structure (Fig. 2.8)**

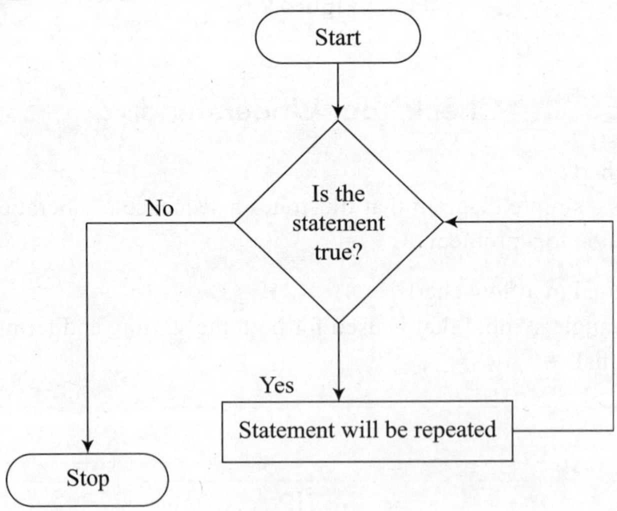

Figure 2.8

- **Sequential Structure (Fig. 2.9)**

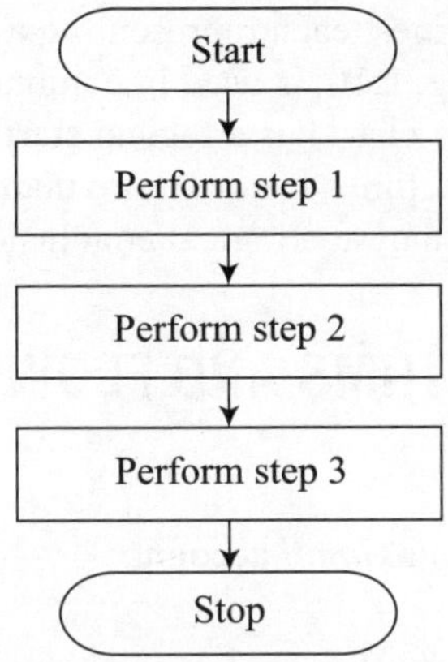

Figure 2.9

An example is shown in Fig. 2.10.

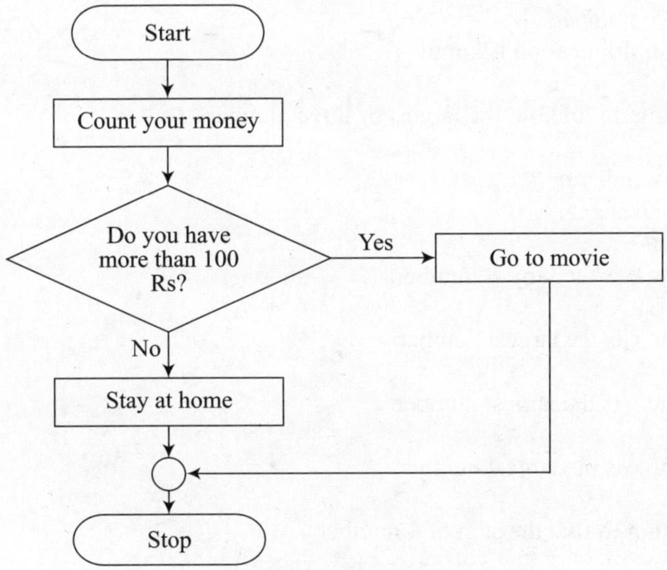

Figure 2.10

Guidelines for Drawing Flow Charts

- Firstly, describe the process to be charted.
- Start with a trigger event. For example, in Fig. 2.10, 'count your money' is the trigger event for starting the process of counting.
- Usually, direction of flow of a process is from left to right or top to bottom.
- Please note that only one flow line should come out from a process symbol.

- Also, only one flow line should enter a decision symbol. However, two or three flow lines can leave the same decision symbol. For example, in Fig. 2.10, decision after the question 'do you have more than 100 rupees?' led to two flow lines, each representing a 'yes' and a 'no', respectively.
- Only one flow line, as shown in Fig. 2.10, is used in conjunction with a terminal symbol.
- It is important to ensure that a flow chart has a logical start and end. A flow chart can have only one start terminal. However, it can sometimes lead to more than one terminal symbols.
- It is also important to stop a flow chart at a logical conclusion.

2.4 EXAMPLES OF ALGORITHMS AND FLOW CHARTS

Examples of Algorithms

A. Write an algorithm to log in to your *Gmail* account.
   1. Go to *www.gmail.com*.
   2. Enter your email id and password.
   3. Click the Sign in button.

B. Write an algorithm to multiply two numbers 5 and 6.
   1. Start.
   2. Read two numbers 5 and 6.
   3. Multiply two numbers, Mul = 5 * 6.
   4. Write "the multiplication is": mul.
   5. Stop.

C. Write an algorithm to find out the largest of three numbers.
   1. Start.
   2. Read three number p, q, r.
   3. If $p > q$, go to step 5.
   4. If $q > r$ then

      write q is the largest number.

      else

      write r is the largest number.
   5. If $p > r$ then

      write p is the largest number.

      else

      write r is the largest number.
   6. Stop.

D. Write an algorithm to find the sum of 4 numbers.
   1. Start.
   2. Sum = 0 and count = 0.
   3. Read the number n.
   4. Now, sum = sum + n and then the counter will be incremented by 1 as count = count + 1.
   5. Now check whether the count is less than 4 or not. If count < 4 then go to step 3 otherwise write sum "the sum is".
   6. Stop.

E. Write an algorithm to calculate the total marks of a student and also check whether the student is pass or fail. The total mark is calculated as the average of five subjects' marks.
   1. Start.

2. Read five subjects' marks *a*1, *a*2, *a*3, *a*4, *a*5.
3. Now, total mark = (*a*1 + *a*2 + *a*3 + *a*4 + *a*5) / 5.
4. If (total mark < 170) then
   write "student is fail".
   else
   write "student is pass".
5. Stop.

F. Write an algorithm to calculate the result when a number is given, if that number is greater than 50 then number must be increased 5 times otherwise the number is decreased by the 10.

1. Start.
2. Read number *P*.
3. If (*P* > 50) then
   write *P* = *P* * 5.
   else
   write *P* = *P* – 10.
4. Write *P*.
5. Stop.

Examples of Flow Charts

A. Draw a flow chart to find the sum of four numbers.

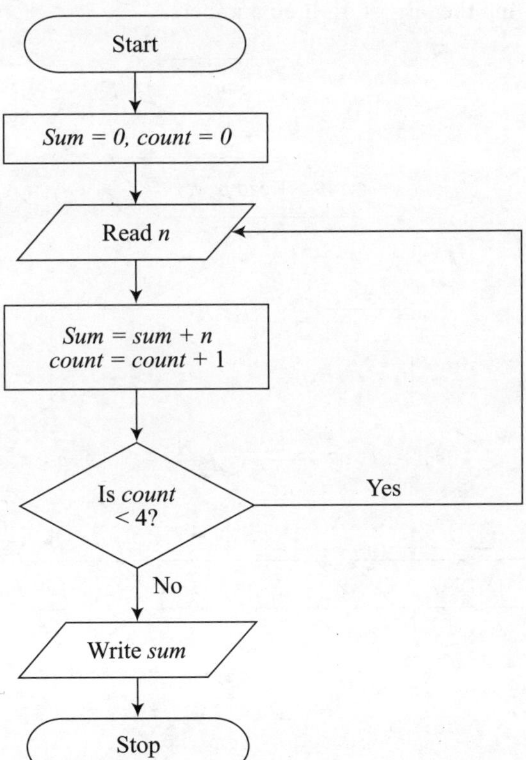

Figure 2.11

B. Draw a flow chart to multiply two numbers 5 and 6.

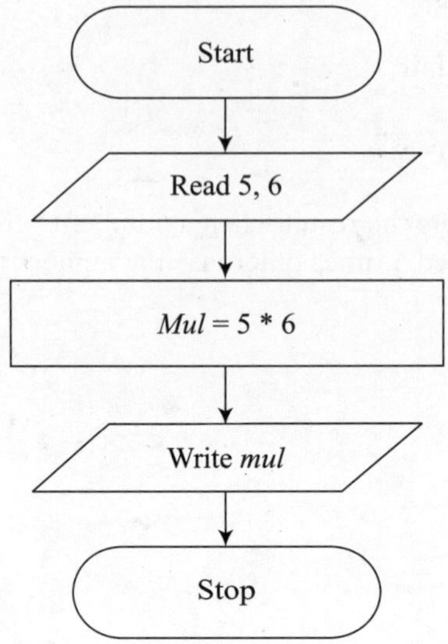

Figure 2.12

C. Draw a flow chart to find the largest of three numbers.

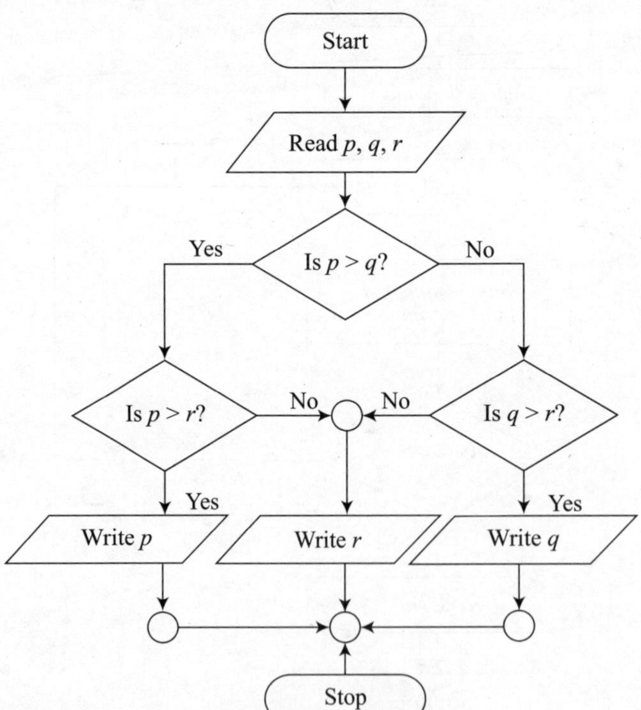

Figure 2.13

D. Draw a flow chart to write the word 'Symbol' 7 times.

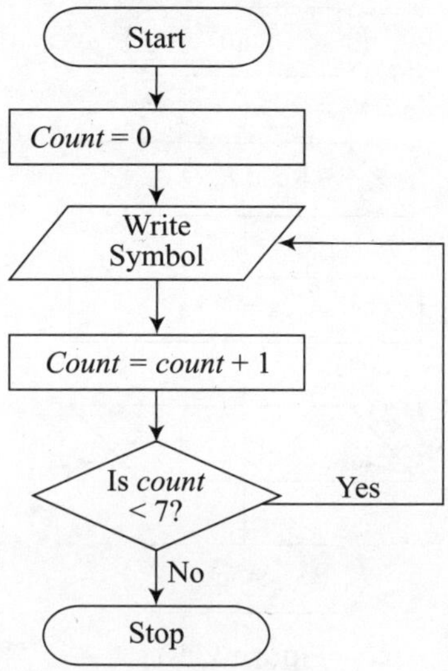

Figure 2.14

E. Draw a flow chart to log in to your *Gmail* account.

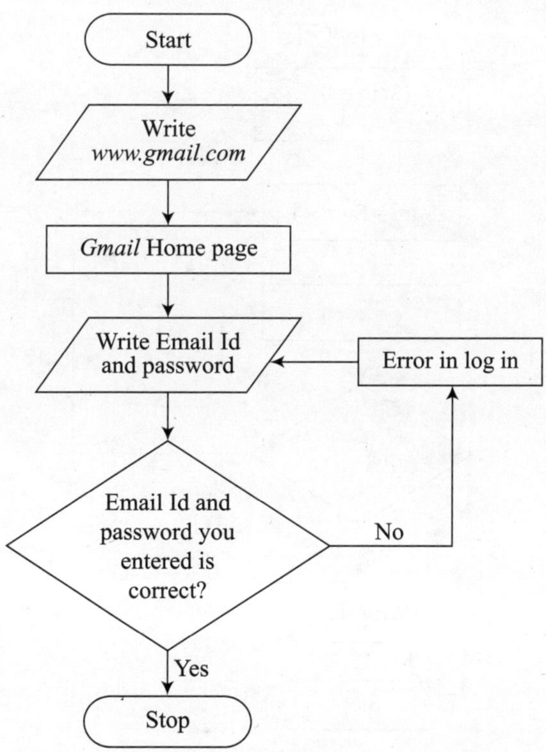

Figure 2.15

F. Draw a flow chart to find the area of rectangle.

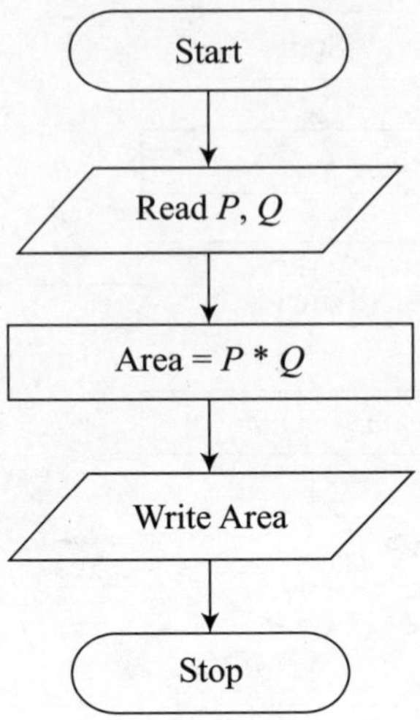

Figure 2.16

G. Draw a flow chart to find the sum of integers 1 to 50.

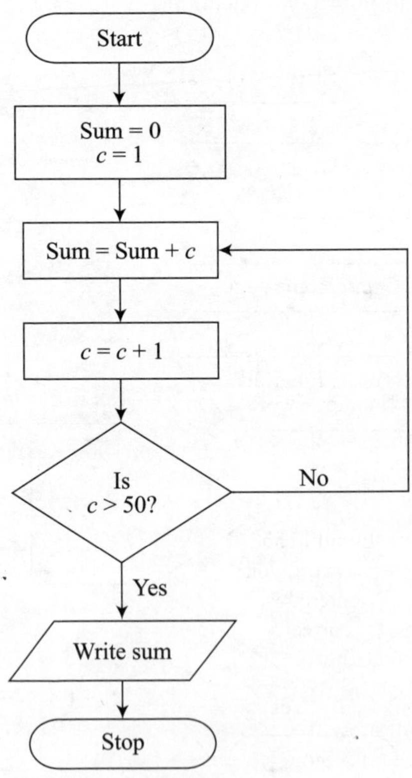

Figure 2.17

ALWAYS REMEMBER

- To analyse a problem, first identify whether the problem is decomposable or not, i.e., it can/cannot be decomposed into sub-problems.
- A problem can be defined as a gap between the actual and desired conditions.
- The process of developing a solution consists of development of a structure chart, a pseudo code and a flow chart.
- A structure chart shows a logical breakdown of a program into different steps. Each step has separate modules that are related to different modules.
- A pseudo code is used to state an algorithm in an English-like syntax.
- An algorithm is a set of instructions used for solving a problem in a step-by-step manner.
- A flow chart is a graphical representation of the logical flow of data.
- A flow chart gives a sequential order of steps that must be followed while designing the whole program.
- A flow chart uses the standard graphical symbols to narrate the sequential processes of a specific module.
- The basic symbols that are used to draw a simple flow chart are as follows:
    1. Terminal symbol
    2. Process
    3. Input/output
    4. Decision
    5. Flow lines
    6. Connector

KEY TERMS

✓ **ALGORITHM:** An algorithm is a finite and ordered sequence of steps.

✓ **DECISION Symbol:** In a flow chart, decision symbol is used to give answers for the questions in the form of either true / false or yes / no.

✓ **FLOW CHART:** A flow chart is a simple diagram which illustrates the sequence of operations to be performed to get to the solution of a problem.

✓ **FLOW LINES:** Flow lines indicate the direction of flow in a flow chart.

✓ **INPUT/OUTPUT:** For input or output in a flow chart, a slanted rectangular symbol called parallelogram is used.

✓ **PROBLEM:** A problem can be defined as a gap between the actual and desired conditions.

✓ **PSEUDO CODE:** A pseudo code is used to state an algorithm in an English-like syntax.

✓ **STRUCTURE CHART:** A structure chart shows a logical breakdown of a program into different steps. Each step has separate modules that are related to different modules.

✓ **TERMINAL:** The rounded rectangle symbol in a flow chart is called a terminal.

REVIEW EXERCISES

Multiple Choice Questions

1. Which procedure is used to solve a problem in a sequence?
   a. Sequence — b. Flow chart
   c. Algorithm — d. Procedure
2. Which symbol is used for a condition statement in a flow chart?
   a.  — b. 
   c. 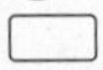 — d. 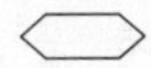
3. When a part of an algorithm is repeated a fixed number of times, what is it called?
   a. Iteration — b. Sequence
   c. Structural — d. Selection
4. What does the symbol 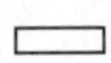 represent in a flow chart?
   a. Terminal — b. Input / output
   c. Connector — d. Process
5. What is used to break the program into logical steps?
   a. Structure chart — b. Flow chart
   c. Pseudo code — d. Algorithm
6. What is the other name of a process map?
   a. Algorithm — b. Flow chart
   c. Problem — d. Structure chart
7. What does a terminal symbol in a flow chart represent?
   a. Input / output — b. Process
   c. Flow lines — d. Condition
8. What are algorithms and flow charts used for?
   a. Better programming — b. Easy testing
   c. Efficient Coding — d. All
9. What is the direction of the flow of process in a flow chart?
   a. Left to top — b. Left to bottom
   c. Left to Right — d. Left to Left
10. How many lines can come out from a process symbol?
    a. One — b. Two
    c. Three — d. None
11. What does a Pseudo code also called?
    a. Structure chart — b. Flow chart
    c. Software language — d. Program design language
12. What should be done first when writing a correct program?
    a. Write Algorithm — b. Write pseudo code
    c. Logic planning — d. Draw flow chart

Short Questions

1. Differentiate between an algorithm and a program?
2. Define a flow chart and list its uses.
3. What are the rules to draw a flow chart?
4. Write an algorithm to make tea.
5. Differentiate between an algorithm and a flow chart?
6. Draw a flow chart to find whether a given number is odd or even.
7. Draw a flow chart to calculate the average of three numbers.
8. What do you mean by problem analysis?
9. What are the methodologies to solve a problem?
10. Briefly describe the basic symbols used to draw a flow chart.
11. Write an algorithm and draw a flow chart to change the temperature from Celsius to Fahrenheit.
12. Write an algorithm to find the area of a circle.

Answers to Multiple Choice Questions

1. c **2.** b **3.** a **4.** d **5.** a **6.** b **7.** a **8.** d **9.** c **10.** a
11. d **12.** c

3 Introduction to Python

3.1 INTRODUCTION

In the previous chapters, we learnt how programming languages and flow charts work. In this chapter, we will learn about the basics of Python, including the declaration of variables and the different data types. We will also learn about the different types of operators supported by Python and the execution of control statements in this language.

Python is a high-level, interpreted, general-purpose, dynamic programming language. Python was conceived in the late 1980s and its usage began from December 1989. It is a widely used programming language. Python possesses a property of code termed *reusability.* The syntax of Python programs can express concepts in fewer lines as compared to programs in C, C++ and JAVA.

Python can be used in multiple programming styles, including Object-Oriented, Functional programming Procedural Programming and Imperative styles. It also supports automatic memory management and has a large standard library and innumerous set of third party libraries. Python can be used on almost every operating system because its interpreter is available for many operating systems.

Python is free and open-source software. Open-source software is a kind of computer software in which the source code of the software is made public, i.e., the copyright holder gives rights to everyone to read, change and distribute the code for any purpose. It generally has a community-based development.

3.2 PYTHON OVERVIEW

Python is a high-level general-purpose programming language. Some of its key features are as follows:

- The code written in Python is automatically compiled to byte code and executed.
- Python can be used as a scripting language, as a language for implementing web applications, etc.
- Extending Python with C or C++ can help in the performance of intensive tasks where speed of execution is a key criterion.
- Python supports many features such as nested code blocks, functions, classes, modules and packages.
- Python makes use of an object-oriented programming approach.

Python has several additional features which are as follows:

- It has many built-in data types: strings, lists, tuples, dictionaries, etc.

- It supports many control statements such as `if, if-else, if-elif-else, while, iterative for, etc.`
- It allows for easier programming with the use of functions, classes, modules and packages.

3.3 GETTING STARTED WITH PYTHON

There are three different ways of starting Python:

1. Running a script written in Python
2. Using a Graphical user interface (GUI) from an Integrated Development Environment (IDE)
3. Employing an interactive approach

The first approach will require a text editor. We will have to create our scripts and then execute them using the text editor. The second approach will require a GUI application, one that comes with the Python installer itself. The third interactive approach is the one we will be using in this book. Python provides us a command line interpreter that we will utilise for this approach.

3.3.1 Installing Python Interpreter

First of all you need to download the Python Installer from the link:

https://www.Python.org/downloads/

> ***Note*** *Python 2.7.x version of python interpreter is being discussed throughout this book. Install Python 2.7.x for better results. Many Examples listed in this book may or may not work under Python 3.x.*

3.3.1.1 Installing on Linux OS

Following steps need to be followed in order to install the Python interpreter in the Linux Machine.

1. Download the .tgz file of Python from the above provided download link.
   http://www.python.org/ftp/python/2.7.11/Python-2.7.11.tgz
2. Unzip the downloaded file.
   tar xvfz Python-2.7.11.tgz
3. Go into the directory.
   cd Python-2.7.11
4. ./configure
5. Build it.
6. make
7. su or sudo su if there is no root user
8. make altinstall

3.3.1.2 Installing on Windows OS

First of all, you need to download the Python Installer from the link: *https://www.Python.org/downloads/*

Next, double click on the installed file. As the installer begins, you will be asked to select the users for whom you want the program to be installed. Choose **Install for all users** and click **Next >** as shown in Fig. 3.1. Please note installing for all users option is recommended.

Figure 3.1

Now, choose the directory where you want to install Python and click **Next>** as shown in Fig. 3.2. It is best to use the default given location.

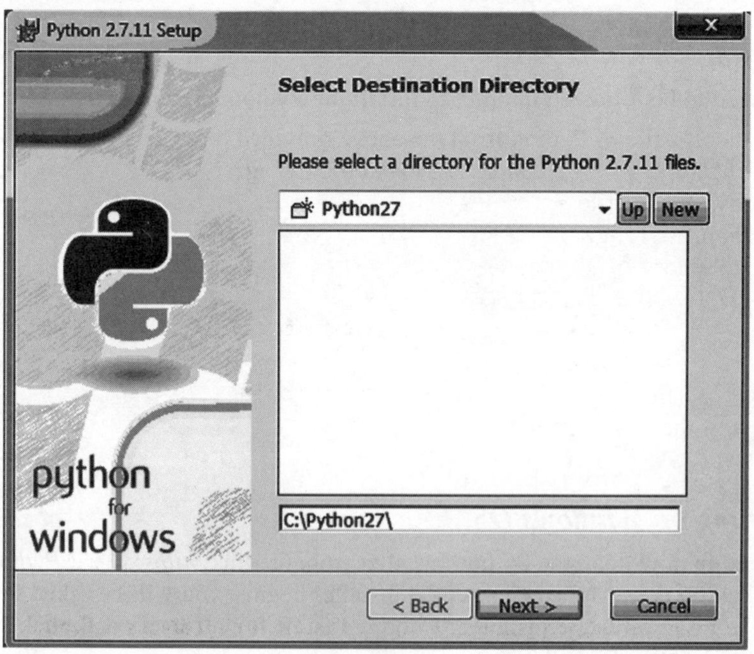

Figure 3.2

You will then be asked to select the package. Click **Next>** as shown in Fig. 3.3.

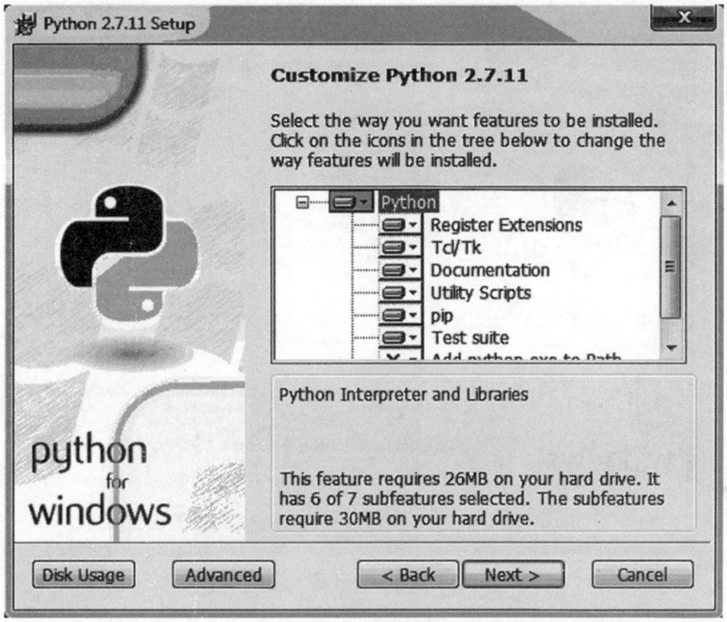

Figure 3.3

Please note that installation takes some time to complete as indicated in Fig. 3.4.

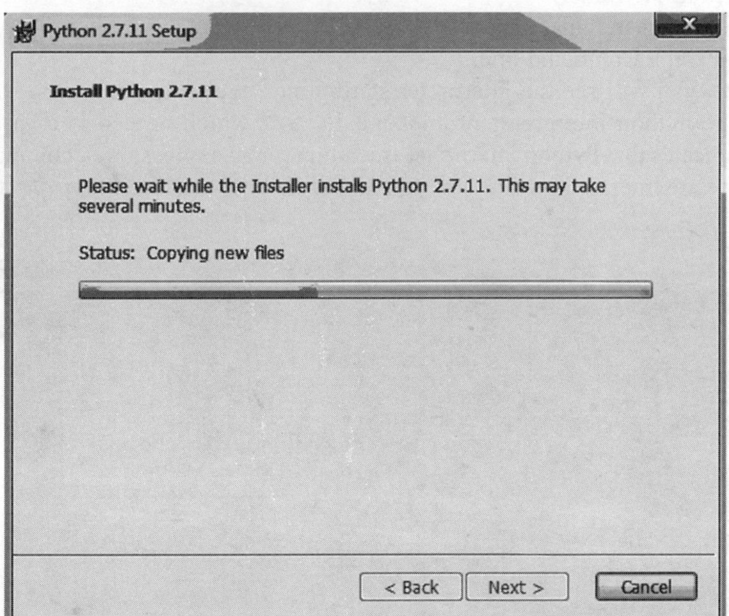

Figure 3.4

Once the installation process is complete, click on **Finish** to exit the installer (Fig. 3.5).

Figure 3.5

Python is now installed in your computer's directory. You need to run Python by following the given steps:

1. Click **START** button.
2. Go to **All Programs**.
3. Search for **Python 2.7** folder.
4. Click **Python** (Command line).

This will start the Python Command line.

Once Python starts, you will see the interpreter startup message, indicating version and platform. You will also be given the python interpreter prompt, i.e., ">>>" which is also known as python chevron prompt. The ">>>"indicates that Python interpreter is waiting for an expression or command. The interactive environment where we are interacting with the Python interpreter is called the *console* or *command shell* as shown in Fig. 3.6.

Figure 3.6

Now, try to interact with the interpreter by entering a simple expression, `8 + 9`, on the console. After entering the expression, press the **Enter** key to get the result.

```
>>> 8+9
17          # Output
>>>
```

The given example shows how Python can also work as a simple calculator.

Now, type the following text at the Python prompts and press **Enter**.

```
>>> print "Hello, Python!"
```

This produces the following result:

```
Hello, Python!      # Output
```

Now, let us try some more examples.

```
>>> Hello
```

After writing `Hello`, when you hit the **Enter** key, an error message will be displayed. This is because Python does not have any `Hello` command and its interpreter is unable to identify the command.

```
>>> Hello
Traceback (most recent call last):              # Output
File "<pyshell#0>", line 1, in <module>
Hello
NameError: name 'hello' is not defined
```

However, if you want to display a message on the console, you will need to keep your message within quotes. This tells the interpreter that the text entered is not a command. Therefore, the interpreter simply echoes the text.

```
>>> 'Hello'
'Hello'            # Output
```

Note *The* `print` *statement is used to display output to the screen. Those of you who are familiar with* **C** *know that the* `printf()` *function produces screen output. Many shell script languages use the* echo *command for program output.*

TIP

The `print` *statement, paired with the string format operator (%), behaves even more like C's* `printf()` *function.*

Check Your Understanding

1. What is Python?

Ans. Python is a high-level, interpreted, interactive and object-oriented scripting language. It is a highly readable language. Unlike other programming languages, Python provides an interactive mode similar to that of a calculator.

3.4 COMMENTS

Just like other programming languages, Python allows you to add comments in the code. Comments are used by the programmer to explain the piece of code to others as well as to himself in a simple language. Every programming language makes use of some special character for commenting, so does Python.

Python uses the hash character (#) for comments. Putting # before a text ensures that the text will not be parsed by the interpreter. Comments do not affect the programming part and the Python interpreter does not display any error message for comments. Comments show up as it is in the programming. It is a good practice to use comments for program documentation in your program so that it becomes easier for other programmers to maintain or enhance the program when required.

Now, take a look at some examples of comments used in Python.

Commenting without the use of Hash mark (#)

```
>>> 8+9 addition
SyntaxError: invalid syntax          # Output
>>>
```

In the above example, 'addition' is written without the Hash mark. As a result, the interpreter accepts the word 'addition' as part of programming. Since 'addition' is not a command in Python, an error message is displayed.

Commenting using Hash mark (#)

```
>>> 8+9 #addition
17          # Output
>>>
```

Now, in this example, 'addition' is written with a Hash mark. Hence, the interpreter understands it as a comment and does not display any error message.

Check Your Understanding

1. What are comments?
Ans. Comments are annotations made by the programmer. These help other programmers in understanding the code.

2. Which character is used for commenting in Python?
Ans. Hash mark (#) is used for commenting in Python.

3.5 PYTHON IDENTIFIERS

A Python identifier is the name given to a variable, function, class, module or other object. An identifier can begin with an alphabet (A – Z or a – z), or an underscore (_) and can include any number of letters, digits, or underscores. Spaces are not allowed.

Python will not accept @, $ and % as identifiers. Furthermore, Python is a case-sensitive language. Thus, **Hello** and **hello** both are different identifiers. In Python, a class name will always start with a capital letter.

Table 3.1 provides examples of valid and invalid names for creating identifiers.

TABLE 3.1 Examples of Valid and Invalid Names for Creating Identifiers

Examples of Identifiers	
Valid	**Invalid**
MyName	My Name (Space is not allowed)
My_Name	3dfig (cannot start with a digit)
Your_Name	Your#Name (Only alphabetic character, Underscore (_) and numeric are allowed

3.6 RESERVED KEYWORDS

Just like other programming languages, Python has a list of reserved words known as keywords. Every keyword has a specific purpose and use. In the upcoming chapters, we will look into the use of these keywords in programming.

A list of reserved keywords in Python:

```
and         del         from        None        True
as          elif        global      nonlocal    try
assert      else        if          not         while
break       except      import      or          with
class       False       in          pass        yield
continue    finally     is          raise
def         for         lambda      return
```

3.7 VARIABLES

3.7.1 Declaring a Variable

A variable holds a value that may change. The process of writing the variable name is called **Declaring the variable**. In Python, variables do not need to be declared explicitly in order to reserve memory spaces as in other programming languages like C, Java, etc. When we initialize the variable in Python, Python Interpreter automatically does the declaration process.

3.7.2 Initializing a Variable

The general format of assignment statement is as follows:

```
Variable = expression
```

The equal sign (=) is known as *Assignment operator*. An `expression` is any value, text or arithmetic expression, whereas `variable` is the name of the variable. The value of the expression will be stored in the variable.

Let us now look at an example of initialising a variable:

```
>>>year=2016
>>> name='Albert'
```

The two given statements reserve two memory spaces with variable names `year` and `name.2016` and `Albert`, are stored respectively, in these memory spaces as shown in Fig. 3.7.

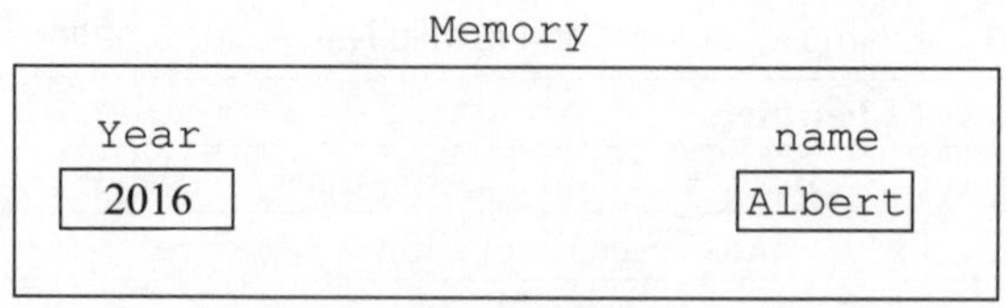

Figure 3.7

> **TIP**
>
> *Whenever you want to display the value of the variables, simply type these variable names on console.*

Let us now look at an example of a variable displaying its value:

```
>>> year
2016                # Output
>>> name
'Albert'            # Output
>>>
```

> **Note** *You can also assign one variable value into another variable. Assign the value of* `name1` *variable into* `name2` *variable.*

Let us now look at an example of assigning one variable value into another:

```
>>> name1='Albert'
>>> name2=name1
>>> name2
'Albert'            # Output
>>>
```

Whenever two values are successively assigned to a variable, the interpreter will forget the previous value assigned to it and store the latest value in the variable memory space.

```
>>> year=2016
>>> year=2017
>>> year
2017                # Output
>>>
```

In the given example, we first assigned `2016` to the variable `year` and then assigned `2017` to the same variable. The interpreter will forget the value 2016 and will display `2017` as the value of `year`.

We can also assign different types of values to the same variable. For example, we can assign a text value where there previously was a numeric value. Even in such a case however, only the last assigned value remains.

Let us now look at an example of assigning different types of values to the same variable:

```
>>> amount=50
>>> amount
50                  # Output
>>> amount='Fifty'
>>> amount
'Fifty'             # Output
>>>
```

3.8 STANDARD DATA TYPES

The data stored in the memory can be of many types. For example, a person's name is stored as an alphabetic value and his address is stored as an alphanumeric value. Sometimes, we also need to store answer in terms of only 'yes' or 'no', i.e., true or false. This type of data is known as *Boolean data.*

Python has six basic data types which are as follows:

1. Numeric
2. String
3. List
4. Tuple
5. Dictionary
6. Boolean

3.8.1 Numeric

Numeric data can be broadly divided into integers and real numbers (i.e., fractional numbers). Integers can themselves be positive or negative. Unlike many other programming languages, Python does not have any upper bound on the size of integers. The real numbers or fractional numbers are called *floating* point numbers in programming languages. Such floating point numbers contain a decimal and a fractional part.

Let us now look at an example that has an integer as well as a real number:

```
>>> num1=2          # integer number
>>>num2=2.5         # real number (float)
>>>num1
2          # Output
>>>num2
2.5        # Output
>>>
```

> **Note** *In all the earlier versions of Python 3, slash (/) operator worked differently. When both numerator and denominator are integers, then the result will be an integer. The slash operator removes the fraction part.*

Let us look at an example of the division operator in all the earlier versions of Python 3:

```
>>> 5/2
2          # Output
>>>
```

The result becomes a floating number when either the numerator or the denominator is a floating number. When both the numerator and the denominator are floating numbers, the result is again a floating number.

Let us look at an example of the division operator in all the earlier versions of Python 3:

```
>>> 5.0/2
2.5        # Output
>>>
```

This operator has been modified in Python 3 and in all the versions after Python 3. The division operator provides accurate results even when both the numerator and the denominator are integers.

Here is an example of the division operator that is used in all the versions after Python 3:

```
>>> 5/2
2.5        # Output
>>>
```

Check Your Understanding

1. What are data types?

Ans. The data you have to manipulate can be in different forms. For example, the name of a person is in string form while his age is in numeric form.

3.8.2 String

Besides numbers, strings are another important data type. *Single quotes* or *double quotes* are used to represent strings. A string in Python can be a series or a sequence of alphabets, numerals and special characters. Similar to C, the first character of a string has an index 0.

There are many operations that can be performed on a string. There are several operators such as slice operator ([] and [:]), concatenation operator (+), repetition operator (*), etc. *Slicing* is used to take out a subset of the string, *concatenation* is used to combine two or more than two strings and *repetition* is used to repeat the same string several times.

Here is an example of string data:

```
>>> sample_string ="Hello"  # store string value
>>> sample_string           # display string value
'Hello'                     # Output
>>> sample_string + "World" # use of + operator
'HelloWorld'                # Output
>>> sample_string * 3       # use of * operator
'HelloHelloHello'           # Output
```

Python also provides slice operators ([] and [:]) to extract substring from the string. In Python, the indexing of the characters starts from 0; therefore, the index value of the first character is 0.

Syntax

```
>>> sample_string[start : end <:step>]  #step is optional
```

Example

```
>>>sample_string="Hello"
>>>sample_string[1]          # display 1st index element.
'e'                          # Output
>>>sample_string[0:2]        # display 0 to 1st index elements
'He'                         # Output
```

Example

```
>>> sample_string = "HelloWorld"
>>> sample_string[1:8:2]       # display all the alternate charactors be-
tween index 1 to 8. ie, 1,3,5,7
'elWr'                         # Output
```

3.8.3 List

List is the most used data type in Python. A list can contain the same type of items. Alternatively, a list can also contain different types of items. A list is an ordered and indexable sequence. To declare a list in Python, we need to separate the items using commas and enclose them within square brackets([]). The list is somewhat similar to the array in C language. However, an array can contain only the same type of items while a list can contain different types of items.

Similar to the string data type, the list also has plus (+), asterisk (*) and slicing [:] operators for concatenation, repetition and sub-list, respectively.

Let us look at an example of the List data type:

```
>>>first=[1,"two",3.0,"four"]        # 1st list
>>>second=["five", 6]                # 2nd list
>>>first                             # display 1st list
[1, 'two', 3.0, 'four']              # Output
>>>first+second                      # concatenate 1st and 2nd list
[1, 'two', 3.0, 'four', 'five', 6]# Output
>>>second * 3                        # repeat 2nd list
['five', 6, 'five', 6, 'five', 6]    # Output
>>>first[0:2]                        # display sublist
[1, 'two']                           # Output
>>>
```

3.8.4 Tuple

Similar to a *list*, a *tuple* is also used to store sequence of items. Like a list, a tuple consists of items separated by commas. However, tuples are enclosed within parentheses rather than within square brackets.

Let us look at an example of the tuple data type:

```
>>>third=(7, "eight",9, 10.0)
>>>third
(7, 'eight', 9, 10.0)    # Output
```

Lists and tuples have the following differences:

- In lists, items are enclosed within *square* brackets [], whereas in tuples, items are enclosed within parentheses ().
- Lists are mutable whereas Tuples are immutable. Tuples are **read only** lists. Once the items are stored, the tuple cannot be modified.

Let us look at an example of list and tuple data type:

```
>>>first[0]="one"
>>>third[0]="seven"
Traceback (most recent call last):    # Output
  File "<pyshell#15>", line 1, in <module>
third[0]="seven"
TypeError: 'tuple' object does not support item assignment
```

TIP

The items cannot be modified in a tuple but the same is not the case with a list.

3.8.5 Dictionary

It is the same as the hash table type. The order of elements in a dictionary is undefined. But, we can iterate over the following:

1. The keys
2. The values
3. The items (key-value pairs) in a dictionary

A Python dictionary is an unordered collection of key-value pairs. When we have the large amount of data, the dictionary data type is used. Keys and values can be of any type in a dictionary. Items in dictionary are enclosed in the curly-braces{} and separated by the comma (,). A colon (:) is used to separate key from value. A key inside the square bracket [] is used for accessing the dictionary items.

Example of dictionary:

```
>>> dict1 = {1:"first line", "second":2}  # declare dictionary
>>> dict1[3] = "third line"               # add new item
>>> dict1                                 # display dictionary
{1: 'first line', 'second': 2, 3: 'third line'}    #Output
>>> dict1.keys()                          # display dictionary keys
[1, 'second', 3]                          # Output
>>> dict1.values()                        # display dictionary values
['first line', 2, 'third line']           # Output
```

3.8.6 Boolean

In a programming language, mostly data is stored in the form of alphanumeric but sometimes we need to store the data in the form of 'Yes' or 'No'. In terms of programming language, Yes is similar to True and No is similar to False.

This True and False data is known as Boolean Data and the data types which stores this Boolean data are known as Boolean Data Types.

Example

```
>>> a = True
>>> type(a)
<type 'bool'>

>>> x = False
>>> type(x)
<type 'bool'>
```

3.8.7 Sets

The lists and dictionaries in Python are known as sequence or order collection of data. However, in Python we also have one data type which is an unordered collection of data known as Set. A Set does not contain any duplicate values or elements.

Union, Intersection, Difference and Symmetric Difference are some operations which are performed on sets.

Union: Union operation performed on two sets returns all the elements from both the sets. It is performed by using & operator.

Intersection: Intersection operation performed on two sets returns all the element which are common or in both the sets. It is performed by using | operator.

Difference: Difference operation performed on two sets set1 and set2 returns the elements which are present on set1 but not in set2. It is performed by using – operator.

Symmetric Difference: Symmetric Difference operation performed on two sets returns the element which are present in either set1 or set2 but not in both. It is performed by using ^ operator.

Example

```
# Defining sets
>>> set1 = set([1, 2, 4, 1, 2, 8, 5, 4])
>>> set2 = set([1, 9, 3, 2, 5])

>>> print set1                          #Printing set
set([8, 1, 2, 4, 5])                    #Output
>>> print set2
set([1, 2, 3, 5, 9])                    #Output

>>> intersection = set1 & set2          #intersection of set1 and set2
>>> print intersection
set([1, 2, 5])                          #Output

>>> union = set1 | set2                 # Union of set1 and set2
```

```
>>> print union
set([1, 2, 3, 4, 5, 8, 9])              #Output

>>> difference = set1 - set2            # Difference of set1 and set2
>>> print difference
set([8, 4])                             #Output

>>> symm_diff = set1 ^ set2             # Symmetric difference of set1 and
                                          set2
>>> print symm_diff
set([3, 4, 8, 9])                       #Output
```

type() Function

type() function in Python programming language is a built-in function which returns the datatype of any arbitrary object. The object is passed as an argument to the type() function. Type() function can take anything as an argument and returns its datatype, such as integers, strings, dictionaries, lists, classes, modules, tuples, functions, etc.

Example

```
>>> x = 10
>>> type(x)
<type 'int'>                            #Output

>>> type('hello')
<type 'str'>                            #Output

>>> import os
>>> type (os)
<type 'module'>                         #Output

>>> tup = (1,2,3)
>>> type(tup)
<type 'tuple'>                          #Output

>>> li = [1,2,3]
>>> type(li)
<type 'list'>                           #Output
```

Check Your Understanding

1. What is a list?

Ans. A list is a dynamic array or sequence that is ordered, indexable and mutable. It is one of the most versatile compound data types of Python. A list is used to store multiple items separated by commas within square brackets [].

2. What is the output of `print list[2]` when list = ['abcd', 2.23, 'john']?

Ans. john

3. What is the main difference between a list and a tuple?

Ans. In a list, items are enclosed within square brackets; tuple is a sequence of items separated by comma and enclosed in parentheses.

Note *Items separated by 'comma' is the signature of tuple not parenthesis*

3.9 OPERATORS

Operators are constructs used to modify the values of operands. Consider the following expression:

```
3 + 4 = 7
```

In the above expression, 3 and 4 are the operands whereas + is operator.
Based on functionality, operators are categories into following seven types:

1. Arithmetic operator
2. Comparison operator
3. Assignment operator
4. Logical operator
5. Bitwise operator
6. Membership operator
7. Identity operator

3.9.1 Arithmetic Operators

These operators are used to perform arithmetic operations such as addition, subtraction, multiplication and division (Table 3.2).

TABLE 3.2 List of Arithmetic Operators

Operator	Description	Example
+	Addition operator to add two operands.	`10+20=30`
–	Subtraction operator to subtract two operands.	`10-20=-10`
*	Multiplication operator to multiply two operands.	`10*20=200`
/	Division operator to divide left hand operator by right hand Operator.	`5/2=2.5`
**	Exponential operator to calculate power.	`5**2=25`
%	Modulus operator to find remainder.	`5%2=1`
//	Floor division operator to find the quotient and remove the fractional part.	`5//2=2`

Example

```
>>> x = 10
>>> y = 12
>>> z = 0

>>> z = x + y
>>> print z
22                                          #Ouput

>>> z = x - y
>>> print z
-2                                          #Ouput

>>> z = x * y
>>> print z
120                                         #Ouput

>>> z = x / y
>>> print z
0                                           #Ouput

>>> z = x % y
>>> print z
10                                          #Ouput

>>> z = x ** y
>>> print z
1000000000000                               #Ouput

>>> z = x // y
>>> print z
0                                           #Ouput
```

3.9.2 Comparison Operators

These operators are used to compare values. Comparison operators are also called relational operators. The result of these operators is always a Boolean value, that is, either true or false. Table 3.3 provides a list of comparison operators.

Table 3.3 List of Comparison Operators

Operator	Description	Example
==	Operator to check whether two operands are equal.	10 == 20, false
!= or <>	Operator to check whether two operands are not equal.	10 !=20, true
>	Operator to check whether first operand is greater than second operand.	10 > 20, false
<	Operator to check whether first operand is smaller than second operand.	10 < 20, true
>=	Operator to check whether first operand is greater than or equal to second operand.	10 >= 20, false
<=	Operator to check whether first operand is smaller than or equal to second operand.	10 <= 20, true

Example

```
>>> x = 10
>>> y = 12
>>> z = 0

>>> if (x == y):
        print "x is equal to y"
    else:
        print "x is not equal to y"

x is not equal to y                     #Output

>>> if (x != y):
        print "x is not equal to y"
    else:
        print "x is equal to y"

x is not equal to y                     #Output

>>> if (x <> y):
        print "x is not equal to y"
    else:
        print "x is equal to y"


x is not equal to y                     #Output
>>> if (x < y):
        print "x is less than y"
    else:
        print "x is not less than y"

x is less than y                #Output

>>> if (x > y):
        print "x is greater than y"
    else:
        print "x is not greater than y"

x is not greater than y         #Output

>>> if (x <= y):
        print "x is either equal to or less than y"
    else:
        print "x is neither equal to nor less than y"

x is either equal to or less than y  #Output

>>> if (x >= y):
```

```
        print "x is either equal to or greater than y"
    else:
        print "x is neither equal to nor greater than y"

x is neither equal to nor greater than y    #Output
```

3.9.3 Assignment Operators

This operator is used to store right side operand in the left side operand. Table 3.4 provides a list of assignment operators.

TABLE 3.4 List of Assignment Operators

Operator	Description	Example
=	Store right side operand in left side operand.	a=b+c
+=	Add right side operand to left side operand and store the result in left side operand.	a+=b or a=a+b
−=	Subtract right side operand from left side operand and store the result in left side operand.	a-=b or a=a-b
*=	Multiply right side operand with left side operand and store the result in left side operand.	a*=b or a=a*b
/=	Divide left side operand by right side operand and store the result in left side operand.	a/b or a=a/b
%=	Find the modulus and store the remainder in left side operand.	a%=b or a=a%b
**=	Find the exponential and store the result in left side operand.	a**=b or a=a**b
//=	Find the floor division and store the result in left side operand.	a//=b or a=a// b

Example

```
>>> x = 10
>>> y = 12

>>> y += x
>>> print y
22                          #Output

>>> y *= x
>>> print y
220                         #Output

>>> y /= x
>>> print y
22                          #Output
```

```
>>> y %= x
>>> print y
2                          #Output

>>> y **= x
>>> print y
1024                       #Output

>>> y //= x
>>> print y
102                        #Output
```

3.9.4 Bitwise Operators

These operators perform bit level operation on operands. Let us take two operands x = 10 and y = 12. In binary format this can be written as x = 1010 and y = 1100. Table 3.5 presents a list of bitwise operators.

Table 3.5 List of Bitwise Operators

Operator	Description	Example
& Bitwise AND	This operator performs AND operation between operands. Operator copies bit if it exists in both operands.	x & y results 1000
| Bitwise OR	This operator performs OR operation between operands. Operator copies bit if it exists in either operand.	x | y results 1110
^ Bitwise XOR	This operator performs XOR operation between operands. Operator copies bit if it exists only in one operand.	x ^ y results 0110
~ bitwise inverse	This operator is a unary operator used to opposite the bits of operand.	~ x results 0101
<< left shift	This operator is used to shift the bits towards left	x << 2 results 101000
<< right shift	This operator is used to shift the bits towards right	x >> 2 results 0010

Example

```
>>> x = 10                 # 10 = 0000 1010
>>> y = 12                 # 12 = 0000 1100
>>> z = 0

# Bitwise AND
>>> z = x & y
>>> print z
8                                # 8 = 0000 1000

# Bitwise OR
```

```
>>> z = x | y
>>> print z
14                                  # 14 = 0000 1110

# Bitwise XOR
>>> z = x ^ y
>>> print z
6                                   # 6 = 0000 0110

# Bitwise inverse
>>> z = ~x
>>> print z
-11                                 # -11 = 1111 0101

# Left shift
>>> z = x << 2
>>> print z
40                                  # 40 = 0010 1000
# Right shift
>>> z = x >> 2
>>> print z
2                                   # 2 = 0000 0010
```

3.9.5 Logical Operators

These operators are used to check two or more conditions. The resultant of this operator is always a Boolean value. Here, x and y are two operands that store either true or false Boolean values. Table 3.6 presents a list of logical operators. Assume x is true and y is false.

TABLE 3.6 List of Logical Operators

Operator	Description	Example
and logical AND	This operator performs AND operation between operands. When both operands are true, the resultant become true.	x and y results false
or logical OR	This operator performs OR operation between operands. When any operand is true, the resultant becomes true.	x or y results true
not logical NOT	This operator is used to reverse the operand state.	not x results false

Example

```
>>> x = True
>>> y = False

>>> print (x and y)
```

```
False                                   #Output

>>> print (x or y)
True                                    #Output

>>> print (not x)
False                                   #Output

>>> print (not y)
True                                    #Output
```

3.9.6 Membership Operators

These operators are used to check an item or an element that is part of a string, a list or a tuple. A membership operator reduces the effort of searching an element in the list. Suppose, *x* stores a value 20 and *y* is the list containing items 10, 20, 30, and 40. Then, *x* is a part of the list *y* because the value 20 is in the list *y*. Table 3.7 gives a list of membership operators.

Table 3.7 List of Membership Operators

Operator	Description	Example
in	Return true, if item is in list or in sequence. Return false, if item is not in list or in sequence.	x in y, results true
not in	Return false, if item is in list or in sequence. Return true, if item is not in list or in sequence.	x not in y, results false

Example

```
>>> x = 10
>>> y = 12
>>> list = [21, 13, 10, 17]

>>> if (x in list):
    print "x is present in the list"
else:
    print "x is not present in the list"

x is present in the list                        #Output

>>> if (y not in list):
    print "y is not present in the list"
else:
    print "y is present in the list"

y is not present in the list                    #Output
```

3.9.7 Identity Operators

These operators are used to check whether both operands are same or not. Suppose, x stores a value 20 and y stores a value 40. Then `x is y` returns `false` and `x not is y` returns `true`. Table 3.8 provides a list of identity operators

Table 3.8 List of Identity Operators

Operator	Description	Example
is	Return true, if the operands are same. Return false, if the operands are not same.	x is y, results false
not is	Return false, if theoperands are same. Return true, if the operands are not same.	x not is y, results true

Example

```
>>> x = 12
>>> y = 12

>>> if ( x is y):
            print "x is same as y"
    else:
            print "x is not same as y"

x is same as y                        #Output

>>> y = 10

>>> if ( x is not y):
            print "x is not same as y"
    else:
            print "x is same as y"

x is not same as y                    #Output
```

3.9.8 Precedence of Operators

When an expression has two or more operators, we need to identify the correct sequence to evaluate these operators. This is because the final answer changes depending on the sequence thus chosen.

Let us look at an example of a mathematical expression:

```
10 + 5 / 5
```

When the given expression is evaluated left to right, the final answer becomes `3`. However, if the above expression is evaluated right to left, the final answer becomes `11`. This shows that changing the sequence in which the operators are evaluated in the given expression also changes the solution. Therefore, in order to remove this problem, a level of precedence is associated with the operators. Precedence is the condition that specifies the importance of each operator relative to the others.

Table 3.9 to display operator precedence from lower precedence to higher:

TABLE 3.9 Operator Precedence

Operator	Description
NOT, OR AND	Logical operators
in , not in	Membership operator
is, not is	Identity operator
=, %=, /=, //=, -=, +=, *=, **==	Assignment operators.
<>, ==, !=	Equality comparison operator
<=, <, >, >=	Comparison operators
^, |	Bitwise XOR and OR operator
&	Bitwise AND operator
<<, >>	Bitwise left shift and right shift
+, -	Addition and subtraction
*, /, %, //	Multiplication, Division, Modulus and floor division
**	Exponential operator

It may happen that an expression has two operators having same precedence. In that case, we use *Associativity* to evaluate the expression. Associativity is nothing but the direction in which we evaluate the operators if they have same precedence.

3.9.9 Associativity

In Table 3.9 (precedence of operators) we can see that many operators are having the same precedence. Hence, associativity decides the order in which the operators with same precedence are executed.

There are two types of associativity. One is left-to-right and other is right-to-left. In left-to-right associativity, the operator of same precedence are executed from the left side first and in right-to-left associativity, the operator of same precedence are executed from the right side first. Most of the operators in Python have left-to-right associativity. Examples for left-to-right associative operators are multiplication, floor division, etc and ** operator is right-to-left associative.

Example

```
>>> 3 * 4 // 6
2                    #Output

>>> 3 * (4 // 6)
0                    #Output

>>> 3 ** 4 ** 2            # 3^16
43046721             #Output

>>> (3 ** 4) ** 2          # 81^2
6561                 #Output
```

Note *The order in which operators are evaluated can be controlled using parentheses, as illustrated in the example. Parentheses have the highest precedence.*

> **Note** *When two operators have the same precedence, then operators are evaluated from left to right direction.*

Let us now look at an example of a mathematical expression with operators having the same precedence:

```
10 * 5 / 5
```

In the above expression, the multiplication operator is evaluated before the division operator is evaluated. Based on the number of operands, operators are classified into following two types:

1. Unary Operator
2. Binary Operator

Unary Operator

Unary operators are operators with only one operand. These operators are basically used to provide sign to the operand.

The format of the unary operator is:

Operator operand

Some unary operators are as follows:

- +
- -
- ~

Example

```
>>> x = 12
>>> +x
12                    #Output
>>> -x
-12                   #Output
>>> ~x
-13                   #Output
```

> **Note** *The* `invert(~)` *operator returns the bit-wise inversion of long integer arguments. The bit-wise inversion of* `y` *can be computed as* `-(y+1)`. *Hence, in the above example, we get the* `~(12)` *as* `-13`.

Binary Operator

Binary operators are operators with two operands that are manipulated to get the result. They are also used to compare numeric values and string values.

The format of binary operator is:

Operand1 **Operator** Operand2

Some binary operators are as follows:

**, *, /, %, +, -, <<,>>, &, | ,^,<,>,<= ,>=, == ,!= ,<>

We saw many examples of binary operators in the section above.

Check Your Understanding

1. What are the different types of operators in Python?

Ans.

- Arithmetic Operator
- Comparison Operator
- Assignment Operator
- Logical Operator
- Bitwise Operator
- Membership Operator
- Identity operator

3.10 STATEMENT AND EXPRESSION

3.10.1 Statement

A statement can be thought as an instruction that can be interpreted by the Python interpreter. In Section 3.9, we came across *print* and *assignment* statements. A statement is interpreted by the interpreter and after execution displays some result (if there is a need for displaying it). For e.g., print statement produces some result to display but it does not happen in case of assignment statement.

A program can contain many statements in sequence. If there are multiple statements, the result is displayed after every statement.

As we move ahead in the chapter, we will study more statements such as `while` statement, `for` statement, `if` statement, `print` statement, etc.

Let us look at an example of the `assignment` statement:

```
>>> message="Hello world"
```

Due to the assignment operator (=), the message variable stores the `Hello world` string.

Let us look at an example of the `print` statement:

```
>>> print 1
      1                 #simply prints 1
>>> x=2
>>>print x
      2                 #prints the value of x
```

3.10.2 Expression

An expression is a combination of variables, operators, values and a reserve keyword.

Whenever you type an expression in the command line, the interpreter evaluates it and produces the result.

Example

```
>>> 1+1
2            # Output
```

Evaluation of Expression

The evaluation of an expression produces a value. In an assignment statement, an expression is always there on the right side.

Let us look at an example of an expression:

```
>>> 2+3
5            # Output
>>>program="Hello Python"
>>>program
'Hello Python'              # Output
>>>print program
Hello Python       # Output
```

An expression is not always a mathematical expression in Python. A value by itself is an expression. In above example, the "Hello Python" is an expression. The interpreter reads the expression and displays the string written in quotes as it is.

> ***Note*** *In the given example, we assigned a value* `"Hello Python"` *to the variable* `program`*. Now, when we type only* `program`*, we get the output* `'Hello Python.'` *This is the term we typed when we assigned a value to the variable. When we use a* `print` *statement with* `program` *it gives the value of the variable, i.e., the value after removing quotes.*

3.11 STRING OPERATIONS

The contiguous set of characters kept within quotation marks in Python is termed string. Either *single quotes* or *double quotes* can be used to represent strings. A string in Python can be a combination of alphabets, numerals and symbols. Mathematical operations cannot be performed on the string even if we have numeral values in it.

There are many operations which can be performed on a string such as slice operator `([]) and [:])`, concatenation operator (+) and repetition operator (*). Slicing is used to take out a subset of the string, concatenation is used to combine two or more than two strings and repetition is used when we want to repeat same string several times.

Let us look at an example of how a string is declared in Python.

```
>>>test="Test string"
```

As mentioned earler, a string supports various types of operations:

3.11.1 Concatenation

The concatenation operation is done with the + operator in Python. Concatenation means joining the strings by linking the last end of the first string with the first end of the second string and so on. Two separate strings transform into one single string after concatenation.

Let us look at an example of concatenation:

```
>>>test="Test string"
>>> "Hello" + test
'HelloTest string'       # Output
>>>
```

3.11.2 Repetition

The repetition operation is performed on the strings in order to repeat the string several times. It is done with * operator.

Let us look at an example of repetition:

```
>>> 'Spam'*3
SpamSpamSpam        # Output
>>>
```

3.11.3 Get Particular Character

To access a single item of the string square brackets[] are used. To access the third element of the string, the string name is typed followed by the [2]. Remember, the index of the string starts with 0 and not 1.

```
>>>test="Test string"
>>>test[3]
't'          # Output
>>>
```

3.11.4 Slicing

In Python, you can extract a substring by using a colon inside the square bracket [:]. The resultant substring is a part of the long string.

```
>>>test="Test string"
>>>test[1:7]# substring between index 1 to 7 (excludes 7)
'est st'          # Output
>>>test[:3]          # substring from index 0 to 3(excludes 3)
'Tes'             # Output
>>>test[2:]          # substring from index 2 to last
'st string'       # Output
>>>
```

Python also provides various in-built commands or methods for string operation (Table 3.10). These methods are used to convert the lower case letter to upper case, to determine the length of string, etc.

Table 3.10 List of in-built commands

Method	Description
`.lower()`	Convert all upper case letters into lower case.
`.upper()`	Convert all lower case letters into upper case.
`.isalpha()`	Return true if string contain only alphabetical characters.
`.isdigit()`	Return true if string contain only digits characters.
`.isspace()`	Return true if string contain space.
`.find("string")`	Return the first index of search string.
`.replace(" old","new")`	Replace the string with other string.
`.count("character")`	Return the occurrence of particular character in string.
`len("string")`	Return the length of string.

Example

```
>>> s = "Hello Python"                #Defining a string
>>> print s.lower()
hello python                          #Converts the string in lower case
>>> print s.upper()
HELLO PYTHON                          #Converts the string in upper case
>>> print s.find("l")
2                                     #returns the index of first 'l'
>>> print s.replace("l","p")
Heppo Python                          #Replace each "l" to "p"
>>> print s.count("o")
2                                     #count the number of "o"
>>> print len(s)
12                                    #Length of the string


>>> s = "Hello"
>>> print s.isalpha()
True                                  #String contains only alphabets
>>> print s.isdigit()
False                                 #String doesn't contain digits
```

Check Your Understanding

1. What is slicing?

Ans. In Python, you can extract a substring by using a colon inside the square bracket [:]. The resultant substring is a part of the long string.

2. What are statement and expression in Python?

Ans. A statement is the instruction that can be interpreted by the Python interpreter. An expression is a combination of variables, operators, values and reserve keyword.

3.12 BOOLEAN EXPRESSIONS

A Boolean expression may have only one of two values: `TRUE` or `FALSE`.

The simplest Boolean expressions in Python are True and False. The following example uses the operator ==, which compares two operands and prints true if they are equal otherwise print false:

```
>>> 5 == 5
True        # Output
>>> 5 == 6
False               # Output
>>> True
True        # Output
>>> False
False               # Output
```

> ***Note*** *We can see in the following example that bool is the name of the class representing Python's Boolean expressions.*

```
>>>type(True)
<type 'bool'>

>>>type(False)
<type 'bool'>
```

3.13 CONTROL STATEMENTS

3.13.1 The `for` Loop

The Python `for` loop is an iterator-based `for` loop. It goes through the elements in any ordered sequence list, i.e., string, lists, tuples, the keys of dictionary and other iterables. In each iteration step, a loop variable is set to a value. The `for` loop in Python is a bit different from the `for` loop in any other programming language you have gone through.

Syntax

```
>>>for x in y :
      Block 1
   else:                        # Optional
      Block 2                   # excuted only when the loop exits normally
```

In the above section, we have seen the syntax of `for` loop. The `for` loop is used to iterate over a sequence. Here, `x` is used to iterate over `y` and when the loop exits normally then the `else` part of the `for` loop executes otherwise not.

Example

```
>>>for letter in 'Python' :
     print 'Current Letter :', letter
Output:
  Current Letter : P
  Current Letter : y
  Current Letter : t
  Current Letter : h
  Current Letter : o
  Current Letter : n
```

Example

```
>>> subjects = ["Maths", "English", "Physics", "Chemistry", "Computer"]
>>> for x in subjects:
     print(x)
```

```
Maths                         #Output
English
Physics
Chemistry
Computer
```

Example

```
>>> for x in range(7):
    print(x)
else:
    print('Else Part')


0
1
2
3
4
5
6
Else Part
```

In the above example, we have printed the value from `0` to `6` by using the `for` loop and an else part having a `print` statement is also been used. In this case, the `for` loop is ended normally then the `else` part also executed but when the loop stops because of `break` statement then the `else` part doesn't execute.

`range()` Function

The `range()` function is a built-in function in Python that helps us to iterate over a sequence of numbers. It produces an iterator that follows arithmetic progression.

Example

```
>>> range(8)
[0, 1, 2, 3, 4, 5, 6, 7]
```

`range(8)` provides a sequence of numbers `0-7`. That is to say, `range(n)` generates a sequence of numbers that starts with `0` and ends with `(n-1)`.

`range()` function can also be passed with two arguments: `begin` and `end`.

Example

```
>>> range(3,9)
[3, 4, 5, 6, 7, 8]
```

We provided the `begin` index with `3` and the `end` index with `9`. Hence, the range function generates a sequence iterator of numbers that starts from `3` and ends at `8`.

Till now, we have seen that all the numbers in the sequence have a difference of `1`. We can also change this difference if we want to. For this purpose, we have to use another parameter, `step`, along with `begin` and `end`.

Example

```
>>> range(3,40, 5)
[3, 8, 13, 18, 23, 28, 33, 38]
```

This range() function gives us a sequence that starts from `3` and ends at `38`; every number in the list has a difference of `5`.

Example

```
>>> subjects = ['maths', 'physics', 'chemistry', 'computer']

>>> for index in range(len(subjects)):
    print 'Current Subject : ', subjects[index]

Current Subject :  maths                    #Output
Current Subject :  physics
Current Subject :  chemistry
Current Subject :  computer
```

In the above example, a list `subjects` is defined which has 4 elements or items in it. Now, it is required to print all the elements in list `subjects` one by one with the `for` loop and taking help of `range()` function. Now, we initialized a `for` loop in next statement which will iterate over the sequence of number given by the `range()` function. In our example, we have used `range(len(subjects))` which means `range(4)` that is because the length of the list `subjects` is 4 which is computed by the function `len`.

3.13.2 `While` Statement

The `while` statement is used when you have a piece of code and you want to repeat it '*n*' number of times or forever. With `while` loop, we have to give a conditional statement that tells the interpreter when the loop will halt.

Syntax

```
>>> while condition :
      block
    else:                  #Optional
      statement
```

Here, `condition` is a statement by which interpreter decides when to halt the loop and `block` is the piece of code that we want to repeat.

Example

Write a while statement that prints integers from zero to 5.

```
>>> count = 0
>>> while count < 6:
      print count
      count += 1

0                             # Output
1
2
3
4
5
```

`break` and `continue` Statements

The `break` and `continue` statements are often useful in a `while` loop as well as in a `for` loop. The `break` statement exits from the loop and transfers the execution from the loop to the statement that is immediately following the loop. The `continue` statement causes execution to immediately continue at the start of the loop, it skips the execution of the remaining body part of the loop.

Example

```
# Print first five even numbers.
>>> count = 2
>>> while True:
     print count
     count = count + 2
     if count >= 12:
            break          # breaks the loop

2                           # Output
4
6
8
10
```

Example

```
# Print first four even numbers.
>>> for i in range(1,10):
```

```
    if i % 2 != 0:
        continue      # if condition becomes true, it skips the print
                        part
    print i
2                           # Output
4
6
8
```

> ***Note*** *If the break statement in a* `for` *loop is executed then the* `else` *part of that for loop is skipped.*

> ***Note*** *The* `break` *and* `continue` *statements are often useful in a* `while` *statement. The* `break` *statement exits from the loop. The* `continue` *statement causes execution to immediately continue at the start of the loop.*

3.13.3 `if elif else` Statement

The `if` statement is known as the decision-making statement in programming languages. With an `if` clause, a condition is provided; if the condition is **True** then the block of statement written in the `if` clause will be executed, otherwise not.

Example

```
>>>var = 100
    if (var ==100) : print "Value of expression is 100"
```

Output:

```
Value of expression is 100
```

An `else` statement can be combined with an `if` statement. It contains the block of code that executes if the conditional expression in the `if` statement resolves to `0` or `FALSE` value. It is an optional statement. Please note there can be at the most one `else` statement following if.

Syntax

```
>>>if expression :
      statement1
      else :
      statement2
```

We can check multiple expressions for `TRUE` with the help of `elif` statement and execute a block of code written just below the `elif` statement whose condition is TRUE.

Similar to `else`, the `elif` statement is optional. However, there can be more than one `elif` statement following an `if`.

Syntax

```
>>>if expression1 :
      statement1
   elif expression2 :
        statement2
   elif expression3 :
        statement3
   else expression4 :
        statement4
```

Check Your Understanding

1. What is a `for` statement?

Ans. The `for` statement in Python differs a bit from what you may be used to in C. In C, `for` loop gives the user the ability to define both the iteration step and the halting condition, but in Python, the `for` statement iterates over the items any ordered sequence (a list or a string), in the order that they appear in the sequence.

3.13.4 Alternative Executions

The alternative execution provides two possibilities. The condition determines which possibility is executed. If the condition is TRUE, the first block is executed but if condition is FALSE, another block of code is executed.

This is the second form of the if statement. The syntax looks like:

```
>>>if x % 2 == 0 : print 'x is even'
   else
print 'x is odd'
```

The condition can be either true or false. So, only one alternative will be executed. The alternatives are called branches, because they are branches in the flow of execution.

3.13.5 Conditional Execution

In programming languages, conditional statements or conditional constructs are the statements that are generally used with some conditions. The actions performed by these conditional statements are entirely dependent on the value of the condition, on whether the value is TRUE or FALSE. The condition usually uses comparisons and arithmetic expressions with variables. These expressions are evaluated to the Boolean values True or False. The statements for the decision-making are called conditional statements or conditional expressions.

The simplest form is the `if` statement:

```
>>>if x > 0 :
   print "x is positive"
```

TIP

The Boolean expression after the `if` statement is called the condition. If the condition is true, then the intended statement is executed. If the condition is not true, the statement is not executed.

Here's an example of the syntax for an `if` statement:

```
>>>if BOOLEAN EXPRESSION:
   STATEMENTS
```

Note *The set of intended statements that follow a conditional statement or a loop statement is called block. Indentation can be done by 'tabs' or 'spaces'. Using 4 spaces for indentation of a block is standard. A statement block inside a compound statement is called the body of the statement.*
The intended statements that follow the conditional statements are called ***block****. The first unintended statement marks the end of the block. A statement block inside the compound statement is called the body of the statement.*

There are no bounds on the number of statements that can appear in the body of an `if` statement, but there has to be at least one statement. Occasionally, it is useful to have a body with no statements. In that case, you can use the pass statement, which does nothing.

```
>>>if True :      # This is always true
      pass        # so this is always executed, but it does nothing
```

3.14 ITERATION – `while` STATEMENT

A `while` loop statement in Python programming language is the command that repeats a piece of code up to several times. The number of times the piece of code is executed depends on the condition expression written with the `while` statement.

Syntax

The syntax of a while loop in Python programming language is as follows:

```
>>> while expression :
        statement(s)
      else:            # Optional
        statement    # executes only when while condition becomes false
```

Here, statement(s) may be a single statement or a block of statements. The condition may be any expression, and whenever the expression resembles a non-zero value, it will be treated as TRUE, otherwise it will be treated as FALSE. The loop iterates while the condition is TRUE.

Unlike other programming languages, `while` loop in Python makes use of an optional `else` clause which is executed when the condition of `while` statement fails.

When the condition becomes false, program control passes to the line immediately following the loop.

Flow Diagram

Figure 3.8 represents a flow diagram.

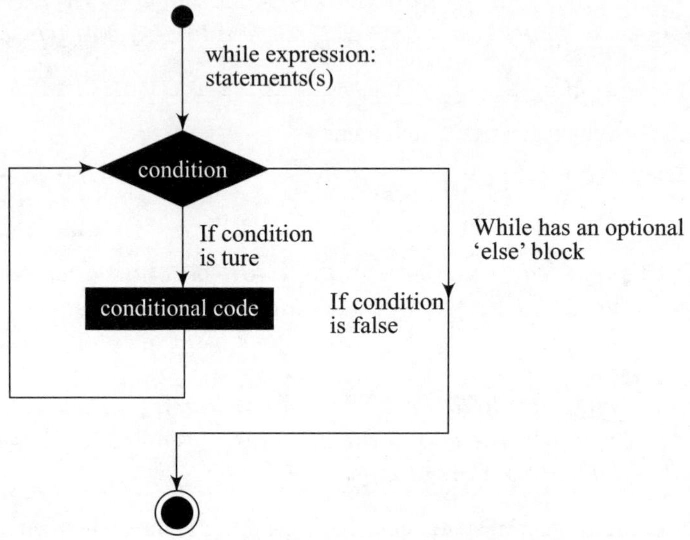

Figure 3.8 Working of a While Loop

Example

```
>>>count = 0
    while (count < 9) :
           print 'The count is :', count
           count = count + 1
```

Output:

```
The count is : 0
The count is : 1
The count is : 2
The count is : 3
The count is : 4
The count is : 5
The count is : 6
The count is : 7
The count is : 8
```

The block here, consisting of the print and increment statements, is executed repeatedly until count is no longer less than 9. With each iteration, the current value of the index count is displayed and then increased by 1.

> ***Note*** *If there is a* `continue` *statement inside a* `while` *loop or a* `for` *loop then also the* `else` *part of that loop is executed.*

3.15 INPUT FROM KEYBOARD

In a programming language, the input from keyboard by user plays the most important role in executing a program. There is hardly any program which executes without some input. The input in many programs is prompted by the user and the user uses the keyboard in order to provide input for the program to execute.

Python programming language also provides the facility to user to provide input from keyboard. That is done by two ways in Python.

3.15.1 `input()` Function

The first function for prompting the input from user in Python is through `input()` function. `input()` function has an optional parameter, which is the prompt string. When the `input()` function is called, in order to take input from the user then the execution of program halts and waits for the user to provide an input. The input is given by the user through keyboard and it is ended by the return key.

`input()` function interprets the input provided by the user, i.e. if user provides an integer value as input then the input function will return this integer value. On the other hand, if the user has input a String, then the function will return a string.

Example

```
>>> name = input("What is your Name?")
>>> print ("Hello " + name + "!")

What is your Name? 'John'                          #Output
Hello John!

>>> age = input("Enter your age? ")
>>> print age

Enter your age? 32                                 #Output
32

>>> hobbies = input("What are your hobbies? ")
>>> print hobby

What are your hobbies? ['playing', 'travelling']  #Output
['playing', 'travelling']

>>> type(name)
<type 'str'>

>>> type(age)
```

```
<type 'int'>

>>> type(hobbies)
<type 'list'>
```

3.15.2 raw_input() Function

`raw_input()` is somewhat different from the `input()` function provided by Python programming language. `raw_input()` also takes the input from the user but it does not interpret the input and also it returns the input of the user without doing any changes, i.e. raw. Afterwards, we can change this raw input into any data type which is needed for our program. In order to take input from the user in desired data type, we can use the casting function with `raw_input()`.

This is the reason, why `raw_input()` is most preferred over the `input()` function.

Example

```
# No casting
>>> age = raw_input("What is Your Age? ")
What is Your Age? 46
>>> type(age)
<type 'str'>                        #Input is stored as string

#Using casting function to convert input to integer
>>> age = int(raw_input("What is your age? "))
What is your age? 46
>>> type(age)
<type 'int'>                        #Input is stored as integer
```

Check Your Understanding

1. What is Alternative Execution?

Ans. The alternative execution provides two possibilities and the condition determines which one is to be executed. This is the second form of the `if` statement.

2. What is the syntax for `ifelse` and `elif` statements?

Ans.

```
>>> if expression1 :
    statement(s)
         elif expression2 :
              statement(s)
         elif expression3 :
              statement(s)
         else expression4 :
              statement(s)
```

ALWAYS REMEMBER

- Python is a high-level general-purpose programming language. The code written in Python is automatically compiled to byte code and executed.
- The `print` statement is used to display the output screen.
- In Python, the Hash character (#) is used for commenting. Codes or texts that come after the hash character are not considered as a part of the program.
- In Python, an identifier (name) must begin with a letter or underscore and can include any number of letters, digits, or underscore.
- Writing the name of a variable is called *declaring a variable* whereas assigning a value to a variable is called *initialising a variable*.
- Python supports six data types which are as follows:
    1. Numeric
    2. String
    3. List
    4. Tuple
    5. Dictionary
    6. Boolean
- The main differences between lists and tuples are that lists are enclosed in brackets ([]) and their elements and size can be changed, while tuples are enclosed in parentheses(()) and cannot be updated. Tuples can be thought of as read-only lists.
- The items cannot be modified in tuple, but can be modified in the list.
- A Python dictionary works on the basis of key-value pairs. Key used in dictionary can be an integer value or a string value.
- On the basis of functionality, operators in Python are categorised into following seven types:
    1. Arithmetic operator
    2. Comparison operator
    3. Assignment operator
    4. Logical operator
    5. Bitwise operator
    6. Membership operator
    7. Identity operator
- A statement is a unit of code that the Python interpreter can execute.
- An expression is a combination of variables, operators, values and reserve keyword.
- A string is a combination of characters (alphabets, digits and symbols). A string value is always enclosed within double or single quotes.
- The concatenation operation is done with the + operator. Concatenation means joining the strings together by linking them end to end.
- The repetition operation is performed on the strings in order to repeat the string several times.
- In Python, you can extract substring by using the colon inside the square bracket [:]. The resultant substring is a part of the long string.

- In Python, `for` statement iterates over the items in a sequence (a list or a string) in the order in which they appear in the sequence.
- Syntax for `while` statement in Python is:

```
>>> while condition :
        Block
```

KEY TERMS

✓ **COMMENT:** The part of the program not executed by the interpreter. It is used by other persons to understand the program thoroughly.

✓ **CONCATENATION:** The process of joining strings end-to-end.

✓ **DICTIONARY:** A mapping of keys to their corresponding values.

✓ **FLOATING POINT:** A type of numeral that has a fractional part.

✓ **HIGH-LEVEL LANGUAGE:** A programming language such as Python that is designed to be easy for humans to read and write.

✓ **INDEX:** An integer value that represents an element in a sequence.

✓ **INTEGER:** A type of numeral that represents whole numbers including negative numbers.

✓ **INTERACTIVE MODE:** A way of using Python language where we type command and expressions.

✓ **INTERPRET:** To execute a program in a high-level language by executing it one line at a time.

✓ **ITEM:** An element or a value in a series.

✓ **ITERATION:** The repetition of a set of statements or a piece of code.

✓ **KEYWORD:** A word that is reserved in a programming language for a specific purpose. We cannot use keywords such as if and else as variable names.

✓ **OPERAND:** The value on which an operator operates.

✓ **SLICE:** A subset or a part of a string.

REVIEW EXERCISES

PROGRAMS

1. Write a Program to find the square root of a number.

Solution.

```
>>> x = int(input('Enter an integer number: '))
>>> sqrt_x = x ** 0.5
>>> print (sqrt_x)

Enter an integer number: 64
8.0                                        #Output
```

2. Write a program to find the area of a Rectangle.

Solution.

```
>>> l = float(input('Enter the length of the Rectangle: '))
>>> b = float(input('Enter the breadth of the Rectangle: '))
>>> area = l * b
>>> print (area)

Enter the length of the Rectangle: 14
Enter the breadth of the Rectangle: 7
98.0                                              #Output
```

3. Write a program to swap the values of two variables.

Solution.

```
>>> num1 = input('Enter the value of num1: ')
>>> num2 = input('Enter the value of num2: ')
>>> temp = num1
>>> num1 = num2
>>> num2 = temp
>>> print "num1 = ", num1
>>> print "num2 = ", num2

Enter the value of num1: 4
Enter the value of num2: 7
num1 =  7                                   #Output
num2 =  4
```

4. Write a program to convert kilogram into pound.

Solution.

```
>>> kg = float(input('Enter the value in kilogram: '))
>>> kg_to_pound = 2.20462
>>> pound = kg * kg_to_pound
>>> print "%0.3f kg = %0.3f pounds" %(kg,pound)
Enter the value in kilogram: 60
60.000 kg = 132.277 pounds                         #Output
```

5. Write a program to find whether a number is even or odd.

Solution.

```
>>> number = int(input("Enter an integer number: "))
>>> if (number % 2) == 0:
     print "Number is even"
else:
     print "Number is odd"

Enter an integer number: 6
Number is even                                 #Output
```

6. Write a program to check the largest among the given three numbers.

Solution.

```
>>> x = int(input("Enter the first number: "))
Enter the first number: 14
>>> y = int(input("Enter the second number: "))
```

```
Enter the second number: 21
>>> z = int(input("Enter the third number: "))
Enter the third number: 10

>>> if (x > y) and (x > z):
    l = x
elif (y > x) and (y > z):
    l = y
else:
    l = z

>>> print "The largest among the three is ",l
The largest among the three is 21                    #Output
```

7. Write a Python program to check if the input year is a leap year or not.

Solution.

```
# Python program to check if the input year is a leap year or not

>>> year = int(input("Enter year: "))
>>> if(year % 4)==0:
    if(year%100)==0:
          if(year%400)==0:
                print (year, ' is  leap year')
          else:
                print (year, ' is not leap year')
    else:
          print (year, ' is  leap year')
else:
    print (year, ' is  leap year')
```

```
Output:
Enter a year: 2016
2016 is leap year

Output:
Enter a year: 1985
1985 not leap year
```

8. Write a Python program to display the Fibonacci sequence for n terms.

Solution.

```
# Program to display the Fibonacci sequence for n terms here n is provided by
the user

# take input from the user
>>> numbers = int(input("Enter the value for x (where x>2) ? "))

# first two terms
>>> x1 = 0
>>> x2 = 1
>>> count = 2
```

```
# check if the number of terms is valid
>>> if numbers <= 0:
   print("Please enter positive integer")
elif numbers == 1:
   print("Fibonacci sequence is: ")
   print(x1)
else:
   print("Fibonacci sequence is: ")
   print(x1,",",x2)
   while count < numbers:
       xth = x1 + x2
       print(xth)
       # update values
       x1 = x2
       x2 = xth
       count += 1
```

Output:

```
Enter the value for n (where n>2)?  10
Fibonacci sequence:
0, 1, 1, 2, 3, 5, 8, 13, 21, 34,
```

9. Write a program to demonstrate While loop with else.

Solution.

```
# Python program to demonstrate
# the while loop and
# else statement

>>> count = 0
>>> while count < 3:
         print("Inside the while loop")
         print (count)
         counter = count + 1
    else:
         print("Inside the else statement")
```

Output:

```
Inside the while loop
0
Inside the while loop
1
Inside the while loop
2
Inside the else
```

10. Write a Python program to print the prime numbers for a user provided range.

Solution.

```
# Python program to print the prime numbers for a user provided range
# input range is provided from the user
>>> low = int(input("Enter Lower range: "))
```

```
>>> up = int(input("Enter upper range: "))
>>> for n in range(low, up+1):
    if n > 1:
            for i in range(2, n):
                    if(n % i) == 0:
                            break
                    else:
                            print(n)
```

Output:

```
Enter lower range: 100
Enter upper range: 173
103
107
109
113
127
131
137
139
149
151
157
163
167
173
```

Multiple Choice Questions

1. Which of the following is not a data type?
   - **a.** String
   - **b.** Numeric
   - **c.** Array
   - **d.** Tuples
2. Which character is used for commenting in Python?
   - **a.** #
   - **b.** !
   - **c.** @
   - **d.** *
3. What is the output of ['name!'] * 2?
   - **a.** ['name!'] * 2
   - **b.** ['name'!, 'name'!]
   - **c.** ['name!', 'name!']
   - **d.** ['name'!] * 2
4. Which is not a reserved keyword in Python?
   - **a.** Insert
   - **b.** Pass
   - **c.** Class
   - **d.** Lambda
5. What is the output of >>> 4+?
   - **a.** 4+
   - **b.** 4
   - **c.** 5
   - **d.** Invalid syntax
6. What will be the output of `str[0:4]` if `str="Hello"`?
   - **a.** 'Hello'
   - **b.** 'H'
   - **c.** 'Hel'
   - **d.** 'Hell'
7. Which of the following is the floor division operator?
   - **a.** /
   - **b.** %
   - **c.** //
   - **d.** \\

8. Which of the following is used to find the first index of search string?
   a. .find("string")
   b. .search("string")
   c. ("string").find
   d. ("string").search
9. Which of the following is used to access single character of string?
   a. [:]
   b. ()
   c. [.]
   d. []
10. What is the order of precedence in Python?
    i. Addition
    ii. Multiplication
    iii. Division
    iv. Subtraction
    v. Exponential
    vi. Parenthesis

    a. ii, i, iii, iv, vi, v
    b. vi, v, iii, ii, i, iv
    c. vi, v, ii, i, iii, iv
    d. ii, vi, iii, i, iv, v
11. Which of the following will be printed?

```
x =4.5
y =2
print x//y
```

    a. 2.0
    b. 2.25
    c. .25
    d. 0.5
12. What gets printed?

```
Nums=set([1,1,2,3,3,3,4])
Print len(nums)
```

    a. 2
    b. 4
    c. 5
    d. 7

Short Questions

1. What is Python? What is Python good for?
2. How can we distinguish between tuples and lists?
3. How can a string be converted to a number?
4. What are comments in Python?
5. What will be the output of the given code?

```
list = ['p', 'r', 's', 't',]
print list[8:]
```

6. Briefly describe the data types in Python.
7. What will be the output of the code `str + "Python" if str = 'Programming!'`?
8. What will be the output of the code `test*5` if `test = (000, 'computer')`?
9. Describe operators in Python.
10. How will you create a dictionary in Python?
11. How will you convert a string to an integer in Python?
12. What are the uses of //, **, *= operators in Python?

Answers to Multiple Choice Questions

1. c **2.** a **3.** c **4.** a **5.** d **6.** a **7.** c **8.** a **9.** d **10.** b
11. a **12.** b

4 FUNCTIONS

4.1 INTRODUCTION

Functions are self-contained programs that perform some particular tasks. Once a function is created by the programmer for a specific task, this function can be called anytime to perform that task.

Suppose, we want to perform a task several times, in such a scenario, rather than writing code for that particular task repeatedly, we create a function for that task and call it when we want to perform the task. Each function is given a name, using which we call it. A function may or may not return a value.

There are many *built-in functions* provided by Python such as `dir()`, `len()`, `abs()`, etc. Users can also build their own functions, which are called *user-defined functions*.

There are many advantages of using functions:

a) They reduce duplication of code in a program.
b) They break the large complex problems into small parts.
c) They help in improving the clarity of code (i.e., make the code easy to understand).
d) A piece of code can be reused as many times as we want with the help of functions.

4.2 BUILT-IN FUNCTIONS

Built-in functions are the functions already defined in the Python programming language; we can directly call them to perform a specific task. Every built-in function in Python performs some particular task. For example, the Math module has some mathematical built-in functions that perform tasks related to mathematics.

In this section, we will see some built-in functions provided in the Python programming language.

4.2.1 Type Conversion

There are some built-in functions in the Python programming language that can convert one type of data into another type. For example, the `int` function can take any number value and convert it into an integer.

Example

```
>>>int(5.5)
5           # Output
>>>int('Python')
Traceback (most recent call last):                # Output
  File "<pyshell#21>", line 1, in <module>
int('Python')
ValueError: invalid literal for int() with base 10: 'Python'
>>>int('5')
5           # Output
```

In the above examples, you can see that in the first case, we took a floating-point number 5.5 that was converted to an integer number 5 by the `int` function. In the second case, we took a string that was not a number and applied `int` function to it, but got an error. This means that a string that is not a number cannot be converted to an integer. However, in the third case, we took a number in string form and converted it to an integer 5 using `int` function.

Similarly, we have a function `float`, which can convert integers and string into floating-point numbers.

Example

```
>>>float(45)
    45.0          # Output
>>> float ('5')
    5.0           # Output
```

Finally, Python has a `str` function that converts the types into strings.

Example

```
>>>str(67)
    '67'          # Output
>>>print('Python version' + 2.7)
TypeError: cannot concatenate 'str' and 'float' objects # Output
>>>print('Python version' + str(2.7))
    Python version2.7         # Output
```

In the example given above, you can see that when we try to concatenate a string and a float object, the interpreter gives an error saying, "`cannot concatenate 'str' and 'float' objects`." Hence, we convert the float object, i.e., 2.7 to a string using the `str` function and then successfully concatenate it with another string.

4.2.2 Type Coercion

Type conversion discussed above is known as explicit conversion.

There is also another kind of type conversion in the Python language, known as implicit conversion. Implicit conversion is also known as type coercion and is automatically done by the interpreter.

Type coercion is a process through which the Python interpreter automatically converts a value of one type into a value of another type according to the requirement.

Example

Suppose we want to calculate an elapsed fraction of an hour. The expression `minutes/60` does integer arithmetic and gives result, even 59 minutes past hour.

One solution is that we convert the `minutes` to a floating-point number using type conversion and do floating-point division:

```
>>>minute=59
>>>float(minute)/60
0.98333333333                # Output
```

Alternatively, we can take advantage of type coercion process in Python. For the mathematical operators, if either operand is a float, the other is automatically converted to float:

```
>>>minute=59
>>>minute/60.0
0.98333333333                # Output
```

Hence, in the example given above, we make the denominator a float number. The Python interpreter automatically converts the numerator into float and does the calculation.

Check Your Understanding

1. What is a function?

Ans. Functions are self-contained programs that perform some particular tasks. Once a function is created by the programmer, this function can be called anytime to perform the specific task.

2. What is Type conversion?

Ans. These are some built-in functions in the Python programming language that can convert one type of data into another type. For example, the `int` function can take any number value and convert it into an integer.

3. Give the syntax required to convert an integer number into string and a float to an integer.

Ans.
```
#integer to string
>>>str(5)
   '5'        # Output
# float to integer
>>>float(5.50)
   5          # Output
```

Note that when a float number is converted to integer, the tractional part is truncated.

4.2.3 Mathematical Functions

In mathematics, we have functions such as `sin` and `log` and we have to evaluate some expressions like `sin(pi/4)` and `log(1/x)`. We follow a process to solve this type of expressions; first, we solve the innermost part of the parenthesis, and then move on to the outer functions.

Python provides us a *Math module* that contains most of the familiar and important mathematical functions. A *module* is a file that contains some predefined Python codes. A module can define functions, classes and variables. It is a collection of related functions grouped together.

Before using a module in Python, we have to import it.

For example, to import the math module, we use:

```
>>> import math
```

This statement creates an object of module named math. Now, if we try to print this object, the interpreter will give some information about it:

```
>>>print math
<module 'math' (built-in)>
```

There are many predefined functions and variables that reside under the module object. To access these functions, we have to write the name of the module followed by a dot (`.`) (this dot is also known as a period) followed by the function name.

Example

```
>>>decibel = 10 * math.log10(18.0)
>>>angle = 2.5
>>>height = math.sin(angle)
```

In the given example, we use two math module functions, `log` and `sin`. In the first statement, the variable `decibel` is set to the `log` of `18 base 10`. If you want to perform `log 18.0` with base `e`, then simply write `log(18.0)`.

The third statement calculates the `sine` of the variable `angle`. `Sin` and other trigonometric functions (i.e., `cos, tan, cosec`, etc.) take the value of angles in radians as arguments. In order to convert degrees to radians, we divide the value in degree by `360` and multiply by `2*pi`.

Example

Find the `cos` of `45`degrees.

```
>>>degree = 45
>>>angle = degree * 2 * math.pi/360.0
>>>math.cos(angle)
0.7071067811865476              # Output
```

In the given example, we use a `math.pi` function in order to get the variable `pi` from the `math` module. The value of this variable is an approximation of π up to 15 digits.

4.2.4 Date and Time

Python provides the built-in modules `time` and `calendar` through which we can handle date and time in several ways. For example, we can use these modules to get the current time and date. In order to use the time module, we need to import it into our program first. Similarly, for working with dates, we have to import the calendar module first.

Examples

Getting current date and time:

```
>>> import time;
>>>
>>> localtime = time.localtime(time.time())
>>> print "Local current time : ", localtime
#Output
Local current time :  time.struct_time(tm_year=2016, tm_mon=5, tm_mday=31,
tm_hour=19, tm_min=21, tm_sec=50, tm_wday=1, tm_yday=152, tm_isdst=0)
```

This example gives us the current time and date. This function returns a time-tuple with nine items. If we want, we can change the format in which the time and date is given.

Getting formatted date and time:
Though we can format time and date according to our interest, the most common method used to get time in readable format is `asctime()`.

```
>>> import time;
>>>
>>> localtime = time.asctime(time.localtime(time.time()))
>>> print "Local current time : ", localtime

Local current time :  Tue May 31 19:28:05 2016    #Output
```

Here, we make use of the `asctime()` function to get a readable format of date and time.

Getting calendar for a month:
Python provides us a calendar module through which we can use yearly and monthly calendars according to our requirement. In the example below, we print a calendar for the month of October, 2015.

```
>>> import calendar

>>> c = calendar.month(2015,10)
>>> print "Calender for October, 2015: \n", c

Calender for October, 2015:              #Output
    October 2015
Mo Tu We Th Fr Sa Su
          1  2  3  4
 5  6  7  8  9 10 11
12 13 14 15 16 17 18
19 20 21 22 23 24 25
26 27 28 29 30 31
```

In the examples discussed above, `localtime()`, `asctime()` and `month()` are built-in functions contained in the modules `time` and `calendar`.

4.2.5 `dir()` Function

`dir()` takes an object as an argument. It returns a list of strings which are names of members of that object. If object is a module, it will list sub-modules, functions provided by, variables, constants, etc. It's a good tool to learn and understand about a module or an object.

Example

```
>>> import math
>>> list = dir(math)
>>> print list
#Output
['__doc__', '__name__', '__package__', 'acos', 'acosh', 'asin', 'asinh',
'atan', 'atan2', 'atanh', 'ceil', 'copysign', 'cos', 'cosh', 'degrees',
'e', 'erf', 'erfc', 'exp', 'expm1', 'fabs', 'factorial', 'floor', 'fmod',
'frexp', 'fsum', 'gamma', 'hypot', 'isinf', 'isnan', 'ldexp', 'lgamma',
'log', 'log10', 'log1p', 'modf', 'pi', 'pow', 'radians', 'sin', 'sinh',
'sqrt', 'tan', 'tanh', 'trunc']
```

In the given example, we give the `math` module as an argument to the `dir()` function and it gives the list of all the functions, modules and variables present in the `math` module.

> **Note** *The module that is passed in the `dir()` function must be imported first.*

4.2.6 `help()` FUNCTION

`help()` function is a built-in function in Python Programming Language which is used to invoke the help system. It takes an object as an argument. It gives all the detailed information about that object like if it's a module, then it will tell you about the sub-modules, functions, variables and constants in details.

Example

```
# import math module
>>> import math
>>> help(math.sin)    #give detailed info about sin function in math module
Help on built-in function sin in module math:

sin(...)
    sin(x)

    Return the sine of x (measured in radians).

>>> help(math.cos)    #give detailed info about cos function in math module
Help on built-in function cos in module math:

cos(...)
    cos(x)

    Return the cosine of x (measured in radians).
```

4.3 COMPOSITION OF FUNCTIONS

Composition is a concept that you might have come across in algebra pre-calculus. The syntax of composition in mathematics is as follows:

```
f(g(x)) = f o g(x),
```

where, `f` and `g` are functions. This means the return value of function `g` is passed into the function `f` as parameters/arguments.

Just as with the mathematical functions, Python functions can also be composed. We can use any kind of expression including arithmetic operators as an argument to a function.

Example

```
>>> x = math.sin(angle + math.pi/4)
```

In the given example, we have used an expression `angle + math.pi/4` as an argument to the function `math.sin`. First, the value of the innermost expression is computed, and then the resulting value is used as the argument for the function `math.sin`.

Similarly, we can also take a function as an argument to another function.

Example

```
>>> x = math.exp(math.log(10.0))
```

Here, the value of the function `math.log(10.0)` is calculated first and then used as the argument for the function `math.exp`.

Check Your Understanding

1. What are mathematical functions? How are they used in Python?

Ans. Python provides us a *math module* containing most of the familiar and important mathematical functions. A *module* is a file that contains some predefined Python codes. A module can define functions, classes and variables. It is a collection of related functions grouped together.

Before using a module in Python, we have to import it.

For example, to import the math module, we use:

```
>>> import math
```

2. Write a program to print the calendar for the month of March, 1991.

Ans.

```
>>> import calendar
>>> c = calendar.month(1991, 3)
>>> print c
     March 1991
```

```
Mo Tu We Th Fr Sa Su
             1  2  3
 4  5  6  7  8  9 10
11 12 13 14 15 16 17
18 19 20 21 22 23 24
25 26 27 28 29 30 31
```

4.4 USER DEFINED FUNCTIONS

Until now, we have seen only the built-in functions of Python, but as with many other languages, Python also allows users to define their own functions. To use their own functions in Python, users have to define the function first; this is known as *Function Definition*. In a function definition, users have to define a name for the new function and also the list of the statements that will execute when the function will be called.

The block of the function starts with a keyword *def* after which the function name is written followed by parentheses. We can also give some input parameters or arguments to a function by placing them within these parentheses. The parameters can also be defined within these parentheses. The block of statements always starts with a colon **(:)**. After writing the code statements, the block is ended with a return statement whose syntax is `return [expression]`. As we have stated earlier, a function may or may not return a value. If you want to return more than one value, separate the values using commas. The default return value is NONE.

Syntax

```
def functionname(parameters):
    "function_docstring"
    statement(s)
    return [expression]
```

In any type of programming language, a docstring is a string literal which is used to document a specific part of the code. It is used just like the comments in the programming language. It does not affect the program execution but it is considered to be a good practice to use docstrings.

Example

```
>>>def print_lines():
...   print "Hello Python!!"
...   print "Welcome to Python Programming!!"
```

The function definition is always preceded by the keyword `def`. In the given example, `print_lines` is the name of the function.

The rules for defining a function name are same as those for variable names: alphabets, numerals and some special characters are allowed. The name of the function cannot start with a number. No keyword can be used as the name of the function. Giving the same name to a variable and a function should be avoided. The parentheses after the function name contain the parameters or arguments. They are optional.

The first line in the definition of function is known as *header* and the rest is abbreviated as *body*. The header line will always end with a *colon*. All the statements meant to execute at the time of function calling are defined in the body part only. We can define any number of statements in the body of the function definition but they have to be ordered from the left margin.

When we type a function definition in interactive mode (command line), the ellipses `(...)` are automatically displayed by the interpreter in the next line to tell us that the definition is not complete yet (as shown in Fig. 4.1).

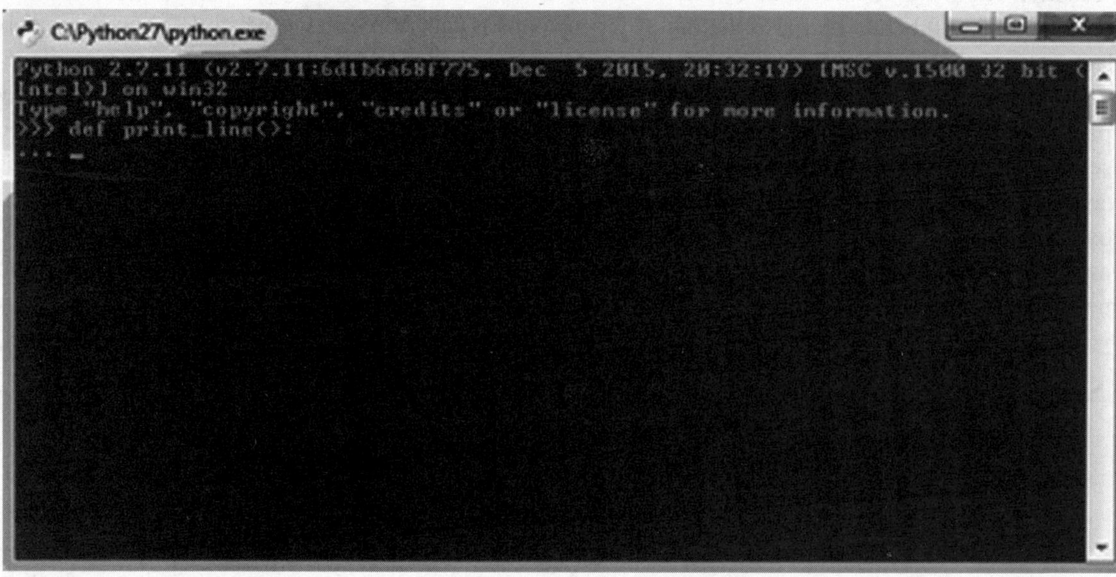

Figure 4.1

In order to end the function definition, we need to enter an empty line.

Example

```
>>>defprint_lines():
... print "Hello Python!!"
... print "Welcome to Python Programming!!"
...
```

When we define a function, Python interpreter also creates a variable with the same name.

```
>>> print print_lines
<functionprint_lines at 0x0294D970>
>>>type (print_line)
<type 'function'>
```

As you can see above, the type of `print_lines` is `'function'` and value is a function object.

In the previous sections, we have seen the calling of the built in function. The calling of the user-defined functions happens in a similar way.

```
>>> print print_lines()
Hello Python!!                                  # Output
Welcome to Python Programming!!                 # Output
```

A function can also be called by another function.

Example

```
>>>defnew_print():
    print_lines()
    print_lines()
>>>new_print()
```

Output:

```
Hello Python!!
Welcome to Python Programming!!
Hello Python!!
Welcome to Python Programming!!
```

In the given example, we created a new function `new_print()` and inside the body of this function, we called the `print_lines()` function twice. Now, when we call `new_print()`, the `print_lines()` function is executed twice. This is how we call a function within another function.

Hence, we can call a function repeatedly when we want to do so and can also call the function from another function. In the example given above, we call `print_lines()` twice inside `new_print()` in order to repeatedly call `print_lines()`.

Now, we combine the code fragments from the above section into a single program:

```
>>> def print_lines():
    print "Hello Python!!"
    print "Welcome to Python Programming!!"

>>> def new_print():
     print_lines()
     print_lines()

>>> new_print()

Hello Python!!                 # Output
Welcome to Python Programming!!
Hello Python!!
Welcome to Python Programming!!
```

As you can see, this whole program has two function definitions: `print_lines()` and `new_print()`. When a function definition is executed, a function object is created. The statements residing inside a function get executed only when the function is called. Outputs are generated only by the function calls and not by the function definitions.

4.5 PARAMETERS AND ARGUMENTS

Parameters and arguments are the values or expressions passed to the functions between parentheses. As we have seen in earlier sections, many of the built in functions need arguments to be passed with them: the `math.cos()` function takes a number, i.e., the value of the angle as an argument. Many functions require two or more arguments to be passed such as the power function in math module `math.pow()`, where we have to pass two arguments, the base and the exponent.

The value of the argument is always assigned to a variable known as parameter. At the time of function definition, we have to define some parameters if that function requires some arguments to be passed at the time of calling.

Example

```
>>>defprint_lines(line):
... print line
... print line
```

In this function we have defined a variable `line` which is a parameter. Now, when the function is called, it prints the value of the parameter `line` twice.

```
>>>print_lines('Hello')
Hello              # Output
Hello              # Output

>>>print_lines(17)
17         # Output
17         # Output

>>>print_lines(math.pi)
3.14159265359          # Output
3.14159265359          # Output
```

We can see that this function works with any type of value that can be displayed.

There can be four types of formal arguments using which a function can be called which are as follows:

1. Required arguments
2. Keyword arguments
3. Default arguments
4. Variable-length arguments

1. Required arguments When we assign the parameters to a function at the time of function definition, at the time of calling, the arguments should be passed to a function in correct positional order; furthermore, the number of arguments should match the defined number of parameters.

Example

```
>>>defprint_lines(str)
... print str
... return;
```

We have defined one parameter `str` to the function `print_lines`. Hence, at the time of calling, we have to pass exactly one argument to the function, otherwise it will produce an error.

```
# function calling here
>>>print_lines();
Traceback (most recent call last):          # Output
  File "<pyshell#18>", line 1, in <module>
print_lines()
TypeError: print_lines() takes exactly 1 argument (0 given)
```

There is an error because we did not pass any argument to the function `print_lines`, while according to the function definition, the function `print_lines` must take exactly one argument.

2. Keyword arguments In keyword arguments, the caller recognises the arguments by the parameter's names. This type of argument can also be skipped or can also be out of order.

Example 1

```
>>>defprint_lines():
... print str
... return
...

# function calling here
>>>print_lines(str = "Hello Python");
Hello Python                # Output
```

Example 2

```
# Function Definition
>>>defprint_info(name, age):
... print "Name: ", name
... print "Age: ", age
... return
...

# function calling
>>>print_info(age=15, name='john');
Name: john         # Output
Age: 15            # Output
```

3. Default arguments In default arguments, we can assign a value to a parameter at the time of function definition. This value is considered the default value to that parameter. If we do not provide a value to the parameter at the time of calling, it will not produce an error. Instead it will pick the default value and use it.

Example

```
# Function definition
>>>defprint_info(name, age=35):
... print "Name: ",name
... print "Age: ", age
... return
...

# function calling
>>>print_info(age=20, name='john');
Name: john              # Output
Age: 20             # Output
>>>
>>>print_info(name='john');
Name: john             # Output
Age: 35             # Output
```

In the given example, we have given a value `35` to the parameter `age`. It is the default value for `age`. Now, in the first function call, we provide the value of `age` as `20`. Hence, the Python interpreter takes the value provided by us and does not use the default value.

However, in the second function call, we do not provide the value for age. Hence, the Python interpreter does not produce any error. Rather it picks the default value from the function definition and displays it. This is how default arguments are used in function calling.

4. Variable-length arguments There are many cases where we are required to process a function with more number of arguments than we specified in the function definition. These types of arguments are known as variable-length arguments. The names for these arguments are not specified in the function definition. Instead we use an asterisk (`*`) before the name of the variable which holds the value for all non-keyword variable arguments.

Syntax

```
def function_name([formal_args] *var_args_tuple):
    "function_docstring"
    function_body
    return[expression]
```

Example

```
# function definition here
>>>defprint_info(arg1,*vartuple):
... print "Result is: "
... print arg1
... for var in vartuple:
...         print var
... return

# function call
>>>print_info(10);
10          # Output
>>>print_info(90,60,40);
90          # Output
60          # Output
40          # Output
```

Check Your Understanding

1. **What are user-defined functions? Give the syntax.**

Ans. Python also allows users to define their own functions. To use their own functions in Python, users have to define the function first; this is known as *Function Definition*. In a function definition, users have to define a name for the new function and also the list of the statements that will execute when the function will be called.

Syntax

```
def functionname(parameters):
    "function_docstring"
    statement(s)
    return [expression]
```

2. **Write a function that takes exactly two arguments. One argument is the name of the student, the other argument is fees and a default fee is 25000. Display at least two outputs in support of your answer.**

Ans.

```
# Function definition
>>>defprint_info(name, fees=25000):
... print "Name: ",name
... print "fees: ", fees
... return
...

# function calling
>>>print_info(fees=20000, name='Jack');
```

```
Name: jack              # Output
Age: 20000              # Output
>>>
>>>print_info(name='john');
Name: john              # Output
Age: 25000              # Output
```

4.6 FUNCTION CALLS

We define a function by giving it a name with some parameters (optional) and then a sequence of statements. Later, we can call the function when we need it. A function is called using the name with which it was defined earlier, followed by a pair of parentheses (()). Any input parameters or arguments are to be placed within these calling parentheses.

All parameters (arguments) which are passed in functions are always passed by reference in Python. This means that if the values of the parameters are changed in the function, it will also reflect the change in the calling function.

Example 1

```
# Function definition here
>>>defprintstring(str):
..."This prints the passed string into this function"#Docstring
... print str;
... return;
# Now we can call printstring function here
>>>printstring("First String");
>>>printstring("Second String");
```

The code given above will produce the following result on execution.

Output:

```
First String
Second String
```

Example 2

Multiplication of two numbers using function.

```
>>>defmult(a,b):
... multiplication = a*b
... return multiplication
# Now calling the function here
>>> a = 4
>>> b = 3
>>> m = mult(a,b) # calling the mult function
>>>print(m)
```

The given code will produce the following result on execution.

```
12          # Output
```

Check Your Understanding

1. **Write the syntax for defining a function.**

Ans.
```
deffunctionname(parameters):
    "function_docstring"
    statement(s)
    return [expression]
```

2. **Write a function which accepts two numbers and returns their sum.**

Ans.
```
>>>def sum(arg1,arg2):
... sum = arg1 + arg2
... return sum
# Now calling the function here
>>> a = 4
>>> b = 3
>>>total = sum(a,b)  # calling the mult function
>>>print(total)
```

4.7 THE `return` STATEMENT

The return statement is used to exit a function. A function may or may not return a value. If a function returns a value, it is passed back by the return statement as argument to the caller. If it does not return a value, we simply write return with no arguments.

Syntax

```
return [expression]
```

Example

```
# function definition here
>>>def div(arg1, arg2):
... division = arg1/arg2
... return division
...

# function call here
>>> arg3 = div(20,10)
>>> print "division: ", arg3
division: 2                # Output
```

In the given example, we define a function `div` that divides one argument by another and stores the result in the variable `division`; then the value of `division` variable is returned by the function to the caller variable `arg3`.

4.8 PYTHON RECURSIVE FUNCTION

Recursion is generally understood to be the process of repeating something in a self-similar way. For example, if an object is placed between two mirrors facing each other, the object will be reflected recursively.

In the programming context, the meaning of recursion remains the same. Here, if a function, procedure or method calls itself, it is called recursive. In Python, we know that a function can call another function, but it is also possible that a function calls itself.

Let us look at an example of a recursive function by computing the factorial of a number. The factorial of any number is defined by multiplying all the integers from 1 to that number. For example, the factorial of 5 is `1*2*3*4*5 = 120.`

Example

```
>>> def fact_rec(x):
     'Recursive function to find the factorial of an integer'
... if x == 1:
...         return 1
... else:
...         return(x * fact_rec(x-1))

>>> fact_rec(4)
24                                  # Output
>>> fact_rec(10)
3628800                             # Output
```

4.9 THE ANONYMOUS FUNCTIONS

The anonymous functions are the functions created using a *lambda* keyword. They are not defined by using *def* keyword. For this reason, they are called anonymous functions.

We can pass any number of arguments to a lambda form functions, but still they return only one value in the form of expression. An anonymous function cannot directly call `print` command as the lambda needs an expression. It cannot access the parameters that are not defined in its own namespace. An anonymous function is a single line statement function.

Syntax

```
lambda [arg1[,arg2,......argn]]:expression
```

The syntax of the lambda function is a single statement.

Example

```
# function definition here
>>>mult = lambda val1, val2: val1*val2;

# function call here
>>> print "value: ", mult(20,40)
Value: 800        # Output
```

In the given example, the `lambda` function is defined with two arguments `val1` and `val2`. The expression `val1*val2` does the multiplication of the two values. Now, in function call, we can directly call the `mult` function with two valid values as arguments and produce the output as above.

Check Your Understanding

1. Define the return statement in a function. Give the syntax.

Ans. The return statement is used to exit a function. A function may or may not return a value. If a function returns a value, it is passed back by the return statement as argument to the caller. If it does not return a value, we simply write return with no arguments.

Syntax

```
return [expression]
```

2. What is an anonymous function? Give the syntax.

Ans. The anonymous functions are the functions created using a *lambda* keyword. They are not defined as all other functions are, i.e., by using *def* keyword. For this reason, they are called anonymous functions.

Syntax

```
lambda [arg1[,arg2,......argn]]:expression
```

The syntax of the `lambda` function is a single statement.

3. Write a function called `ninelines` that uses a function `threelines` to print nine blank lines. Print twenty seven new lines using this.

Ans.

```
# function definition here
>>>defthreelines():
...     print     # prints one newline
...     print
...     print
```

```
>>>defninelines():
...     threelines()        # prints three new lines
...     threelines()
...     threelines()

# function call here to print 27 lines
>>>ninelines()      # prints nine new lines
>>>ninelines()
>>>ninelines()
```

4.10 WRITING PYTHON SCRIPTS

As discussed in Chapter 3, the first and most common way to use python is to write code into a file and run the file as a script using python interpreter. Any text editor can be used to create the script file, in which any valid python statements can be written. Python script is usually saved with extension '.py'. Python code in a file is also called a module. Just placing loose python statements into text file and executing it will work, but the good structure of a python file looks like as follows:

Filename : example.py

```
#! /usr/bin/python
# Comment section.

"""
    Docstring section
"""

# import section
Import os
Import sys

# from import section
from math import sin

def main():
    " docstring for main function "
    # the code for solving the problem goes here.

# This section is the standard way to invoke the main function. It makes
the code reusable.
if __name__ == '__main__':
      main()
```

The first line starts with #! Is known as 'interpreter descriptor' or 'shebang' as short form of 'sharp bang'. It is added to have compatibility with linux or unix based systems. In unix based systems, this line identifies which interpreter to be used to execute this script. But in windows the file is identified as a python script by extension '.py'

Comment section starts with a '#' which is optional. This is where you can put details about script. You can add any number of lines which starts with '#' here.

Docstring is the section where you document your script. In this section you can write documentation for the script, such as how to use your script or any other information that users should know to use your script. It can span into multiple lines. Documentation tools picks docstrings automatically to create documentation for the module.

Import section and from import section is the right place for adding import statements for importing needed other modules or functions into this script.

`main()` is a good place to put all the high level code for solving the problem. The last section will be common in all script. It invokes the main function only if the module is executed as a script. It prevents the execution of main function when the module is imported in other scripts.

For example, a script to find the logarithm of a number may look like as follows. Let's call it logme.py

```
#! /usr/bin/python
# Program for finding out Logarithm of a given number

"""
    Program for finding Logarithm of a number.
    Usage:

    $ python logme.py
    Welcome, this script allows you to find log of a number!
    Enter a number: 100
    Log of 100 is 2.0
    Thank you!

"""

from math import log10

def main():
    "reads a number from user and finds log of it"

    print "Welcome, this script allows you to find log of  a number!"

    try:
        number = int(raw_input("Enter a number: "))
    except ValueError:
        print "Error: given input is not valid, please enter a number."
        return

    result = log10(number)
    print "Log of {num} is {res}".format(num=number, res=result)
```

```
    print "Thank you!"

if __name__ == '__main__':
    main()

#The End!



To execute the file,

For windows:
1.   Open cmd
2.   Change directory to python folder. (Usually with in C drive)
     C:\> cd C:\Python27\
3.   Run python script example.py
      C:\Python27\> python path\to\logme.py

For linux or unix:
1.   Open terminal
2.   Run python script example.py
       $ python path/to/logme.py
```

ALWAYS REMEMBER

- Functions are self-contained programs that perform some particular tasks.
- There are many *built-in functions* provided by Python such as `dir()`, `len()`, `abs()`, etc., and users can also make their own functions which are known as *user-defined functions.*
- The block of the function starts with a keyword *def* after which we write our function name followed by parentheses.

Syntax

```
deffunctionname(parameters):
    "function_docstring"
    statement(s)
    return [expression]
```

- A function is called using the name with which it was defined earlier, followed by a pair of parentheses (()).

- Type coercion is a process through which Python interpreter automatically converts a value of one type into a value of another type according to the requirement.
- Python provides a *Math module* that contains most of the familiar and important mathematical functions.
- A *module* is a file that contains some predefined Python codes. A module can define functions, classes and variables. It is a collection of related functions grouped together.
- For importing the math module, we use:

```
>>> import math
```

- To use their own functions in Python, users have to define the functions first; this is known as *Function Definition*.
- The anonymous functions are the functions that are created using a *lambda* keyword. They are not defined as other functions are, i.e., by using *def* keyword.
- Parameters and arguments are the values or expressions that are passed to the functions between the parentheses.
- There are four types of formal arguments using which a function can be called.
  - Required arguments
  - Keyword arguments
  - Default arguments
  - Variable-length arguments
- In keyword arguments, the caller recognises the arguments by the parameter's names. This type of argument can also be skipped or can also be out of order.
- In default arguments, we can assign a value to a parameter at the time of function definition that will be considered the default value to that parameter.

KEY TERMS

✓ **FUNCTION:** Functions are self-contained programs that perform some particular tasks.

✓ **FUNCTION OBJECT:** A value created by the definition of a function. A variable which is the name of the function refers to the function object.

✓ **HEADER:** The very first line of the function definition.

✓ **BODY:** The block of statements inside the function definition.

✓ **PARAMETER:** The variables used to pass some values to a function, defined between parentheses.

✓ **FUNCTION CALL:** It is a statement which executes the function.

✓ **ARGUMENT:** It is a value which is provided at the time of function calling. It is specified within parentheses.

✓ **RETURN VALUE:** The value returned by the function as output to the caller.

✓ **MODULE:** A file that contains a collection of related functions and definitions.

✓ **IMPORT STATEMENT:** It is a type of statement used to import various modules in Python.

REVIEW EXERCISES

PROGRAMS

1. Write a function to find the HCF of some given numbers.

Solution.

```
>>> def hcf(a, b):
        if a > b:
                small = b
        else:
                small = a
        for i in range (1, small + 1):
                if((a % i == 0) and (b % i == 0)):
                        hcf = i
        return hcf
>>> hcf(20,40)
20                                      #Output
>>> hcf(529,456)
1                                       #Output
```

2. Write a function to display the factors of a given number.

Solution.

```
>>> def factors(a):
        for i in range (1, a + 1):
                if a % i == 0:
                        print(i)

>>> factors(70)
1                               #Output
2
5
7
10
14
35
70
```

3. Write a function to find the ASCII value of the character.

Solution.

```
>>> def ascii_val_of(a):
        print ("The ASCII value of '" + a + "' is", ord(a))

>>> ascii_val_of('A')
("The ASCII value of 'A' is", 65)       #Output
>>> ascii_val_of(' ')               #Finding Ascii value of space
("The ASCII value of ' ' is", 32)       #Output
```

4. Write a function to convert a decimal number to its binary, octal and hexadecimal equivalents.

Solution.

```
>>> def bin_oct_hex(a):
     print(bin(a), "binary equivalent")
     print(oct(a), "octal equivalent")
     print(hex(a), "hexadecimal equivalent")

>>> bin_oct_hex(10)             #Finding binary, octal, hex value of 10
('0b1010', 'binary equivalent')                  #Output
('012', 'octal equivalent')
('0xa', 'hexadecimal equivalent')
```

5. Write a function to display Fibonacci sequence using recursion.

Solution.

```
>>> def fib_rec(x):
     if x <= 1:
            return x
     else:
            return(fib_rec(x-1) + fib_rec(x-2))

# Take input for number of terms from user
>>> num_terms = int(input("How many terms? "))
>>> for i in range(num_terms):
     print(fib_rec(i))

How many terms? 12              #Fibonacci Sequence up to 12 terms
0                               #Output
1
1
2
3
5
8
13
21
34
55
89
```

6. Write a function to find the sum of several natural numbers using recursion.

Solution.

```
>>> def sum_rec(n):
     if n <= 1:
            return n
     else:
            return n + sum_rec(n-1)

>>> sum_rec(3)             #Sum of first 3 natural numbers
6                          #Output
>>> sum_rec(25)   #Sum of first 25 natural numbers
325                        #Output
```

7. A Python Program that demonstrates the built-in functions

Solution.

```
# Python program to demonstrate built in functions
#We consider this variable to be the controller of the loop.
# value 1 denotes the loop.
# other than 1 means do not loop.
lp = 1
#the choice variable is used to read the menu choices:
ch = 0
while lp == 1:
    #print what options you have
    print "Welcome to Chap4.py"
    print "your options are:"
    print " "
    print "1) Demonstrate conversion"
    print "2) Integer to float conversion"
    print "3) Mathematical Functions "
    print "4) Date and time"
    print "5) Quit Chap4.py"
    print " "
    ch = input("Enter the option (1-5): ")
    if ch == 1:
        # Read the decimal number from the user
       decnum = int(input("Enter the value of an integer: "))
       print "The decimal value of",decnum,"is:"
       print bin(decnum),"in binarynumber."
       print oct(decnum),"in octalnumber."
       print hex(decnum),"in hexadecimalnumber."
    elif ch == 2:
        decnum2 = int(input("Enter the value of an integer: "))
        fltnum2 = float(decnum2)
        print "float value is", fltnum2
    elif ch == 3:
        import math
        num3 = float(input("enter n in float:"))
        print "Floor value is:",math.floor(num3)
        print "Round value is :",round(num3)
        print "Ceil value is :",math.ceil(num3)
        decnum3 = int(input("Enter the value of an integer: "))
        print "Absolute value is",abs(decnum3)
        print "Square root is",math.sqrt(decnum3)
    elif ch == 4:
        import datetime
        today = datetime.date.today()
        print today
        print 'ctime:', today.ctime()
        print 'tuple:', today.timetuple()
        print 'ordinal:', today.toordinal()
        print 'Year:', today.year
```

```
        print 'Mon :', today.month
        print 'Day :', today.day
    elif ch == 5:
        lp = 0
    print "Thankyou for using Chap4.py!"
```

Output:

```
Welcome to Chap4.py
your options are:

1) Demonstrate conversion
2) Integer to float conversion
3) Mathematical Functions
4) Date and time
5) Quit Chap4.py

Enter the option (1-5): 1
'0b10000', 'in binarynumber.'
'020', 'in octalnumber.'
'0x10', 'in hexadecimalnumber.'
Welcome to Chap4.py
your options are:

1) Demonstrate conversion
2) Integer to float conversion
3) Mathematical Functions
4) Date and time
5) Quit Chap4.py

Enter the option (1-5): 2
Enter the option (1-5): 2
Enter the value of an integer: 15
float value is 15.0
Welcome to Chap4.py
your options are:

1) Demonstrate conversion
2) Integer to float conversion
3) Mathematical Functions
4) Date and time
5) Quit Chap4.py

Enter the option (1-5): 3
enter n in float:115.369369
Floor value is: 115.0
Round value is : 115.0
Ceil value is : 116.0
Enter the value of an integer: 15
Absolute value is 15
Square root is 3.87298334621
```

```
Welcome to Chap4.py
your options are:

1) Demonstrate conversion
2) Integer to float conversion
3) Mathematical Functions
4) Date and time
5) Quit Chap4.py

Enter the option (1-5):4
2016-07-03
ctime: Sun Jul  3 00:00:00 2016
tuple: time.struct_time(tm_year=2016, tm_mon=7, tm_mday=3, tm_hour=0,
tm_min=0, tm_sec=0, tm_wday=6, tm_yday=185, tm_isdst=-1)
ordinal: 736148
Year: 2016
Mon : 7
Day : 3

Welcome to Chap4.py
your options are:

1) Demonstrate conversion
2) Integer to float conversion
3) Mathematical Functions
4) Date and time
5) Quit Chap4.py

Enter the option (1-5): 5
Thankyou for using Chap4.py!
```

8. A python program to print the current directory

Solution.

```
import os
import sys
# provide the current directory path
addr = "/var/python/sample/"
dirs = os.listdir( addr )
# We use the for loop to print the files and assuming multiple
for file in dirs:
   print file
```

Output:

```
Chapter3.doc
Examples-chapter3.py
Chapter4.py
Sample.py
```

9. A Python program to implement recursion for factorial of a number that demonstrates the user defined function and return statement.

Solution.

```
# Python program to find the factorial of a number using recursion

>>> def fact(n):
    if n == 1:
            return n
    else:
            return n * fact(n-1)


>>> num = int(input("Enter a number: "))
Enter a number: 9
>>> if num < 0:
    print "Factorial for negative values not exist"
elif num == 0:
    print "Factorial is 1"
else:
    print "Factorial of ",num," is ",fact(num)
```

Output:

```
Enter a number: 6
Factorial of 6 is 720
Enter a number: -21
Factorial for negative values not exist
Enter a number: 1
Factorial of 1 is 1
```

Multiple Choice Questions

1. What are the advantages of using functions?
   - **a.** Reduce duplication of code
   - **b.** Clarity of code
   - **c.** Reuse code
   - **d.** All
2. Which keyword is used to define the block of statement in the function?
   - **a.** `Function`
   - **b.** `def`
   - **c.** `func`
   - **d.** `pi`
3. What does the block of statement always starts with?
   - **a.** (:)
   - **b.** (;)
   - **c.** [:]
   - **d.** [;]
4. Which file contains the predefined Python codes?
   - **a.** Function
   - **b.** Pi
   - **c.** module
   - **d.** lambda
5. A function is called using the name with which it was defined earlier, followed by:
   - **a.** { }
   - **b.** ()
   - **c.** <>
   - **d.** [ ]

6. What is the use of the return statement?
   - **a.** exit a function
   - **b.** null value
   - **c.** initiate a function
   - **d.** none
7. Which keyword is used to create an anonymous function?
   - **a.** `Def`
   - **b.** `lambda`
   - **c.** `func`
   - **d.** `pi`
8. What does the following code do?
   ```
   def p(q, r, s): pass
   ```
   - **a.** defines a function, which does nothing
   - **b.** defines an empty list
   - **c.** defines a function with parameter
   - **d.** defines an empty string
9. Which command cannot be called directly by an anonymous function?
   - **a.** `Scan`
   - **b.** `Def`
   - **c.** `exit`
   - **d.** `print`
10. What will be the output of the following code?
    ```
    definputDevice():
          print('Keyboard')
    inputDevice()
    inputDevice()
    ```
    - **a.** `'Keyboard' 'Keyboard'`
    - **b.** `'Keyboard'`
    - **c.** `Keyboard Keyboard`
    - **d.** `Keyboard`
11. What will be the output of the following code?
    ```
    defsqr(a):
          return a * a
    a = sqr(4)
    ```
    - **a.** 4
    - **b.** 16
    - **c.** 8
    - **d.** none

Short Questions

1. What is a function in Python? What are the advantages of using a function?
2. What is the difference between user-defined function and built-in function?
3. Write a function which accepts three numbers and returns their multiplication.
4. Write a function which can take any number value and convert it into an integer, float and string.
5. What will be the output of the code given below?
   a. `str(54.0)`
   b. `print('Python version' + 7)`
6. What do you mean by mathematical functions and how can they be used in Python? Explain with the help of examples.
7. Briefly explain the types of formal arguments using which a function can be called.
8. Write a function that takes exactly two arguments. One argument is the name of the employee, and the other argument is the PF. The default PF is 30000. Display at least two outputs in support of your answer.
9. How are parameters passed in Python? By value or by reference.
10. What are anonymous functions in Python?

11. What is type coercion in Python? Explain with the help of an example.
12. Write a function called `sixteenlines` that uses `fourlines` to print sixteen blank lines. Print sixty four new lines using this.

Answers to Multiple Choice Questions

1. d **2.** b **3.** a **4.** c **5.** b **6.** a **7.** b **8.** a **9.** d **10.** c
11. b

5 Strings and Lists

5.1 STRINGS

Strings are one of the most popular data types in Python. Strings are created by enclosing various characters within quotes. Python does not distinguish between single quotes and double quotes. Creating strings is very simple in Python.

Example

```
>>> var1 = 'Hello Python!'
>>> var2 = "Welcome to Python Programming!"
>>> var3 = """This is triple quoted string"""
>>> print var1
Hello Python                        # Output
>>> print var2
Welcome to Python Programming       # Output
>>> print var3
This is triple quoted string        # Output
```

Strings are of literal or scalar type. The Python interpreter treats them as a single value.

> ***Note*** *Strings are immutable. If you want to change an element of a string, you have to create a new string.*

TIP

Triple quoted strings can span to multiple lines.

Example

```
>>> var = """Welcome            # String written in multiple lines
to
Python
Programming"""
>>> print var
Welcome                          # Output
to
Python
Programming
```

5.1.1 Compound Data Type

Until now, we have mostly looked at two kinds of data types: int and float. Strings are very different from these since strings are made up of smaller pieces/characters. The data types that are made up of smaller pieces are known as *compound data types*.

Strings, in Python, can be used as a single data type, or, alternatively, can be accessed in parts. This makes strings really useful and easier to handle in Python.

TIP

In order to access a part of the string, a square bracket operator `([])` *must be used.*

Example

```
>>> string = "hello"
>>> letter = var[4]
>>> print letter
o                          # Output
```

In the given example, `hello` is stored in a variable `string`. Then the element of the `string` variable with index number 4 is stored in the `letter` variable. As we know, in programming, every index starts with 0. Hence, index 4 means the 5th letter of the string. The 5th `letter` of the string `hello` is `o`. Hence, o is displayed in output.

Example

Let us now look at an example of how to get the first letter of the string:

```
>>> letter = string[0]
>>> print letter
h                          # Output
```

The first letter of the string, i.e., 'h' is displayed by the interpreter.

5.1.2 `len` Function

`len` is a built-in function in Python. When used with a string, `len` returns the length or the number of characters in the string.

Example

```
>>> var = "Hello Python!"
>>> len(var)
13                          # Output
```

Here, we took a string `'Hello Python!'` and used the `len` function with it. The `len` function returned the value `13` because not only characters, but also special characters and blank spaces are considered in the string. Therefore, the *blank space* and *exclamation mark* in our string will also be counted as elements.

Example

Access the last letter of our string with the help of length.

```
>>>length = len(var)
>>> last = [length - 1]
>>> print last
!                           # Output
```

In this example, we store the length of the string in a variable `length` to access the last element of our string. To access the last element, we need the index of last element which is `12` and not 13 because the index of the string starts with 0 not 1, as we discussed earlier. This is the reason we subtracted 1 from the length of the string in order to get the last element index.

Alternatively, we can also use negative indices for accessing the string from last. So, the expression `var [-1]` yields the last letter of the string and `var [-2]` yields the second last letter and so on.

Example

```
>>> var = "Hello world"
>>> last = var[-1]
>>> second_last = var[-2]
>>> print last
d                           # Output
>>> print second_last
l                           # Output
```

Check Your Understanding

1. What is a String in Python?

Ans. Strings are one of the most popular data types in Python. Strings are created by enclosing various characters within quotes. Python does not distinguish between single quotes and double quotes.

2. What is the work of `len` function? Give one example.

Ans. `len` is a built-in function in Python programming language. When used with a string, `len` returns the length or the number of characters in the string.

```
>>> x = 'My name is Anil'
>>> len(x)
15
```

5.1.3 String Slices

A piece or subset of a string is known as slice. Slice operator is applied to a string with the use of square braces (`[]`). Operator `[n:m]` will give a substring which consists of letters between `n` and `m` indices, including letter at index `n` but excluding that at `m`, i.e. letter from nth index to `(m-1)`th index.

Similarly, operator `[n:m:s]` will give a substring which consists of letters from nth index to `(m-1)`th index, where `s` is called the step value, i.e. after letter at `n`, that at `n+s` will be included, then `n+2s`, `n+3s`, etc…

Example

```
>>> var = 'Hello Python'
>>> print var[0:4]
Hell                        # Output
>>> print var[6:12]
Python                      # Output
```

In the above example, you can see that in the first case the slice is `[0:4]`, which means that it will take the 0th element and will extend to the 3rd element, while excluding the 4th element. Similarly, in the second case where slice is `[6:12]`, it will consider the 6th element and extend to the 11th element.

Example

```
>>> alphabet = "abcdefghij"
>>> print alphabet[1:8:3]
beh                         # Output
>>> print alphabet[1:8:2]
bdfh                        # Output
```

In the above example, you can see that in the first case the slice is `[1:8:3]`, which means that it will take the element at 1st index which is `b` and will extend till the 7th element. Since step is 3, it will print 1st element, then 4th element and then 7th element. i.e. `beh`. Similarly, in second case where slice is `[1:8:2]`, it will print 1st , 3rd, 5th, 7th elements, i.e. `bdfh`.

Now, if we do not give any value for the index before the colon, i.e., `n`, then the slice will start from the first element of the string. Similarly, if we do not give any value for the index, i.e., `m` after the colon, the slice will extend to the end of the string.

Example

```
>>> var = 'banana'
>>> var[:4]
'bana'                              # Output
>>> var[4:0]
'na'                                # Output
```

Similarly, if we don't give any value at both the sides of the colon, i.e., values for `n` and `m` are not given then it will print the whole string.

```
>>> var[ : ]
'banana'                            # Output
```

Now, if the second index, i.e., `m`, is smaller than the first index, i.e., `n`, then output will be an empty string represented by two single quotes:

```
>>> var = 'banana'
>>> var[4:3]
''                                  # Output
```

Now, if we give the value of step as -1 and no value for `n` and `m`, then it will print the string in reverse order. For example,

```
>>> var = 'banana'
>>> var[ : : -1]
'ananab'                            # Output
```

Note *An empty string has length o. Though it does not contain any character, it is still a string.*

5.1.4 Strings are Immutable

Strings are immutable which means that we cannot change any element of a string. If we want to change an element of a string, we have to create a new string.

Example

```
>>> var = 'hello python'
>>> var[0] = 'p'
```

Output:

```
TypeError: 'str' object does not support item assignment
```

Here, we try to change the 0th index of the string to a character `p`, but the Python interpreter generates an error.

Now, the solution to this problem is to generate a new string rather than change the old string.

Example

```
>>> var = 'hello python'
>>> new_var = 'p' + var[1:]
>>> print new_var
pello python                                # Output
```

Note that we cut the slice from the original string and concatenate it with the character we want to insert in the string. It does not have any effect on the original string.

5.1.5 String Traversal

Traversal is a process in which we access all the elements of the string one by one using some conditional statements such as for loop, while loop, etc. String traversal is an important pattern since there will be many situations in different programs where we need to visit each element of the string and do some operations, continuing till the end of the string.

Example

Let us try the traversal of string using `while` loop

```
>>> i=0
>>> while i < len(var):    # string was assigned In the example given above
... letter = var[i]
... print letter
... i = i + 1
```

Output:

```
h
e
l
l
o

p
y
t
h
o
n
```

In the given example, we take a variable `i` and initialise it to `0`. Then, we begin a `while` loop with the condition `i < len(var)`. At one point of time, the index becomes equal to the length of the string. As a result, the condition of while loop becomes `false` and it halts. The last character is displayed with the index `len(var)-1`, which will be the last character of the string. Thus, our whole string is traversed and displayed.

Now, let us try the same thing with a `for` loop,

```
>>> for char in var:
... print char
h
e
l
l
o

p
y
t
h
o
n
```

TIP

Each time in the -`for` loop, the next character in the string will be assigned to the variable `char`. The loop halts when the last character is processed.

Check Your Understanding

1. You have been given a string 'I live in Cochin. I love pets.' Divide this string in such a way that the two sentences in it are separated and stored in different variables. Print them.

Ans.

```
>>> var = 'I live in Cochin. I love pets.'
>>> var1 = var[:17]
>>> var2 = var[18:30]
>>> print var1
I live in Cochin.          # Output
>>> print var2
I love pets.          # Output
```

2. Define Traversing of strings. Give one example.

Ans. Traversal is a process in which we access all the elements of the string one by one using some conditional statements such as for loop, while loop, etc.

```
>>> var = 'jack john'
>>> i=0
>>> while i < len(var):
...             x = var[i]
...             print x
...             i=i+1
```

Output:

j
a
c
k

j
o
h
n

Searching within Strings Let us take an example of searching a character in a string.

```
>>> def find(string, char)
... index = 0
... while index < len(string):
...         if string[index] == char:
...                 return index
...  index = index + 1
... return -1
```

Here, we define a function `find` that takes a string and a character as input (`string` and `char` respectively in the example). A `while` loop traverses the string until the end and compares every element of the string with the character passed by the user. If it matches any element of the string then the index of that element is returned by the function. Otherwise, it returns `-1`.

> ***Note*** *The `return` statement in a while loop works in the same way as the `break` function does. If the result is found, then it will break the loop and return the result back to the function.*

5.1.6 Escape Characters

The backslash character `(\)` is used to escape characters. It converts difficult-to-type characters into a string. Let us understand the concept of escaping characters with an example. Suppose, we want to print a string with double quotes or single quotes. Usually, when we use single or double quotes with the string, Python neglects them and prints only the string. What should we do if we want the quotation marks in the output? Then we will need to make use of the escaping character concept.

Example

```
>>>print "I am 6'2\" tall."  # escape double quotes inside string
I am 6'2" tall.         # Output
```

Note that we use a backslash operator before the 2nd double quotation marks. As a result, the Python interpreter understands that the quotation marks are a part of the string and should be displayed in output.

Table 5.1 shows various common escape characters.

TABLE 5.1 List of Escape Characters

Escape Sequence	Meaning
`\newline`	Ignored
`\\`	Backslash (`\`)
`\'`	Single quote (`'`)
`\"`	Double quote (`"`)
`\a`	ASCII Bell (BELL)
`\b`	ASCII Backspace (BS)
`\f`	ASCII Formfeed (FF)
`\n`	ASCII Linefeed (LF)
`\r`	ASCII Carriage return (CR)
`\t`	ASCII Horizontal tab (TAB)
`\v`	ASCII Vertical tab (VT)
`\ooo`	ASCII Character with octal value `ooo`
`\xhhh...`	ASCII Character with hex value `hh...`

5.1.7 String Formatting Operator

The strings in Python have a unique built-in operation: the `%`operator (modulo). This is also called the String Formatting operator and is similar to the formatting operator used in C language.

Example

```
>>> print "My name is %s and age is %d years." %('John', 26)
My name is John and age is 26.          # Output
```

Table gives the list of symbols that can be used with `%`.

TABLE 5.2 List of Symbols Used with `%` Operator

Format Symbol	Conversion
`%c`	Character
`%s`	String conversion via `str()` prior to formatting
`%i`	Signed decimal integer
`%d`	Signed decimal integer
`%u`	Unsigned decimal integer

%o	Octal integer
%x	Hexadecimal integer (lowercase letters)
%X	Hexadecimal integer (uppercase letters)
%e	Exponential notation (with lowercase 'e')
%E	Exponential notation (with uppercase 'E')
%f	Floating point real number
%g	The shorter of %f and %e
%G	The shorter of %f and %E

The following example elaborates the usage of different string formatting operators

```
>>>print ("the first letter of %s is %c" %('python','p'))
>>>print("The sum = %d" %(-15))
>>>print("The sum = %i" %(-15))
>>>print("The sum = %u" %(15))
>>>print("%o is the octal equivalent of %d" %(9,9))
>>>print("%x is the hexadecimal equivalent of %d" %(12,12))
>>>print("%X is the hexadecimal equivalent of %d" %(12,12))
>>>print("%e is the exponential equivalent of %f" %(8.98354,8.98354))
>>>print("%E is the exponential equivalent of %f" %(8.98354,8.98354))
```

The output of the above program will be:

```
the first letter of python is p
The sum = -15
The sum = -15
The sum = 15
11 is the octal equivalent of 9
c is the hexadecimal equivalent of 12
C is the hexadecimal equivalent of 12
8.983540e+00 is the exponential equivalent of 8.983540
8.983540E+00 is the exponential equivalent of 8.983540
```

5.1.8 String Formatting Functions

Python includes many built-in functions for strings as shown in Table 5.3.

TABLE 5.3 Built-in functions for strings

Sr. No.	Functions with description
1.	`capitalize()` Makes the first letter of the string capital.
2.	`center(width,fillchar)` Returns a space-padded string with the original string centered to a total width columns.
3.	`count(str,beg=0,end=len(string))` Counts the number of times `str` occurs in the string or in a substring provided that starting index is `beg` and ending index is `end`.

4.	`decode(encoding='UTF-8',errors='strict')` Decodes the string using the codec registered for encoding.
5.	`encode(encoding='UTF-8',errors='strict')` Returns encoded string version of string; on error, default is to raise a `ValueError` unless errors are given with `'ignore'` or `'replace'`.
6.	`endswith(suffix,beg=0,end=len(string))` Determines whether string or a substring of string ends with `suffix`, returning `True` if so and `False` otherwise.
7.	`expandstab(tabsize=8)` Expands tab in string to multiple spaces.
8.	`find(str,beg=0,end=len(string))` Determine whether the `str` occurs in the string or in a substring of string provided that the starting index is `beg` and the ending index is `end`. If the string is found, it returns the `index` otherwise returns `-1`.
9.	`index(str,beg=0,end=len(string))` Acts in the same way as `find();` if `str` is not found, it raises an exception.
10.	`isalnum()` If string has at least one character and all characters are alphanumeric, then it returns `True` and `False` otherwise.
11.	`isalpha()` If string has at least one character and all characters are alphabetic, it returns `True` and `False` otherwise.
12.	`isdigit()` If string contains only numbers, then it returns `True` and `False` otherwise.
13.	`islower()` If string has at least one cased character and all cased characters are in lower case, then it returns `True` and `False` otherwise.
14.	`isnumeric()` If a Unicode string contains only numeric characters, then it returns `True` and `False` otherwise.
15.	`isspace()` If string contains only whitespace characters, then it returns `True` and `False` otherwise.
16.	`istitle()` If string is properly "titlecased", then it returns `True` and `False` otherwise.
17.	`isupper()` If string has at least one cased character and all cased characters are in upper case, then it returns `True` and `False` otherwise.
18.	`join(seq)` Concatenates the string representations of elements in sequence `seq` into a string with separator string.
19.	`len(string)` It returns the length of the string.
20.	`ljust(width[,fillchar])` It returns the padded string with spaces with the original string left-justified to a total of width columns.
21.	`lower()` It converts all the uppercase letters into lowercase in a string.
22.	`lstrip()` It removes all the leading whitespaces in a string.
23.	`maketrans()` It returns a translation table that is to be used in translate function.

24.	`max(str)` It returns the maximum alphabetic characters in a string `str`.
25.	`min(str)` It returns the minimum alphabetic characters in a string `str`.
26.	`replace(old,new[,max])` Replaces all occurrences of old in string with new or at most `max` occurrences if `max` provided.
27.	`rfind(str,beg=0,end=len(string))` It works same as `find()` but it searches backward in a string.
28.	`rindex(str,beg=0,end=len(string))` It works same as `index()` but it searches backward in a string.
29.	`rjust(width,[,fillchar])` It returns a space-padded string with the original string right-justified to a total of width columns.
30.	`rstrip()` It removes all trailing whitespaces in a string.
31.	`split(str="",num=string.count(str))` It splits string according to delimiter `str` and returns list of substrings; split into at most `num` substrings if provided.
32.	`splitlines(num=string.count('\n'))` It splits string at all NEWLINEs and returns a list of each line with NEWLINEs removed.
33.	`startswith(str,beg=0,end=len(string))` It determines whether a string or a substring of string begins with substring `str`; returning `True` if so and `False` otherwise.
34.	`strip([chars])` It performs both `lstrip()` and `rstrip()` on string.
35.	`swapcase()` It inverts case for all characters in the string.
36.	`title()` It returns "titlecased" version of string, that is, all words start with uppercase and the rest are in lowercase.
37.	`translate(table,deletechars="")` It translates string according to translation table `str` which is of 256 chars, removing those in the `del` string.
38.	`upper()` Converts all lowercase characters into uppercase.
39.	`zfill(width)` It returns the string left padded with zeros to a total of width characters; intended for numbers, `zfill()` retains any sign given (less one zero).
40.	`isdecimal()` If a Unicode string contains only decimal characters, then it returns `True` if so and `False` otherwise.

Check Your Understanding

1. What are escape characters?

Ans. The backslash character (\) is used to escape characters. It converts difficult-to-type characters into a string. For example, we need the escaping character concept when we want to print a string with double quotes or single quotes. When single or double quotes are used with the string, Python normally neglects them and prints only the string.

2. What do %s, %d, %x and %e stand for?

Ans. %s = String conversion via `str()` prior to formatting
%d = Signed decimal integer
%x = Hexadecimal integer (lowercase letters)
%e = Exponential notation (with lowercase 'e')

5.2 LISTS

5.2.1 Values and Accessing Elements

Like strings, lists are also a series of values in Python. In a string, all the values are of character type but in a list, values can be of any type. The values in a list are called elements or items.

A list is a collection of items or elements; the sequence of data in a list is ordered. The elements or items in a list can be accessed by their positions, i.e., indices. We have already studied the index in the strings section.

Like all other variables, lists are also defined before they are used. There are several ways of defining or creating a list. The most convenient way is using square brackets (`[]`).

Example

```
>>> list1 = [2,-1,0,-2,8]
>>> list2 = ['crunchy chocolate', 'hello', 'python programming']
```

The first line list contains only the numerals that are integers. The second line list contains strings. However, it is not necessary that the lists have homogenous data type elements.

There can be elements of different data types in the list:

```
>>> list3 = ['python', 5.5, 8]
```

The list given above contains three different types of elements: string, float and integer. A list-type data item can also be defined inside a list:

```
>>> list4 = ['python', 5.6, [20,40]]
```

Here, a list is contained in another list. Alternatively, we can say that a list is **nested** within another list.

Copying the List

We can make a duplicate or copy of an existing list. The general syntax in the beginner's mind can come like using the assignment operator; we can copy a list into another. For example,

```
>>> list_original = [1,2,3,4]
>>> list_copy = list_original
```

Although, this statement doesn't have any syntax error and also it works, but this is not the correct way to copy of a list. Let's understand why this is not a correct way and what is the correct way then?

Basically, what the statement `list_original = [1,2,3,4]` does is that it makes a variable named `list_original` and it points to the list `[1,2,3,4]` and by the statement `list_copy = list_original`, we are not copying the list but we are just making another variable named `list_copy` and attach it to the list pointed by `list_original`. Hence, logically both variables are pointing to the same list. But by making a duplicate of a list, we mean that two different lists but they contain same elements. This is illustrated in Fig. 5.1.

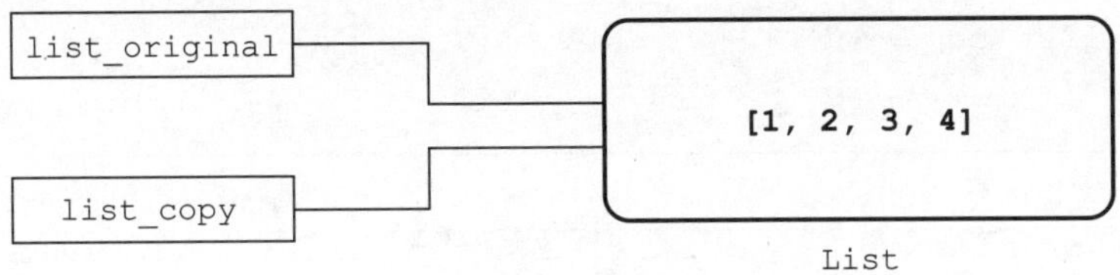

Figure 5.1

In the figure, we can see that both variables are pointing to the same list.

If we modify `list_original`, then the modification will also take place in `list_copy` and vice versa. For Example,

```
>>> list_original.append(10)
>>> print list_original
[1, 2, 3, 4, 10]
>>> print list_copy
[1, 2, 3, 4, 10]
```

Now, after understanding the concept of how the list is stored in Python, we will understand the correct way of making copy of an existing list.

There are two ways to make copy of a list.

1. Using `[ : ]` operator
2. Using built-in copy function

Using [:] operator

```
>>> list_original = [1,2,3,4]
>>> list_copy = list_original[ : ]          # Using [:] operator
>>> print list_copy
[1, 2, 3, 4]
```

Now, let us make changes in original list and we will see whether the changes take place in copied list also or not.

```
>>> list_original.append(10)       # Adding element to original
>>> print list_original
[1, 2, 3, 4, 10]                   # original list changed
>>> print list_copy
[1, 2, 3, 4]                       # copied list is unaffected
```

Hence, when we make changes in the original list, the copied list was unaffected by the changes.

Using built-in function

Python has a built-in copy function which can be used to make copy of an existing list. In order to use the copy function, first we have to import it.

Example

```
>>> from copy import copy                     #Import library
>>> list_original = [1,2,3,4]
>>> list_copy = copy(list_original)           #Copying list
>>> print list_copy
[1, 2, 3, 4]
```

TIP

An empty list can also be created using enclosing brackets with no elements inside them.

```
>>> a = []
```

The above statement assigns an empty list to a variable `a`.

We can print a list by assigning it to a variable:

```
>>> list = [10,20,30,'hello']        # assign the list
>>> print list                       # printing a list
[10, 20, 30, 'hello']                # Output
```

5.2.2 Lists are Mutable

Lists are mutable. The value of any element inside the list can be changed at any point of time. The elements of the list are accessible with their index value. The index always starts with `0` and ends with `n-1`, if the list contains `n` elements. The syntax for accessing the elements of a list is the same as in the case of a string. We use square brackets around the variable and index number.

Example

```
>>> list = [10,20,30,40]
>>> list[1]
20          # Output
```

In the given example, we access the 2nd element of the list that has 1 as index number and the interpreter prints 20.

Now, if we want to change a value in the list given above:

```
>>> list[3] = 50
>>> print list
[10,20,30,50]              # Output
```

Note that the value of the 4th element is changed to 50.

The index number written within the square brackets indicates the distance from the beginning of the list. Hence, the expression `list[0]` indicates the starting element (a distance zero from the beginning) and `list[1]` indicates the second element (a distance of one from the beginning). This concept is illustrated in Fig. 5.2.

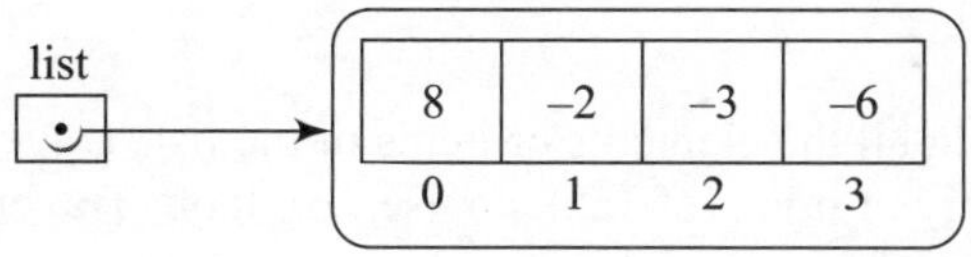

Figure 5.2 A View of a List

In Fig. 5.2, the numbers below each list element indicate the index of that element. Indices in a list work in the same way as in strings:

- Any integer expression can be used as an index number.
- If any element that does not exist in the list is accessed, there will be an `IndexError`.
- If the indices are given in negative, then counting happens from the end of the list. (backward)

> ***Note*** *Every element or item inside a list always has an index number through which it is accessed.*

Check Your Understanding

1. What is a list? How are the values of a list accessed?

Ans. Just like a string, a list is also a series of values in Python. In a string, all the values are of character type, but in lists, values can be of any type. The values in a list are called elements or items. A list is a collection of items or elements; the sequence of data in a list is ordered and can be accessed by their positions, i.e., indices.

Example

```
>>> list = [1,2,3,4]
>>> list[1]
2          # Output
>>> list[3]
4          # Output
```

2. What do you mean by "Lists are mutable"?

Ans. Lists are mutable means that we can change the value of any element inside the list at any point of time. The elements inside the list are accessible with their index value. The index will always start with `0` and end with `n-1`, if the list contains `n` elements.

Example

```
>>> list = [1,2,3,4]
>>> list[2] = 6
>>> print list
[1,2,6,4]          # Output
```

5.2.3 Traversing a List

Traversing a list means accessing all the elements or items of the list. Traversing can be done by using any conditional statement of Python, but it is preferable to use `for` loop. Traversing in list is done in the same way as in string.

Example

```
>>> list = ['a','b','c','d']
>>> for x in list:
...     print x
```

Output:

```
a
b
c
d
```

In the example, we define a list of some elements. Using `for` loop, the list is traversed and all the elements of the list are printed.

The `for` loop is used mostly when we want to read the elements of the list. However, in order to write to a list, we need to access the indices of the elements in a list. The following example traverses the list and also adds 4 to every element of the list.

```
>>> list = [10,20,30,40]
>>> for i in range(len(list)):
...         list[i] = list[i] + 4
>>> print list
[14,24,34,44]              # Output
```

Here, we make use of the `range` and `len` functions on a list, where `len` returns the length of the list and `range` returns the list of indices. Hence, for each iteration of the loop, the variable `i` gets the index of the next element and the statement defined in the body of `for` loop reads the old value at the index `i` and assigns it a new value.

5.2.4 Deleting Elements from List

Python provides many ways in which the elements in a list can be deleted. In this section, we will learn the methods of deleting elements from a list.

1. pop Operator If we know the index of the element that we want to delete, then we can use the `pop` operator.

```
>>> list = [10,20,30,40]
>>> a = list.pop(2)
>>> print list
[10,20,40]              # Output
>>> print a
30                      # Output
```

The `pop` operator deletes the element on the provided index and stores that element in a variable for further use.

2. `del` Operator The `del` operator deletes the value on the provided index, but it does not store the value for further use.

```
>>> list = ['w','x','y','z']
>>> del list(1)
>>> print list
['w', 'y', 'z']                # Output
```

3. `remove` Operator We use the `remove` operator if we know the item that we want to remove or delete from the list (but not the index).

```
>>> list = [10,20,30,40]
>>> list.remove(10)
>>> print list
[20,30,40]                     # Output
```

Note *In order to delete more than one value from a list,* `del` *operator with* `slicing` *is used.*

```
>>> list = [1,2,3,4,5,6,7,8]
>>> del list[1:3]
>>> print list
[1,4,5,6,7,8]              # Output
```

Check Your Understanding

1. What do you understand by traversing a list? Give an example.

Ans. Traversing of the list refers to accessing all the elements or items of the list. Traversing can be done using any conditional statement of Python, but it is preferable to use `for` loop.

Example

```
>>> list = [1,2,3]
>>> for x in list:
...     print x
```

Output:

```
1
2
3
```

2. What is the `pop` operator?

Ans. If the index of the element we want to delete is known, we can use the `pop` operator. The `pop` operator deletes the element on the provided index and stores that element in a variable for further use.

5.2.5 Built-in List Operators

1. Concatenation The concatenation operator works in lists in the same way it does in a string. This operator concatenates two strings. This is done by the + operator in Python.

Example

```
>>> list1 = [10,20,30,40]
>>> list2 = [50,60,70]
>>> list3 = list1 + list2
>>> print list3
[10,20,30,40,50,60,70]            # Output
```

In the given example, there are two lists, `list1` and `list2`. Here, `list1` and `list2` are concatenated using + operator between them and the resulting list is stored in the variable `list3`. Now, when we print `list3`, it gives the concatenation of `list1` and `list2`.

2. Repetition The repetition operator works as suggested by its name; it repeats the list for a given number of times. Repetition is performed by the * operator.

Example

```
>>> list1 = [1,2,3]
>>> list1 * 4
[1,2,3,1,2,3,1,2,3,1,2,3]         # Output
>>> [2] * 6
[2,2,2,2,2,2]                     # Output
```

In the given example, the list `[1,2,3]` was repeated 4 times and the list `[2]` was repeated 6 times.

3. `In` Operator The `In` operator tells the user whether the given string exists in the list or not. It gives a Boolean output, i.e., `True` or `False`. If the given input exists in the string, it gives `True` as output, otherwise, `False`.

Example 1

```
>>> list = ['Hello', 'Python', 'Program']
>>> 'Hello' in list
True        # Output
>>> 'World' in list
False             # Output
```

Example 2

```
>>> list = [10,20,30,40]
>>> 10 in list
True# Output
>>> 50 in list
False             # Output
```

5.2.6 Built-in List Methods

Python includes many built-in methods for use with list as shown in Table 5.4.

TABLE 5.4 List of built-in list methods

Sr. No.	Method	Description
1.	`cmp(list1,list2)`	It compares the elements of both the lists, `list1` and `list2`.
2.	`len(list)`	It returns the length of the string, i.e., the distance from starting element to last element.
3.	`max(list)`	It returns the item that has the maximum value in a list.
4.	`min(list)`	It returns the item that has the minimum value in a list.
5.	`list(seq)`	It converts a tuple into a list.
6.	`list.append(item)`	It adds the item to the end of the list.
7.	`list.count(item)`	It returns number of times the item occurs in the list.
8.	`list.extend(seq)`	It adds the elements of the sequence at the end of the list.
9.	`list.index(item)`	It returns the index number of the item. If item appears more than one time, it returns the lowest index number.
10.	`list.insert(index,item)`	It inserts the given item onto the given index number while the elements in the list take one right shift.
11.	`list.pop(item=list[-1])`	It deletes and returns the last element of the list.
12.	`list.remove(item)`	It deletes the given item from the list.
13.	`list.reverse()`	It reverses the position (index number) of the items in the list.
14.	`list.sort([func])`	It sorts the elements inside the list and uses compare function if provided.

1. `append` Method This method can add a new element or item to an existing list.

Example

```
>>> list = [1,2,3,4,]
>>> list.append(0)
>>> print list
[1,2,3,4,0]                # Output
```

2. `extend` Method This method works like concatenation. It takes a list as an argument and adds it to the end of another list.

Example

```
>>> list1 = ['x','y','z']
>>> list2 = [1,2,3]
>>> list1.extend(list2)
>>> print list1
['x', 'y', 'z', 1, 2, 3]              # Output
```

In this example, list1 is modified by adding list2 at the end of it while list2 is left as it is.

3. sort Method This method arranges the list in ascending order.

Example

```
>>> list=[4,2,5,8,1,9]
>>> list.sort()
>>> print list
[1, 2, 4, 5, 8, 9]                # Output
```

Note *Not all the list methods return anything.*

Check Your Understanding

1. **What are concatenation operator and in operator?**

Ans. Concatenation Operator:

The concatenation operator works in the same way in lists as it does in strings. This operator concatenates two strings. Concatenation is done by the + operator in Python.

in Operator:

The in operator works on lists. It tells the user whether the given string exists in the list or not. It gives a Boolean output, i.e., True or False. If the given input exists in the string, it gives True as output, otherwise, False.

2. **Give examples for len, max and min methods.**

Ans.

```
>>> list = [789, 'abcd','jinnie',1234]
>>> len(list)
 4              # Output
>>> max(list)
 'jinnie'              # Output
>>> min(list)
 789            # Output
```

ALWAYS REMEMBER

- Strings are created by enclosing various characters within quotes.
- Strings are immutable. This means that if you want to change an element of the string, you have to create new string.
- To access a part of the string, we use a square bracket operator ([]).

- `len` is a built-in function in Python, which when used with a string, returns the length or the number of characters in the string.
- Traversal is a process in which we access all the elements of the string one by one using some conditional statements such as for loop, while loop, etc.
- The `return` statement in a while loop works in the same way as the `break` function does. If the result is found then it will break the loop and return the result back to the function.
- The backslash character `(\)` is used to escape characters. It converts difficult-to-type characters into a string.
- The strings in Python have one unique built-in operation: the `%`operator (modulo).
- A list is a collection of items or elements; the sequence of data in a list is ordered.
- The elements or items in a list can be accessed by their positions, i.e., indices.
- An empty list can also be created by enclosing brackets with no elements inside them.
- Lists are mutable which means that we can change the value of any element inside the list at any point of time.
- If we know the index of the element that we want to delete then we can use the `pop` operator.
- If we know the item that we want to remove or delete from the list (but not the index) then we use `remove` operator.
- The repetition operator works in the way its name suggests; it repeats the list a given number of times. Repetition is performed by the `*` operator.
- `extend` method works in a way similar to concatenation. It takes a list as an argument and adds this list to the end of another list.
- `sort` method arranges the list in ascending order.
- `append` method can add a new element or item to an existing list.

KEY TERMS

✓ **SEQUENCE:** It is an ordered set or series, where each value has an index.
✓ **ITEM:** An item is a value in the sequence.
✓ **SLICE:** A slice is a part of the string determined by range of indices.
✓ **EMPTY STRING:** A string with no character having 0 length is empty string.
✓ **IMMUTABLE:** It is the property by which the value in a sequence cannot be changed.
✓ **SEARCH:** It is a pattern of traversal where an item is found in the sequence.
✓ **LIST:** It is a series or a sequence of different data items.
✓ **ELEMENT:** An element is a value in the list, also called item.
✓ **INDEX:** It is an integer value that indicates the position of an element in a list.
✓ **LIST TRAVERSAL:** Accessing all the items in a list.
✓ **OBJECT:** It is something a variable can refer to. An object has a type and value.
✓ **EQUIVALENT:** It means having equal values.
✓ **IDENTICAL:** It means same objects (which implies equivalence).

✓ **REFERENCE:** The mapping between a variable and its value is called reference.
✓ **DELIMITER:** It is a character or string used to specify where a string must be split.

REVIEW EXERCISES

PROGRAMS

1. Write a program to find duplicate characters in a given string.

Solution.

```
>>> str = 'java'
>>> first_time = []
>>> dup = []
>>> for i in str:
     if i not in first_time:
            first_time.append(i)
     else:
            if i not in dup:
                   dup.append(i)
     print "".join(dup)

a                #Output
```

2. Write a program to check whether a string is a palindrome or not.

Solution.

```
>>> str1 = raw_input("Enter a String: ")
>>> reversed_str = str(reversed(str1))
>>> if str1 == reversed_str:
        print "String is Palindrome"
else:
        print "String is not a Palindrome"
```

3. Write a program to remove punctuations from a string.

Solution.

```
>>> punc = '''!()-[]{};:'"\.,<>/@?$#^&*%_~'''
>>> str = input("Enter a String: ")
>>> no_punc = ""
>>> for char in str:
     if char not in punc:
            no_punc = no_punc + char
     print(no_punc)

Enter a String: '~~(#)[Hey!: how}^ are#*$ y*@o#u'
Hey how are you          #Output
```

4. Write a program to transpose a matrix.

Solution.

```
>>> a = [[4, 8],
         [3, 19],
         [15, 6]]
>>>
>>> trans = [[0, 0, 0],
           [0, 0, 0]]
>>>
>>> for i in range(len(a)):
        for j in range(len(a[0])):
                trans[j][i] = a[i][j]

>>> for k in trans:
        print(k)


[4, 3, 15]          #Output
[8, 19, 6]
```

5. Write a program to add two metrices.

Solution.

```
>>> a = [[4, 8, 18],
          [3, 19, 12],
          [15, 6, 9]]
>>>
>>> b = [[8, 32, 23],
          [12, 1, 15],
          [5, 12, 3]]
>>>
>>> sum_of_mat = [[0, 0, 0],
                     [0, 0, 0],
                     [0, 0, 0]]
>>>
>>> for i in range(len(a)):
        for j in range(len(a[0])):
                sum_of_mat[i][j] = a[i][j] + b[i][j]

>>> for k in sum_of_mat:
        print(k)


[12, 40, 41]                      #Output
[15, 20, 27]
[20, 18, 12]
```

6. Write a python program to demonstrate various strings functions and operations

Solution.

```
# Python program to demonstrate various string functions and operations
>>> str = "python program"
```

```
>>> str2 = 'string operations'
>>> print "In this line we display the single quotes ' '"
>>> print "length of the strings: str and str2"
>>> print len(str)
>>> print len(str2)
>>> print "First occurrences of o in str and r in str2 is"
>>> print str.index("o")
>>> print str2.index("r")
>>> print "number of occurrences in str and str2 are"
>>> print str.count("o")
>>> print str2.count("i")
>>> print "str string slice operations"
>>> print str[2:9]
>>> print str[2:9:2]
>>> print str[2:7]
>>> print str[2:9:1]
>>> print str[::-1]
>>> print "str2 string slice operations"
>>> print str2[1:6]
>>> print str2[2:8:2]
>>> print str2[2:8]
>>> print str2[2:8:1]
>>> print str2[::-1]
>>> print "strings str and str2 in upper case"
>>> print str.upper()
>>> print str2.upper()
>>> print "strings str and str2 in lower case"
>>> print str.lower()
>>> print str2.lower()
>>> print "str and str2 string functions starts with"
>>> print str.startswith("python")
>>> print str2.startswith("Hello")
>>> print "str and str2 ends with"
>>> print str.endswith("asdfasdfasdf")
>>> print str2.endswith("operations")
>>> print "str and str2 split operations"
>>> strsplit = str.split(" ")
>>> print strsplit
>>> strsplit2 = str2.split(" ")
>>> print strsplit2
>>> print "string concatenation"
>>> print str + str2
```

Output:

```
In this line we display the single quotes ' '
Length of the strings: str and str2
14
17
First occurrences of o in str and r in str2 is
4
```

```
2
number of occurrences in str and str2 are
2
2
str string slice operations
thon pr
to r
thon
thon pr
margorp nohtyp
str2 string slice operations
tring
rn
ring o
ring o
snoitarepo gnirts
strings str and str2 in upper case
PYTHON PROGRAM
STRING OPERATIONS
strings str and str2 in lower case
python program
string operations
str and str2 string functions starts with
True
False
str and str2 ends with
False
True
str and str2 split operations
['python', 'program']
['string', 'operations']
string concatenation
python programstring operations
```

7. Write a Python Program to demonstrate List functions and operations

Solution.

```
# Python program to demonstrate list functions and operations
>>> lst1 = ['java', 'cloud', 1995, 2010];
>>> lst2 = [3, 6, 9, 12, 15 ];
>>> lst3 = ["p", "q", "r", "s"]
>>> print "various list operations"
>>> print "lst1[0]: ", lst1[0]
>>> print "list split operations"
>>> print "lst2[1:5]: ", lst2[1:5]
>>> print"value available at index 2 :"
>>> print lst1[2]
>>> print "Insert elements into the list"
>>> lst1[2] = 2001;
>>> print "New value in lst1 at index 2 is"
>>> print lst1[2]
```

```
>>> print "Modified lst1"
>>> print lst1
>>> print "delete from lst1"
>>> del lst1[2];
>>> print "After deletion at index:2 is"
>>> print lst1
>>> print "len() on lst"
>>> print len(lst1)
>>> print "Max() and Min() on lst for numeric"
>>> print max(lst1)
>>> print min(lst1)
>>> print "sum() on numeric lsts"
>>> print sum(lst2)
>>> print "Avg() on numeric lsts"
>>> print sum(lst2)/len(lst2)
>>> print "del() for multiple elements in the lst"
>>> del lst1[1:4]
>>> print "modified lst1"
>>> print lst1
>>> print "remove() on lst3"
>>> lst3.remove('p')
>>> print "sort() on lst2"
>>> print lst2
>>> lst2.sort()
>>> print "After sort()"
>>> print lst2
>>> print "Append() on lst2"
>>> lst2.append('18')
>>> print "lst2 after append", lst2
>>> print "split operations"
>>> lst1[2:4]
>>> lst2[1:5]
>>> lst3[2:]
>>> print "lst1 split"
>>> print lst1
>>> print "lst2 split"
>>> print lst2
>>> print "lst3 split"
>>> print lst3
>>> print " for loop on lsts"
>>> for i in range(len(lst2)):
    lst2[i] = lst2[i] * 3
>>> print lst2
>>> print "Creating list in another way"
>>> a = 'python'
>>> b = list(a)
>>> print a
>>> print b
>>> c = 'welcome to python programming'
>>> print c
```

```
>>> d = c.split()
>>> print d
>>> print "slice of d"
>>> print d[1:3]
>>> print d[:2]
>>> h = 'python-program-is-easy'
>>> print h
>>> delim = '-'
>>> h.split(delim)
>>> print "After split and delim"
>>> print h
>>> delim = '***'
>>> delim.join(h)
>>> print "join () on lsts"
>>> print h
>>> print "cmp () on lsts"
>>> print cmp(lst1, lst2)
>>> print cmp(lst2, lst1)
>>> lst4 = lst3 + [786];
>>> print cmp(lst3, lst4)
>>> print "Max values"
>>> print "Max value element : ", max(lst1)
>>> print "Max value element : ", max(lst2)
>>> print "Max value element : ", max(lst3)
>>> print "Min() values of lsts"
>>> print "min value element : ", min(lst1)
>>> print "min value element : ", min(lst2)
>>> print "min value element : ", min(lst3)
>>> print "new lst5 from existing lst2"
>>> lst5 = list(lst2)
>>> print "pop on lst"
>>> print"list elements", lst5
>>> print "lst2", lst2.pop()
>>> print "lst2:", lst2.pop(2)
>>> print "reverse() on lst"
>>> lst2.reverse()
>>> print "sort() on lst"
>>> print lst2
>>> lst2.sort()
>>> print "After sort", lst2
>>> print "end of chap5"
```

Output:

```
various list operations
lst1[0]:  java
list split operations
lst2[1:5]:  [6, 9, 12, 15]
value aviliable at index 2 :
1995
Insert elements into the list
```

```
New value in lst1 at index 2 is
2001
Modified lst1
['java', 'cloud', 2001, 2010]
delete from lst1
After deletion at index:2 is
['java', 'cloud', 2010]
len() on lst
3
Max() and Min() on lst for numeric
java
2010
sum() on numeric lsts
45
Avg() on numeric lsts
9
del() for multiple elements in the lst
modified lst1
['java']
remove() on lst3
sort() on lst2
[3, 6, 9, 12, 15]
After sort()
[3, 6, 9, 12, 15]
Append() on lst2
lst2 after append [3, 6, 9, 12, 15, '18']
split operations
lst1 split
['java']
lst2 split
[3, 6, 9, 12, 15, '18']
lst3 split
['q', 'r', 's']
 for loop on lsts
[9, 18, 27, 36, 45, '181818']
Creating list in another way
python
['p', 'y', 't', 'h', 'o', 'n']
welcome to python programming
['welcome', 'to', 'python', 'programming']
slice of d
['to', 'python']
['welcome', 'to']
python-program-is-easy
After split and delim
python-program-is-easy
join () on lsts
python-program-is-easy
cmp () on lsts
1
```

```
-1
-1
Max values
Max value element :  java
Max value element :  181818
Max value element : s
Min() values of lsts
min value element :  java
min value element :  9
min value element :  q
new lst5 from exisiting lst2
pop on lst
list elements [9, 18, 27, 36, 45, '181818']
lst2 181818
lst2: 27
reverse() on lst
sort() on lst
[45, 36, 18, 9]
After sort [9, 18, 36, 45]
end of chap5
```

Multiple Choice Questions

1. Which type of operator will we use to access a part of the string?

a. `{ }` **b.** `[ ]`
c. `<>` **d.** `( )`

2. What will be the output of the given code?

```
>>>"h"+"lm"
```

a. `h` **b.** `"hlm"`
c. `lm` **d.** `hlm`

3. What will be the output of the given code?

```
>>>str1 = 'hello world'
>>>str2 = 'computer'
>>>str1 [-2]
```

a. `e` **b.** `ld`
c. `l` **d.** `er`

4. Which operator is used to represent escape character?

a. `\` **b.** `\\`
c. `\'` **d.** `/`

5. What will be the output of the given code?

```
>>> string = "Hello COMPUTER!"
>>> len(string)
```

a. 14 **b.** 15
c. 13 **d.** 16

6. What will be the output of `len([4, 5, 7, 9])`.

a. 1 **b.** 9
c. 4 **d.** 3

7. What will be the output of the given code?

```
>>>"python!"[3:]
```

a. `hon!`
b. `hon`
c. `"hon"`
d. `"hon!"`

8. Which of the following functions checks whether all the characters in a string are whitespaces?

a. `isnumeric()`
b. `swapcase`
c. `istitle()`
d. `isspace()`

9. Which operator is known as String Formatting operator in Python?

a. `\\`
b. `\`
c. `%`
d. `**`

10. Which one of the following functions replaces all occurrences of old substring in string with new string?

a. `replace(new, old[,max])`
b. `replace(old, new[,max])`
c. `replace(old, new[max])`
d. `replace(new, old[max])`

11. If we do not give any value for the index before the colon, which element of the string will the slice start from?

a. First
b. Zero
c. Second
d. Last

12. If we do not give any value for the index after the colon, which element of the string will the slice go up to?

a. Third
b. First
c. Fourth
d. Last

13. If the second index is smaller than the first index, what will be the output?

a. String itself
b. Null
c. Empty string
d. First Character

14. What will be the output of the given code?

```
>>>str = "*"
>>>seq = ("hello","world")
>>>print (str.join(seq))
```

a. `"hello"*"world"`
b. `hello*world`
c. `hello world`
d. error

15. What will be the output of the given code?

```
>>>str = "John is good student"
>>>print (str.split(' ',2))
```

a. `['John', 'is', 'good student']`
b. `['John', 'is', 'good', 'student']`
c. `['John is', 'good student']`
d. `['John is', 'good', 'student']`

16. What will be the output of the given code?

```
>>>print('wxyZ!56'.swapcase())
```

a. `WXYZ!`
b. `WXYz56@`
c. `Wxyz`
d. `WXYz!56`

17. What will be the output of the given code?

```
>>>print ('john' boy, good' .title())
```

a. `John boy good`
b. `John Boy good`
c. `John Boy Good`
d. none

18. Which of the following will separate all the items in list?

a. `*`
b. `,`
c. `;`
d. `&`

19. What is the repetition operator in lists?

a. `*`
b. `,`
c. `;`
d. `&`

20. Which of the following functions will sort a list?

a. `list.sort`
b. `list.sort([func])`
c. `list.sort[func]`
d. `list.sort(func)`

21. What will be the output of the given code?

```
list = ['john', 'book', 123, 3.45, 105, 'good']
>>>print (list[4:])
```

a. `[3.45, 105, 'good']`
b. `['john', 'book', 123, 3.45]`
c. `[105, 'good']`
d. `[123, 3.45]`

22. What will be the output of the given code?

```
list = ['john', 'book', 123, 3.45, 105, 'good']
>>>print (list[2:5])
```

a. `[123, 3.45, 105]`
b. `['book', 123, 3.45, 105, 'good']`
c. `['john', 'book', 'good']`
d. `[123, 3.45, 105, 'good']`

23. Which of the following functions will give the total length of a list?

a. `Len`
b. `len(list)`
c. `max(len)`
d. `max len(list)`

24. What will be the output of the given code?

```
list = [2356, 325.8, 3450, 1897]
>>>print("minimum value in:", list, "is", min(list))
```

a. 3450
b. 1897
c. 2356
d. 325.8

25. What will be the output of the given code?

```
list("hi")
```

a. `['hi']`
b. `["hi" ]`
c. `['h', 'i']`
d. `hi`

26. Which of the following functions will be used to shuffle a list?

a. `random.shufle(list)`
b. `list.shuffle()`
c. `shuffle(list)`
d. `shuffle.list()`

27. What will be the output of the given code?

```
list=[1, 2, 3, 4, 10]
>>>print (list[-1])
```

a. 1
b. 10
c. 4
d. Error

28. What will be the output of the given code?

```
list=[1, 2, 3, 4, 10]
>>>print (list[:-1])
```

a. `[4, 3, 2, 1]` b. `10`
c. `[1, 2, 3, 4]` d. error

29. Which of the following functions will be used to add a new element to a list?

a. `list.append(obj)` b. `list.add(obj)`
c. `list.append()` d. `list.add()`

30. Which of the following functions will be used to insert 8 to the forth position in the list?

a. `list.insert(8, 4)` b. `list.add(4, 8)`
c. `list.add(8, 4)` d. `list.insert(4, 8)`

31. What will be the output of the given code?

```
list=[1, 2, 3, 4, 10]
>>>del list[3]
>>>print(list)
```

a. `[1, 2, 4, 10]` b. `[1, 2, 3, 10]`
c. `[1, 2, 4]` d. error

32. Which of the following functions is used to remove string "python" from the list?

a. `list.remove(python)` b. `list.delete("python")`
c. `list.remove("python")` d. `list.del`

33. Which of the following functions is used to return a tuple to a list?

a. `list(seq)` b. `seq(list)`
c. `list(tuple)` d. `tuple(list)`

Short Questions

1. What is string in Python? Why is `len` function used in string?
2. How we can access the last letter of the string with the help of length? Explain with an example.
3. What is the_`slice` operator? Explain with an example.
4. Write a program to search a character in a string.
5. What will be the output of the given code?

```
>>> string = "computer"
>>> letter = string[6]
>>> print letter
```

6. What will be the output of the given code? Give the reason.

```
>>> string = 'keyboard'
>>> string[6:4]
```

7. Write a Python program to get a single string from two given strings separated by a space, and swap the first two characters of each string.
8. What will be the output of the given code?

```
>>>str1 = "Hello World!"
>>>str2 = 'Welcome to Programming'
```

```
>>>print (str1 [4])
>>>print (str1 * 5)
>>>print (str2 * 3)
>>>print (str1 [6:])
>>>print (str2 [14:])
>>>print (str1 [5:10])
>>>print (str2 + "Python")
```

9. What will be the output of the given code?

```
>>> print("%o is the octal equivalent of %d" %(6,6))
>>> print ("the fourth letter of %s is %c"      %('programming','i'))
>>> print("The sum = %d" %(-5))
>>> print("%X is the hexadecimal equivalent of %d" %(14,14))
>>> print("%x is the hexadecimal equivalent of %d" %(13,13))
```

10. What will be the output of the given codes?

a)
```
>>>str = "This is my first python program. My first Python program is
simple.
>>>print (str.replace('first', 'second')
>>>print (str.replace('first', 'second', 2)
```

b)
```
>>>s = "I am learning Python and it is simple to learn.
>>>print ('Maximum character is:' max(s))
>>>print ('Minimum character is:' min (s))
```

c)
```
>>>str = "This is my first python program. My first Python program is
simple.
>>>print (str.count('o',0,28))
>>>print(str.count('o',0,60))
```

d)
```
>>>str = "Welcome to programming in python"
>>>print (str.find('gramm',0,31))
>>>print (str.find('thing'))
```

e)
```
>>>str = "Welcome to programming in python"
>>>print (str.index('gramm',0,31))
>>>print (str.index('thing'))
```

f)
```
>>>str = "Welcome to programming in python"
>>>print (str.startswith('in',8,25))
>>>str = "Welcome to programming in python"
>>>print (str.startswith('in',23,31))
```

g)
```
>>>str = "Welcome to programming in python"
>>>print (str.endswith('in',8,25))
>>>str = "Welcome to programming in python"
>>>print (str.endswith('in',0,31))
```

11. What is a list? Explain with an example.

12. How can we add an element in the list? Write a program to insert 32 to the fourth position in the given list [1, 4, 23, 56, 90].

13. What will be the output of the given codes?

a)
```
>>>list = ['hey', 234, 1.32, 'book', 100]
>>>print("item at position 3=", list[3])
>>>list[3]=432
>>>print("item at position 3=", list[3])
>>>print("item at position 1 and 2 is", list[1], list[2])
>>>list [1] = 'hi'; list[2] = 340
>>>print("item at position 1 and 2 is", list[1], list[2])
```

b)
```
>>>list = ['hey', 234, 1.32, 'book', 100]
>>>print(list)
>>>del list[4]
>>>print("list after deletion:", list)
>>>print(list * 3)
>>>print(list + list)
```

c)
```
>>>tuple = ['hey', 234, 1.32, 'book', 100]
>>>print("list:", list(tuple))
```

d)
```
>>>list = ['hey', 234, 1.32, 'book', 100]
>>>print("old list before append:", list)
>>>list.append(387)
>>>print("new list after append:", list)
```

e)
```
>>>list = ['hey', 234, 1.32, 'book', 234, 100, 234]
>>>print("the number of times", 234, "appears in", list, "=", list.
count(234))
```

f)
```
>>>list = ['hey', 234, 1.32, 'book']
>>>list.remove('hey')
>>>print(list)
```

g)
```
>>>list = ['hey', 234, 1.32, 'book', 100]
>>>print(list.index(100))
>>>list = ['hey', 234, 1.32, 'book', 100]
>>>print(list.index('john'))
```

14. Write a program to reverse a list.

15. What will be the output of the given code?
```
>>>list=input("Enter a list(space separated):")
>>>list = list(map(int,list.split()))
>>>print("maximum element in a list:", max(list))
```

16. Write a Python program that accepts numbers separated by commas. Produce a list with those numbers.

17. Suppose there is a list containing the names of animals. Write a Python program that will display only the first and last animal names from the given list.

18. Write a Python program that displays the smallest number from the list.

19. What will be the output of the given code?
```
>>>values = input("input some comma separated numbers:")
>>>list = values.split(",")
>>>print ('list":',list)
```

20. What will be the output of the given code?

```
>>>list = ['hey', 234, 1.32, 'book', 100]
>>>print ('list before poping:",list)
>>>list.pop(-1)
>>>print("list after poping:", list)
```

Answers to Multiple Choice Questions

1. b	**2.** d	**3.** c	**4.** a	**5.** b	**6.** c	**7.** a	**8.** d	**9.** c	**10.** b
11. a	**12.** d	**13.** c	**14.** b	**15.** a	**16.** d	**17.** c	**18.** b	**19.** a	**20.** b
21. c	**22.** a	**23.** b	**24.** d	**25.** c	**26.** a	**27.** b	**28.** c	**29.** a	**30.** d
31. b	**32.** c	**33.** a							

6 TUPLES AND DICTIONARIES

6.1 TUPLES

In Python Programming, tuples are just like the lists we have seen in earlier chapters. Tuples are the sequence or series values of different types separated by commas (,). Just like strings and lists, values in tuples can also be accesed by their index values, which are integers starting from 0. The main difference between lists and tuples is that in case of a list, a value in the list can be replaced with another anytime after its creation. Whereas in tuples, the values in it cannot be replaced with another, once tuples are created. List allows us to add new items to it. But tuple does not allow us to add new items, once it is created.

Example

The names of the months in a year can be defined in a tuple:

```
>>> months = ('January', 'February', 'March', 'April', 'May', 'June',
'July', 'August', 'September', 'October', 'November', 'December')
```

6.1.1 Creating Tuples

Creating tuples is easy in Python. In order to create a tuple, all the items or elements are placed inside parentheses separated by commas and assigned to a variable. The parentheses, at the time of creating a tuple, is not necessary, but it is a good practice to use parentheses. Tuples can have any number of different data items (that is, integer, float, string, list, etc.).

Examples

1. A tuple with integer data items

```
>>> tuple = (4,2,9,1)
>>> print tuple
(4,2,9,1)          # Output
```

2. A tuple with items of different data types

```
>>>tuple_mix = (2,30,"Python",5.8,"Program")
>>>print tuple_mix
(2, 30, 'Python', 5.8, 'Program')              # Output
```

3. Nested tuple

```
>>>nested_tuple = ("Python", [1,4,2],["john",3.9])
>>> print nested_tuple
('Python', [1, 4, 2], ['john', 3.9])           # Output
```

4. Tuple can also be created without parenthesis

```
>>>tuple =4.9,6,'house'
>>>print tuple
(4.9, 6, 'house')          # Output
```

Note *Creating a tuple with one element is somewhat different. When we are creating a tuple with one element, we need to add a final comma after the item or element in order to complete the assignment of the tuple.*

Example

```
>>>tuple = ("home")
>>>type(tuple)
<type 'str'>               # Output
```

In the above assignment statement, we are trying to create a tuple with only one item, but when we print its type in Python interpreter, the type is not `tuple` but `str`.

Now, consider the following code:

```
>>>tuple = ("home",)
>>>type(tuple)
<type 'tuple'>             # Output
```

Here, we added a final comma after the element `"home"` and the python interpreter takes the tuple as the type `tuple`.

This can also be done without parentheses:

```
>>>tuple = "home",
>>>type(tuple)
<type 'tuple'>             # Output
```

6.1.2 Accessing Values in Tuples

In order to access the values in a tuple, it is necessary to use the index number enclosed in square brackets along with the name of the tuple.

Example 1: Using square brackets

```
>>>tup1 = ('Physics','chemistry','mathematics')
>>>tup2 = (10,20,30,40,50)
>>>print tup1[1]
Chemistry          # Output
>>>print tup2[4]
50                 # Output
>>>print tup1[0]
Physics            # Output
>>> print tup2[0]
10                 # Output
```

Note *We can also use slicing in order to print the continuous values in a tuple.*

Example 2: Using slicing

```
>>>tup1 = ('Physics','chemistry','mathematics')
>>>tup2 = (10,20,30,40,50)
>>>tup2[1:4]
(20, 30, 40)                    # Output
>>>tup1[:1]
('Physics',)                    # Output
>>>tup1[:2]
('Physics', 'chemistry')        # Output
```

In the Example 1, we can see that the output does not comprise any braces, that is, because a single element or item is being retrieved from the tuple whereas in the Example 2 above, tuples are cutting into parts i.e. slicing. The output is also a tuple which we get after slicing and the tuples in Python programming language are written in parentheses.

TIP

As with the lists and strings, we can access the elements of the tuple. However, unlike strings and lists, we cannot update or delete the values in the tuple—tuples are immutable.

Check Your Understanding

1. **What is a tuple and how is it created in Python?**

Ans. In Python programming, tuples are just like the lists we have seen in earlier chapters. Tuples are the sequence or series of different types of values separated by commas. Creating tuples is pretty easy in Python. In order to create a tuple, all the items or elements are placed inside parentheses separated by commas and assigned to a variable. Tuples can have any number of different data items (i.e., integer, float, string, list, etc.).

2. How are the values in a tuple accessed?

Ans. In order to access the values in a tuple, we need to use the index number enclosed in square brackets along with the name of the tuple.

Example

```
>>>tuple = (10,20,30,40)
>>>tuple[1]
20          # Output
>>>tuple[3]
40          # Output
```

6.1.3 Tuples are Immutable

Tuples are immutable. The values or items in the tuple cannot be changed once it is declared. If we want to change the values, we have to create a new tuple.

Example

```
# declaring a tuple
>>>tup = (12, 15, "Python", 2.3)
# change the 3rd element "Python" to "Hello"
>>>tup[2] = "Hello"
TypeError: 'tuple' object does not support item assignment
```

In the given example, a tuple `tup` is declared with some items. Now, if we try changing the 3rd element `"Python"` to `"Hello"` using the assignment operator, the Python interpreter generates an error. From this example, it is clear that the values of tuple elements cannot be changed afterwards.

6.1.4 Tuple Assignment

Tuple assignment is a very attractive and powerful feature in Python. It allows the assignment of values to a tuple of variables on the left side of the assignment from the tuple of values on the right side of the assignment.

The number of variables in the tuple on the left of the assignment must match the number of elements/items in the tuple on the right of the assignment.

Example

```
# creating a tuple
>>>Anil = ('221','Anil','Rahul','Delhi',1971,'Jaipur Gwalior')
# tuple assignment
>>>(id,fst_name,lst_name,city,year_of_birth,birth_place) = Anil
```

Here, we created a tuple named `john`, with 7 elements inside it. Now, in the next statement, the value of each element of this tuple is assigned to the respective variables. It can be seen that the number of variables to the left of assignment is seven and the number of items in the tuple is also seven; hence, the number of values are matching and the assignment is successful.

Now,

```
>>>print id
221          # Output
>>>print fst_name
John         # Output
>>>print year_of_birth
1971         # Output
>>>print birth_place
atlanta Georgia             # Output
```

In the assignment statement, each variable is assigned with a value that was inside the tuple and can be accessed individually. If we had used the traditional assignment procedure, it would have been done in 7 lines of statement. With the help of tuple assignment, it is done in a one-line statement.

Similarly, sometimes we need to swap the values of two variables in the program. With the traditional approach, this can be done by using a temporary variable for swapping the values of two variables.

Example

```
>>>temp = x
>>> x = y
>>> y = temp
```

In order to swap the values of variables `x` and `y`, we need a temporary variable `temp`. However, this problem can be solved much more conveniently with tuple assignment.

```
>>>x = 3
>>>y = 4
>>>x , y = y , x            # Using tuple assignment
>>>print x
4            # Output
>>>print y
3            # Output
```

Hence, with the use of tuple assignment approach, there is no need to use any temporary variable to swap values of two variables. All it takes is one simple statement.

Note *The number of variables on the left side of the assignment must match the number of values on the right side of the assignment.*

```
>>>x,y = 1,2,3,4
Traceback (most recent call last):             # Output
  File "<pyshell#62>", line 1, in <module>
x,y = 1,2,3,4
ValueError: too many values to unpack
```

6.1.5 Tuples as Return Values

Tuples can also be returned by the function as return values. Generally, the function returns only one value but by returning tuple, a function can return more than one value.

For example, if we want to compute a division with two integers and want to know the quotient and the remainder, both the quotient and the remainder can be computed at the same time. Two values will be returned, i.e., quotient and remainder, by using the tuple as the return value of the function.

Example

```
>>>defdiv_mod(a,b):                    # defining function
... quotient = a/b
... remainder = a%b
... return quotient,remainder # function returning two values

# function calling
>>>x = 10
>>>y = 3
>>>t = div_mod(x,y)
>>>print t
(3, 1)                # Output
>>>type(t)
<type 'tuple'>                 # Output
```

In the given example, we have defined the function `div_mod`, which calculates the quotient and remainder. It returns two values, the quotient and the remainder respectively. Now, at the time of calling the function, a tuple needs to store the values returned by the function. Hence, we have taken a variable that calls the function `div_mod` and stores the values `(3,1)`, which, in our example, are quotient and remainder respectively.

When we tried to see the type of the variable `t`, it was tuple.

We can also use the tuple assignment approach in order to print the quotient and the remainder separately.

```
>>>quot, rem = div_mod(10,3)
>>> print quot
3           # Output
>>> print rem
1           # Output
```

Here, we have taken two variables at the left side which are `quot` and `rem`. Now, when the function `div_mod` returns the values of quotient and remainder, the values will be stored in `quot` and `rem` respectively.

Now, we will see an example of a function that returns tuple as return value.

Example

```
>>>defmax_min(t):
...     return max(t),min(t)
```

max and min are the built-in functions in Python which return the maximum and minimum elements from a sequence. We have defined a function max_min that returns both the values.

```
>>>a = (10,3,2,100,72,67)
>>>max_min(a)
(100, 2)            # Output
```

6.1.6 Variable-length Argument Tuples

Variable number of arguments can also be passed to a function. A variable name that is preceded by an asterisk (*) collects the arguments into a tuple.

Example

```
>>>def traverse(*t):
...           i=0
...           while i<len(t):
...           print t[i]
...           i=i+1
>>>traverse(1,2,3,4,5)
```

Output:

```
1
2
3
4
5
```

In the given example, we have defined a function traverse with argument *t, which means it can take any number of arguments and will print each of them one by one.

Similarly, we know that the opposite of collect is scatter. In order to pass a series of arguments to a function, we need to simply use * before the arguments.

For example, the function div_mod that was discussed in earlier section takes exactly two arguments; but it does not work when we pass a tuple to it.

```
>>>t = (10,3)
>>>div_mod(t)
Traceback (most recent call last):                # Output
  File "<pyshell#142>", line 1, in <module>
div_mod(t)
TypeError: div_mod() takes exactly 2 arguments (1 given)
```

To make it work with a tuple, it is necessary to scatter the values of the tuple.

```
>>>div_mod(*t)
(3, 1)              # Output
```

We use * before t while passing an argument to the function div_mod. It scatters the values (10, 3) in two values; the function accepts these arguments and gives the result.

TIP

When the asterisk (`*`) is used before the arguments at the time of function definition, it collects all the calling function arguments in a tuple and when it is used at the time of calling, it scatters the values of the tuple.

Check Your Understanding

1. An email address is provided: `hello@python.org` . Using tuple assignment, split the username and domain from the email address. (Hint : use split method)

Ans.
```
>>>addr = 'hello@python.org'
>>>usrname, domain = addr.split('@')
>>>print usrname
Hello          # Output
>>>print domain
    python.org        # Output
```

2. Write a function called `sumall` that takes any number of arguments and returns their sum.

Ans.
```
>>> def sumall(*t):
...    i=0
...    sum=0
...    whilei<len(t):
...    sum = sum + t[i]
...    i = i + 1
... return sum

>>>sumall(1,2,3,4,5,6,7)
28             # Output
```

3. Write a function called `circleinfo` which takes the radius of circle as argument and returns the area and circumference of the circle.

Ans.
```
>>>defcircleinfo(r):
...    c=2 * 3.14159 * r
...    a=3.14159 * r * r
...  return (c,a)

>>>circleinfo(10)
 (62.8318, 314.159)        # Output
```

6.1.7 Basic Tuples Operations

1. Concatenation The concatenation operator works in tuples in the same way as it does in lists. This operator concatenates two tuples. This is done by the + operator in Python.

Example

```
>>>t1 = (1,2,3,4)
>>>t2 = (5,6,7,8)
>>>t3 = t1 + t2
>>>print t3
(1, 2, 3, 4, 5, 6, 7, 8)                    # Output
```

In this example, there are two tuples, `t1` and `t2`. Tuples `t1` and `t2` are concatenated using `+` operator between them and the resulting tuple is stored in the variable `t3`. Now, when we print `t3`, it gives the concatenation of `t1` and `t2`.

2. Repetition The repetition operator works as its name suggests; it repeats the tuples a given number of times. Repetition is performed by the`*` operator in Python.

Example

```
>>>tuple = ('ok',)
>>>tuple * 5
('ok', 'ok', 'ok', 'ok', 'ok')          # Output
>>>('Hello',) * 3
('Hello', 'Hello', 'Hello')             # Output
```

Note that, the tuple `('ok',)` was repeated 5 times and the tuple `('Hello',)` was repeated 3 times.

3. `in` Operator The `in` operator also works on tuples. It tells user that the given element exists in the tuple or not. It gives a Boolean output, that is, TRUE or FALSE. If the given input exists in the tuple, it gives the TRUE as output, otherwise FALSE.

Example 1

```
>>>tuple = (10,20,30,40)
>>>20 in tuple
True                # Output
>>>50 in tuple
False               # Output
```

Example 2

```
>>>tuple = ('anil', 'rahul', 'rohan')
>>> 'james' in tuple
False               # Output
>>> 'rohan' in tuple
True         # Output
```

4. Iteration Iteration can be done in tuples using `for` loop. It helps in traversing the tuple.

Example

```
>>>tuple = (1,2,3,4,5,6)
>>>for x in tuple:
... print x
```

Output:

```
1
2
3
4
5
6
```

6.1.8 Built-In Tuple Functions

Python includes many built-in functions that can be executed on tuples. Some of them are described in Table 6.1.

TABLE 6.1 Built-in Functions

S.No.	Function	Description
1.	`cmp(tuple1, tuple2)`	It compares the items of two tuples.
2.	`len(tuple)`	It returns the length of a tuple.
3.	`zip(tuple1, tuple2)`	It 'zips' elements from two tuples into a list of tuples.
4.	`max(tuple)`	It returns the largest value among the elements in a tuple.
5.	`min(tuple)`	It returns the smallest value among the elements in a tuple
6.	`tuple(seq)`	It converts a list into a tuple.

Example

```
>>> tuple1 = ('physics','chemistry','mathematics')
>>> tuple2 = (10,20,30,40,50)
>>>cmp(tuple1,tuple2)
1          # Output
>>>cmp(tuple2,tuple1)
-1         # Output
>>>len(tuple1)
3          # Output
>>>len(tuple2)
5          # Output
>>>zip(tuple1,tuple2)
[('physics', 10), ('chemistry', 20), ('mathematics', 30)]       # Output
>>>max(tuple1)
'physics'        # Output
>>>max(tuple2)
50         # Output
>>>min(tuple1)
'chemistry'            # Output
>>>min(tuple2)
10         # Output
```

In the above example, `physics` is `max` element of `tuple1` because if we compare the first letter of all the words in the `tuple` then `p` is greater than `c` and `m`. Hence, the comparison stops here and `physics` is declared as the `max` element of the tuple. Similarly, `chemistry` is the `min` element of this tuple.

> ***Note*** *`zip` is a built-in function that takes two or more sequences and "zips" them into a list of tuples where each tuple contains one element from each sequence.*

TIP

When there are different numbers of elements in the tuples i.e. if the length of the tuples are not same then the resulting tuple after applying the `zip` function will have the length of shorter tuple.

Example

```
>>> s = ('Hello')                    # Length is 5
>>> t = ('Python')                   # Length is 6
>>> zip(s,t)
[('H', 'P'), ('e', 'y'), ('l', 't'), ('l', 'h'), ('o', 'o')]
    # Resulting tuple has length 5 equal to s
```

Check Your Understanding

1. **What are concatenation and iteration? Give one example of concatenation.**

Ans. Concatenation:

The concatenation operator works in tuples in the same way as in lists. This operator concatenates two tuples. Concatenation is done by the + operator in Python.

Example

```
>>>t1 = (10,20,30)
>>>t2 = (50,60)
>>>t3 = t1 + t2
>>>print t3
(10, 20, 30, 50, 60)            # Output
```

Iteration:

Iteration is done in tuples using `for` loop. It helps in traversing the tuple.

2. **Give one-one example for `zip`, `max` and `min` methods.**

Ans.
```
>>>tuple1 = ('a','b','c')
>>>tuple2 = (1,2,3)
>>>max(tuple2)
```

```
  3            # Output
>>>min(tuple1)
  'a'          # Output
>>>zip(tuple1,tuple2)
  [('a', 1), ('b', 2), ('c', 3)]          # Output
```

6.2 DICTIONARIES

The Python dictionary is an unordered collection of items or elements. All other compound data types in Python have only values as their elements or items whereas the dictionary has a key: value pair. Each value is associated with a key. In the list and the tuple, there are indices that are only of integer type but in dictionary, we have keys and they can be of any type.

Dictionary is said to be a mapping between some set of keys and values. Each key is associated to a value. The mapping of a key and value is called as a key-value pair and together they are called one item or element.

A key and its value are separated by a colon `(:)` between them. The items or elements in a dictionary are separated by commas and all the elements must be enclosed in curly braces. A pair of curly braces with no values in between is known as an empty dictionary.

The values in a dictionary can be duplicated, but the keys in the dictionary are unique.

6.2.1 Creating a Dictionary

Creating a dictionary is simple in Python. The values in a dictionary can be of any data type, but the keys must be of immutable data types (such as string, number or tuple).

Example

Empty Dictionary

```
>>> dict1 = {}
>>>print dict1
{}          # Output
```

Dictionary with integer keys

```
>>> dict1 = {1:'red',2:'yellow',3:'green'}
>>>print dict1
{1: 'red', 2: 'yellow', 3: 'green'}          # Output
```

Dictionary with mixed keys

```
>>> dict1 = {'name' : 'jinnie', 3:['Hello',2,3]}
>>>print dict1
{3: ['Hello', 2, 3], 'name': 'jinnie'}          # Output
```

In the above examples, we have seen many types of ways for creating a dictionary in Python programming language. One thing to be noticed in initialization of dictionary is that the values of keys can be given in any order but on printing the dictionary, it prints the sorted order of keys. This is because the dictionary has an internal mechanism to sort the keys and then print them.

Note *Python also provides a built-in function* `dict()` *for creating a dictionary:*

Example

```
>>> d1 = dict({1:'red', 2:'yellow', 3:'green'})
>>> d2 = dict([(1,'red'), (2,'yellow'),(3,'green')])
>>> d3 = dict(one=1, two=2, three=3)
>>> print d3
{'three': 3, 'two': 2, 'one': 1}
```

In the above example, three dictionaries `d1, d2 and d3` are initialized using the built-in `dict` function in the Python programming language.

6.2.2 Accessing Values in a Dictionary

In order to access the elements from a dictionary, we can use the value of the key enclosed in square brackets. Python also provides a `get()` method that is used with the key in order to access the value. There is a difference in both the accessing methods. When the key is not found in the dictionary, it returns `none` instead of `KeyError`.

```
>>> dict1 = {'name' : 'John', 'age' : 27}
>>> dict1['name']
'John'              # Output
>>> print dict1['name']
John        # Output
>>> print dict1['age']
27          # Output
>>> dict1.get('name')
'John'              # Output
>>> print dict1.get('name')
John        # Output
>>> dict1.get('age')
27          # Output
```

TIP

When we try to access a key that does not exist in the dictionary, an error occurs.

```
>>> print dict1['address']
Traceback (most recent call last):          # Output
  File "<pyshell#19>", line 1, in <module>
    print dict1['address']
KeyError: 'address'
>>> dict1.get('address')
```

`get()` method returns None, which means nothing, when there is no value in the dictionary stored against the given key. `get()` also allows us to specify custom default value.

Example

```
>>> dict1 = {'name' : 'John', 'age' : 27}
>>> dict1.get("address",0)              # Default value is 0
0
```

Here, we have searched for a key `'address'` which is not present in the dictionary. `get()` function therefore gives the default value which is 0.

Check Your Understanding

1. **What is a Dictionary in Python?**

Ans. Python dictionary is an unordered collection of items or elements. All other compound data types in Python have only values as their elements or items whereas the dictionary has a key: value pair, i.e., each value is associated with a key. In the list and the tuple, there are indices that are only of integer type, but in the dictionary, we can have keys of any type.

2. **Give one example of accessing the value in dictionary.**

Ans.
```
>>> dict1 = {1:'a',2:'b',3:'c'}
>>> dict1[1]
  'a'           # Output
>>> dict1[2]
  'b'           # Output
>>> dict1[3]
  'c'           # Output
```

6.2.3 Updating Dictionary

Dictionaries in Python are mutable. Unlike those in tuple and string, the values in a dictionary can be changed, added or deleted. If the key is present in the dictionary, then the associated value with that key is updated or changed; otherwise a new key: value pair is added.

Example

```
>>> dict1 = {'name' : 'John', 'age' : 27}
>>> dict1['age'] = 30   # updating a value
>>> print dict
{'age': 30, 'name': 'John'}             # Output
>>> dict1['address'] = 'Alaska'         # adding a key: value
>>>print dict1
{'age': 30, 'name': 'John', 'address': 'Alaska'}        # Output
```

Note that we tried to reassign the value `'30'` to the key `'age'`, Python interpreter first searches the key in the dictionary. In our example, the key `'age'` exists. Hence, the value of `'age'` is updated to `30`. However, in the next statement, it does not find the key `'address'`; hence, the key: value `'address': 'Alaska'` is added to the dictionary.

6.2.4 Deleting Elements from Dictionary

The items or elements from a dictionary can be removed or deleted by using `pop()` method. `pop()` method removes that item from the dictionary for which the key is provided. It also returns the value of the item.

Furthermore, there is a `popitem()` method in Python. `popitem()` method is used to remove or delete and return an arbitrary item from the dictionary.

The `clear()` method removes all the items or elements from a dictionary at once. When this operation is performed, the dictionary becomes an empty dictionary.

Python also provides a `del` keyword, which deletes the dictionary itself. When this operation is performed, the dictionary is deleted from the memory and it ceases to exist.

Example

```
>>>dict_cubes = {1:1, 2:8, 3:9, 4:64, 5:125, 6:216}

>>>dict_cubes.pop(3)          # remove a particular item
9        # Output
>>>dict_cubes
{1: 1, 2: 8, 4: 64, 5: 125, 6: 216}         # Output

>>>dict_cubes.popitem()       # remove an arbitrary item
(1, 1)           # Output
>>>dict_cubes.popitem()
(2, 8)           # Output
>>>dict_cubes
{4: 64, 5: 125, 6: 216}       # Output

>>>deldict_cubes[6]           # delete a particular item
>>>dict_cubes
{4: 64, 5: 125}        # Output

>>>dict_cubes.clear()         # remove all items
>>>dict_cubes
{}       # Output

>>>deldict_cubes              # delete the dictionary itself
>>> print dict_cubes
Traceback (most recent call last):         # Output
  File "<pyshell#40>", line 1, in <module>
printdict_cubes
NameError: name 'dict_cubes' is not defined
```

We have seen many examples of deleting items from a dictionary. When the `clear()` method was used, all the items were removed and an empty dictionary was left. When the `del` method was used, the dictionary was deleted from the memory.

6.2.5 Properties of Dictionary Keys

The values in the dictionary do not have any restrictions; any data type can be used here, including string, integer, any user-defined object, python object, etc. However, such is not the case with the keys.

Keys have some restrictions while defining them. There are two important points to be kept in mind about keys which are as follows:

1. One key in a dictionary cannot have two values, i.e., duplicate keys are not allowed in the dictionary; they must be unique. Whenever duplicate keys are assigned values in a dictionary, the latest value is considered and stored whereas the previous one is lost.

Example

```
>>> dict1 = {'Name':'John','Age':30,'Name':'Jinnie'}
>>> print dict1['Name']
Jinnie              # Output
```

In the above example, two values have been assigned to the same key `'Name'`. However, when we print the dictionary, only the latest one, i.e., `'Jinnie'` is stored whereas `'John'` is lost.

2. Keys are immutable, i.e., we can use string, integers or tuples for dictionary keys, but something like `['key']` is not valid.

Example

```
>>> dict1 = {['Name']:'John','Age':30}


Traceback (most recent call last):
  File "<pyshell#46>", line 1, in <module>
    Dict1 = {['Name']:'John','Age':30}
TypeError: unhashable type: 'list'
```

Note that when we tried to input a key `['Name']`, Python interpreter gives an error message.

Check Your Understanding

1. **What are the different methods used in deleting elements from dictionary?**

Ans. `pop()` method removes that item from the dictionary for which the key is provided. It also returns the value of the item.

`popitem()` method is used to remove or delete and return an arbitrary item from the dictionary.

`clear()` method removes all the items or elements from a dictionary at the same time.

Python also provides a `del` keyword that deletes the dictionary itself.

2. **What are the two properties of `key` in the dictionary?**

Ans. 1. One key in a dictionary cannot have two values, i.e., duplicate keys are not allowed in the dictionary; they must be unique.

2. Keys are immutable, i.e., we can use string, integers or tuples for dictionary keys, but cannot use something like `['key']`.

6.2.6 Operations in Dictionary

1. Traversing We have learnt about traversing strings, lists and tuples in the previous sections. Now, we will learn traversing in a dictionary. Traversing in dictionary is done on the basis of keys. For this, `for` loop is used, which iterates over the keys in the dictionary and prints the corresponding values using keys.

Example

We will define a function `print_dict`. Whenever a dictionary is passed as an argument to this function, it will print the keys and values of the dictionary.

```
>>>defprint_dict(d):
... for c in d:
...        print c,d[c]

>>> dict1 = {1:'a',2:'b',3:'c',4:'d',5:'e',6:'f',7:'g',8:'h'}
>>> print_dict(dict1)
```

Output:

```
1 a
2 b
3 c
4 d
5 e
6 f
7 g
8 h
```

This example prints the key: value pairs in the dictionary `dict`.

Note *Traversing in the dictionary is done on the basis of keys because they are unique.*

2. Membership Using the membership operator (`in` and `not in`), we can test whether a key is in the dictionary or not. We have seen the `in` operator earlier as well in the list and the tuple. It takes an input key and finds the key in the dictionary. If the key is found, then it returns True, otherwise, False.

Example

```
>>>cubes = {1:1, 2:8, 3:27, 4:64, 5:125, 6:216}
>>>3 in cubes
True        # Output
>>>7 not in cubes
True        # Output
>>>10 in cubes
False            # Output
```

6.2.7 Built-In Dictionary Methods

There are some built-in methods which are included in Python given in Table 6.2.

Table 6.2 Built-In Dictionary Methods

Sr.No.	Function	Description
1.	`all(dict)`	It is a Boolean type function, which returns True if all keys of dictionary are true (or the dictionary is empty).
2.	`any(dict)`	It is also a Boolean type function, which returns True if any key of the dictionary is true. It returns false if the dictionary is empty.
3.	`len(dict)`	It returns the number of items (length) in the dictionary.
4.	`cmp(dict1,dict2)`	It compares the items of two dictionaries.
5.	`sorted(dict)`	It returns the sorted list of keys.
6.	`str(dict)`	It produces a printable string representation of the dictionary.
7.	`dict.clear()`	It deletes all the items in a dictionary at once.
8.	`dict.copy()`	It returns a copy of the dictionary.
9.	`dict.fromkeys()`	It creates a new dictionary with keys from sequence and values set to value.
10.	`dict.get(key, default=None)`	For `key` key, returns value or default if key not in dictionary.
11.	`dict.has_key(key)`	It finds the key in dictionary; returns True if found and false otherwise.
12.	`dict.items()`	It returns a list of entire key: value pair of dictionary.
13.	`dict.keys()`	It returns the list of all the keys in dictionary.
14.	`dict.setdefault (key, default=None)`	Similar to `get()`, but will set `dict[key]=default` if `key` is not already in dict.
15.	`dict.update(dict2)`	It adds the items from `dict2` to `dict`.
16.	`dict.values()`	It returns all the values in the dictionary.

Example

```
>>>cubes = {1:1, 2:8, 3:27, 4:64, 5:125, 6:216}
>>>all(cubes)
True        # Output
>>>any(cubes)
True        # Output
>>>len(cubes)
6           # Output
>>>sorted(cubes)
[1, 2, 3, 4, 5, 6]          # Output
>>>str(cubes)
'{1: 1, 2: 8, 3: 27, 4: 64, 5: 125, 6: 216}'          # Output
```

Check Your Understanding

1. What are the different operations performed on the dictionary?

Ans. (i) Traversing:

Traversing in dictionary is done on the basis of keys. We use `for` loop which iterates over the keys in the dictionary and prints the corresponding values using keys.

(ii) Membership:

Using the membership operator (`in` and `not in`), we can test whether a key is in the dictionary or not. It takes an input key and finds the key in the dictionary. If the key is found, then it returns True, otherwise False.

2. Give examples for `all`, `any`, `len` and `sorted` methods in dictionary.

Ans.

```
>>> dict1 = {8:'a',3:'b',5:'c',7:'d'}
>>> all(dict1)
    True                # Output
>>> any(dict1)
    True                # Output
>>> len(dict1)
    4              # Output
>>> sorted(dict1)
    [3, 5, 7, 8]              # Output
```

ALWAYS REMEMBER

- Tuples are the sequences of different types of values.
- Elements are separated by commas inside the parentheses and are assigned to a variable to create a tuple.
- Tuples can be created with or without parentheses.
- Nested tuples can be created.
- To complete the assignment of the tuple, a final comma must be added after the element.
- In order to access the values in a tuple, it is necessary to use the index number enclosed in square brackets along with the name of the tuple.
- Slicing can be used to print the continuous values in a tuple.
- Tuples are immutable and thus the elements or values cannot be modified.
- Assignment of values to a tuple of variables on the left side of assignment from the tuple of values on the right side of the assignment is allowed.
- A function returns only one value, but by returning tuple, a function can return more than one value.
- Asterisk (`*`) is used before the arguments at the time of function definition. This means that it collects all the calling function arguments in a tuple. When it is used at the time of calling, it scatters the values of the tuple.
- A dictionary is a mapping between some set of keys and values. Each key is associated with a value. The mapping of a key and value is called a key-value pair and together they form one item or element.

- The values in a dictionary are not unique and can be duplicated, but the keys in the dictionary are unique.
- The value of the key enclosed within square brackets is used to access the elements from a dictionary. An alternative method of accessing the elements is the `get()` method, which is used with the key.
- The difference between the accessing methods of dictionary is that when the key is not found in dictionary, it returns `none` instead of `KeyError`.
- Dictionaries are mutable and thus the elements or values can be modified.
- Four methods are used to delete the elements from the dictionary:
  1. `pop()`
  2. `popitem()`
  3. `clear()`
  4. `del`

KEY TERMS

✓ **TUPLE:** Tuples, just like lists, are the sequence or series of different types of values that are separated by commas (,).

✓ **TUPLE ASSIGNMENT:** It allows assignment of values to a tuple of variables on the left side of assignment from the tuple of values on the right side of the assignment.

✓ **VARIABLE-LENGTH ARGUMENT TUPLES:** A variable number of arguments can also be passed to a function. A variable name which is preceded by an asterisk (`*`) collects the arguments into a tuple.

✓ **CONCATENATION:** This operator works in tuples in the same way as in lists. This operator concatenates two tuples. This is done by the + operator in Python.

✓ **REPETITION:** This operator repeats the tuples a given number of times. Repetition is performed by `*` operator.

✓ **`in` OPERATOR:** This operator tells the user whether the given element exists in the tuple or not. It gives a Boolean output, i.e., TRUE or FALSE.

✓ **ITERATION:** Iteration can be done in tuples using `for` loop. It helps in traversing the tuple.

✓ **`len(tuple)`:** It returns the length of the tuple.

✓ **`cmp(tuple1, tuple2)`:** It compares the items of two tuples.

✓ **`max(tuple)`:** It returns the largest value among the elements in a tuple.

✓ **`min(tuple)`:** It returns the smallest value among the elements in a tuple.

✓ **`tuple(seq)`:** It converts a list into a tuple.

✓ **`zip(tuple1, tuple2)`:** It 'zips' elements from two tuples into a list of tuples.

✓ **DICTIONARY:** The Python dictionary is an unordered collection of items or elements. The dictionary has a key: value pair.

✓ **KEY:** It is used to get the value in the dictionary.

✓ **KEY-VALUE:** This pair represents the items in the dictionary.

1. **`dict()`:**This function is used to create a dictionary.

2. **`get()`:** This method is used with the key to access the value in a dictionary.
3. **`pop()`:** This method removes the item from the dictionary and returns the value of the item.
4. **`popitem()`:** This method is used to delete and return an arbitrary item from the dictionary.
5. **`clear()`:** This method removes all the items from the dictionary.
6. **`del`:** It is used to delete the dictionary itself.

✓ **IMMUTABLE:** It is the type in which elements cannot be modified. Tuples are immutable.

✓ **MUTABLE:** It is the type in which elements are modified. Dictionaries are mutable.

1. **`len(dict)`:** It returns the number of items (length) in the dictionary.
2. **`cmp(dict1,dict2)`:** It compares the items of two dictionaries.
3. **`sorted(dict)`:** It returns the sorted list of keys.
4. **`str(dict)`:** It produces a printable string representation of dictionary.

REVIEW EXERCISES

PROGRAMS

1. Given an integral number n, write a program to generate a dictionary that contains (i, i*i) such that i is an integral number between 1 and n (both included). The program should then print the dictionary.

Suppose the following input is supplied to the program:

7

Then, the output should be:
{1:1, 2:4, 3:9, 4:16, 5:25, 6:36, 7:49}

Solution:

```
>>>n = int(raw_input())
>>>d = dict()
>>>for i in range(1,n+1):
    d[i] = i*i
    print d
```

2. Define a function that prints a dictionary where the keys are numbers between 1 and 4 (both included) and the values are cubes of the keys.

Solution:

```
>>>def dictionary():
    n=dict()
    n[1]=1**3
    n[2]=2**3
    n[3]=3**3
    n[4]=4**3
    print n

>>>dictionary()
{1: 1, 2: 8, 3: 27, 4: 64}          #Output
```

3. Consider the tuple (1,3,5,7,9,2,4,6,8,10). Write a program to print half its values in one line and the other half in the next line.

Solution:

```
>>>tup = (1,3,5,7,9,2,4,6,8,10)
>>>tup1 = tup[:5]
>>>tup2 = tup[5:]

>>>print tup1
(1,3,5,7,9)                #Output
>>> print tup2
(2,4,6,8,10)               #Output
```

4. Consider the tuple (12, 7, 38, 56, 78). Write a program to print another tuple whose values are even numbers in the given tuple.

Solution:

```
>>> tup = (12,7,38,56,78)
>>> even_list = list()
>>> for i in tup:
     if i % 2 == 0:
            even_list.append(i)
     print tuple(even_list)

(12, 38, 56, 78)                        # Output
```

5. Define a function that prints a tuple whose values are the cube of a number between 1 and 15 (both included).

Solution:

```
>>> def printTup():
     l = list()
     for i in range(1,16):
            l.append(i**3)
     print tuple(l)

>>> printTup()
(1, 8, 27, 64, 125, 216, 343, 512, 729, 1000, 1331, 1728, 2197, 2744,
3375)                    # Output
```

6. Write a python program to demonstrate tuples functions and operations

Solution:

```
# python program to demonstrate tuples and their basic operations
# zero element tuple
tpl = ();
print "tpl is empty", tpl
tpl1 = (1, 2, 3, 5, 7, 11 );
tpl2 = ('aaa','pqr', 'uvw', 'zzz');
print "displaying the elements in tuple1", tpl1
print "displaying the elements in tuple2", tpl2
# create a new tuple from the exisitng
print "creating tpl3 from tpl1 and tpl2"
```

```
tpl3 = tpl1 + tpl2;
print "displaying the elements in tuple3"
print tpl3
print "Display the lengths of the tuple"
print (len(tpl1))
print (len(tpl2))
print "Max and Min functions on tuple"
print (max(tpl1))
print (max(tpl2))
print (min(tpl1))
print (min(tpl2))
# Search for a value using in.
print "using in for tpl3 and tpl2"
if "uvw" in tpl3:
    print("uvw found")
# Search for a value not present.
if "9" not in tpl2:
    print("9 not found")
print "Using the index on the tuples"
# Print all the tuple elements from the index 1 or more.
print(tpl3[1:])
# print only one element for the index 1.
print(tpl2[:1])
# prin the values from index 3 to 9.
print(tpl3[3:9])
# Get index of element with value "python" in tuple4.
tpl4 = ("aaa", "sss", "www", "python", "program")
print "prin the index value of 3 in tpl1"
index = tpl4.index("python")
print(index, tpl4[index])
#print "unsucessful index of a tuple tpl3"
#inx1 = tpl3.inx1("python") generates AttributeError: 'tuple' object has no
attribute 'inx'
#print(inx1, tpl3[inx1])
print "count function on tuple"
print(tpl2.count(1))
print(tpl3.count(3))
print "when there are not same elements"
print (tpl3.count(30))
print "Using compare over tupless tpl1 tpl2 and tpl3"
print cmp(tpl1, tpl2)
print cmp(tpl2, tpl1)
print cmp(tpl1, tpl3)
print cmp(tpl3, tpl2)
print "Implementing tuple() method"
lst = tuple(tpl3)
print "lst elements : ", lst
print "Deleting the elements in a tuple"
del tpl3;
```

```
# when the tuple is deleted we get an error when displaying
print "After deleting tuple3 : "
print tpl3
```

Output:

```
tpl is empty ()
displaying the elements in tuple1 (1, 2, 3, 5, 7, 11)
displaying the elements in tuple2 ('aaa', 'pqr', 'uvw', 'zzz')
creating tpl3 from tpl1 and tpl2
displaying the elements in tuple3
(1, 2, 3, 5, 7, 11, 'aaa', 'pqr', 'uvw', 'zzz')
Display the lengths of the tuple
6
4
Max and Min functions on tuple
11
zzz
1
aaa
using in for tpl3 and tpl2
uvw found
9 not found
Using the index on the tuples
(2, 3, 5, 7, 11, 'aaa', 'pqr', 'uvw', 'zzz')
('aaa',)
(5, 7, 11, 'aaa', 'pqr', 'uvw')
print the index value of python in tpl4
prin the index value of 3 in tpl1
(3, 'python')

when there are not same elements
0
Using compare over tupless tpl1 tpl2 and tpl3
-1
1
-1
-1
Implementing tuple() method
lst elements :  (1, 2, 3, 5, 7, 11, 'aaa', 'pqr', 'uvw', 'zzz')
Deleting the elements in a tuple
After deleting tuple3 :
Traceback (most recent call last):
  File "main.py", line 33, in <module>
    print tpl3
NameError: name 'tpl3' is not defined
```

Note *When a tuple does not exist we get a name error and when an element does not exist inside a tuple with an index method an error is generated. We need to be more conscious in using the index method over tuples.*

7. Write a Python Program to demonstrate the Dictionaries functions and operations

Solution:

```
# python program to demonstrate the Dictionaries functions and operations
dicti = {'Lang': 'Python', 'Chap': 6, 'Topic': 'Program'}
print "dicti['Lang']: ", dicti['Lang']
print "dicti['Chap']: ", dicti['Chap']
dicti = {'Lang': 'Python', 'Chap': 6, 'Topic': 'Program'}
# updating the existing entry of a dictionary
dicti['Chap'] = 8;
# Adding a new element into a dictionary
dicti['Topic'] = "Dictionary topic";
print "dicti['Chap']: ", dicti['Chap']
print "dicti['Topic']: ", dicti['Topic']
# deleting the element with the key 'Lang'
del dicti['Lang'];
print dicti
# removing the dictionary elements
dicti.clear();
# delete entire dictionary
del dicti ;
dicti1 = {'Lang': 'Python', 'Chap': 11};
dicti2 = {'Lang': 'c', 'Chap': 15};
dicti3 = {'Lang': 'java', 'Chap': 35};
dicti4 = {'Lang': 'perl', 'Chap': 25};

print "dicti1['Chap']: ", dicti1['Chap']
# Uisng the dictionary keys
print "dicti2['Lang']: ", dicti2['Lang']
print "compare() on dictionaries"
print "Return Value : %d" %  cmp (dicti1, dicti2)
print "Return Value : %d" %  cmp (dicti2, dicti3)
print "Return Value : %d" %  cmp (dicti1, dicti4)
print "len() on dictionaries "
print "Length : %d" % len (dicti1)
print "str() on dictionaries"
print "Equivalent String : %s" % str (dicti1)
print "type() on dictionaries"
print "Variable Type : %s" %  type (dicti1)
print "Start Len : %d" %  len(dicti1)
print "clear() on dictionaries"
dicti1.clear()
print "End Len : %d" %  len(dicti1)
print "copy () on dictionaries"
dicti5 = dicti1.copy()
print "seq on dictionaries"
seq = ('lang', 'chap', 'program')
dicti6 = dicti6.fromkeys(seq)
print "New Dictiionary : %s"
print  str(dicti6)
dicti7 = dicti6.fromkeys(seq, 10)
```

```
print "New Dictiionary : %s"
print  str(dicti7)
print "New Dictiinary : %s"
print  str(dicti7)
seq = ('lang', 'chap', 'program')
dicti8 = dicti7.fromkeys(seq)
print "New Dictiionary : %s" %  str(dicti8)
dicti9 = dicti8.fromkeys(seq, 10)
print "New Dictiionary : %s" %  str(dicti9)
print "Value : %s" %  dicti9.get('Chap')
print "Value : %s" %  dicti9.get('Education', "Never")
print "Value : %s" %  dicti9.has_key('Chap')
print "Value : %s" %  dicti9.has_key('Program')
print "Value : %s" %  dicti9.items()
print "Value : %s" %  dicti9.keys()
print "Value : %s" %  dicti9.setdefault('Chap', None)
print "Value : %s" %  dicti9.setdefault('Program', None)
dicti5.update(dicti2)
print "Value : %s" %  dicti5
print "Value : %s" %  dicti5.values()
```

Output:

```
dicti['Lang']:
Python
dicti['Chap']:
6
dicti['Dictionary']:
Traceback (most recent call last):
 dicti['Chap']:
8
dicti['Topic']:
Dictionary topic
{'Topic': 'Dictionary topic', 'Chap': 8}
dicti1['Chap']:  11
dicti1['Topic']:
Traceback (most recent call last):
  Line 27, in <module>
    print "dicti1['Topic']: ", dicti1['Topic']
KeyError: 'Topic'
dicti2['Lang']:  c
cmp () on dictionaries
Return Value : -1
Return Value : -1
Return Value : -1
len() on dictionaries
Length : 2
str() on dictionaries
Equivalent String : {'Lang': 'Python', 'Chap': 11}
type() on dictionaries
Variable Type : <type 'dict'>
```

```
Start Len : 2
clear() on dictionaries
End Len : 0
copy () on dictionaries
seq on dictionaries
New dictionaries : % s
{'lang': None, 'chap': None, 'program': None}
New Dictiionary : %s
{'lang': 10, 'chap': 10, 'program': 10}
New Dictiinary : %s
{'lang': 10, 'chap': 10, 'program': 10}
New Dictiionary : {'lang': None, 'chap': None, 'program': None}
New Dictiionary : {'lang': 10, 'chap': 10, 'program': 10}
Value : None
Value : Never
Value : False
Value : False
Value : [('lang', 10), ('chap', 10), ('program', 10)]
Value : ['lang', 'chap', 'program']
Value : None
Value : None
Value : {'Lang': 'c', 'Chap': 15}
Value : ['c', 15]
```

> ***Note*** *When we execute the following lines of code in the program*
>
> ```
> print "dicti['Dictionary']: ", dicti['Dictionary']
> ```
>
> *the following errors are occurred*
>
> ```
> Line 9, in <module>
>     print dicti['Dictionary']
> KeyError: 'Dictionary' those lines can be edited for hassle free program.
> ```
>
> *When we add this line to the program*
>
> ```
> print "dicti1['Topic']: ", dicti1['Topic']
> ```
>
> *The following errors are occurred*
>
> ```
> line 25, in <module>
>     print "dicti1['Topic']: ", dicti1['Topic']
> KeyError: 'Topic'
> ```
>
> *These errors are provided to the user only for implementation purpose.*

Multiple Choice Questions

1. Which of the following sequence data type is similar to the tuple?
   a. Dictionaries **b.** List
   c. String **d.** function
2. In which operator are tuples enclosed?
   a. { } **b.** [ ]
   c. <> **d.** ( )

3. Which of the following is a Python tuple?
   - a. `[7, 8, 9]`
   - b. `{7, 8, 9}`
   - c. `(7, 8, 9)`
   - d. `<7, 8, 9>`
4. What will be the output of the following code?
```
>>>tuple = (‘john’, 100, 345, 1.67, ‘book’)
>>>print(tuple[0])
```
   - a. `John`
   - b. `0`
   - c. `Book`
   - d. error
5. What will be the output of the following code?
```
>>>tuple = (‘john’, 100, 345, 1.67, ‘book’)
>>>print(tuple[2:4])
```
   - a. `(345, 1.67, ‘book’)`
   - b. `(100, 345, 1.67)`
   - c. `(345, 1.67)`
   - d. `(100, 345)`
6. Which of the following will not be correct if `tuple = (10, 12, 14, 16, 18)`?
   - a. `print(min(tuple))`
   - b. `print(max(tuple))`
   - c. `tuple[4] = 20`
   - d. `print(len(tuple))`
7. What will be the output of the following code?
```
>>>tuple = (‘john’, 100, 345, 1.67, ‘book’)
>>>print(tuple[3:])
```
   - a. `(1.67, ‘book’)`
   - b. `(345, 1.67)`
   - c. `(‘john’, 100, 345)`
   - d. `(345, 1.67, ‘book’)`
8. What will be the output of the following code?
```
>>>tuple = (1, 5, 8, 9)
>>>print(tuple[1:-1])
```
   - a. `(1, 5, 8)`
   - b. `(1, 5)`
   - c. `(5, 8, 9)`
   - d. `(5, 8)`
9. Which of the following statements is used to delete an entire tuple?
   - a. `Remove`
   - b. `exit`
   - c. `del`
   - d. `backspace`
10. What will be the output of the following code?
```
>>>tuple1 = (3, 5, 7, 9)
>>>tuple2 = (3, 5, 9, 7)
>>>tuple1 < tuple2
```
   - a. Error
   - b. False
   - c. True
   - d. Null
11. Which of the following functions in Python is used to convert a string into a tuple?
   - a. `tuple(str)`
   - b. `str(tuple)`
   - c. `repr(tuple)`
   - d. `list(tuple)`
12. Which of the following data types does not belong to Python?
   - a. String
   - b. Tuple
   - c. Dictionary
   - d. Structure
13. Which of the following functions will return a list into a tuple?
   - a. `tuple(list)`
   - b. `len(tuple)`
   - c. `tuple(seq)`
   - d. `append(tuple)`

14. Which core data type in Python is an unordered collection of key-value pairs?
    a. Tuple
    b. dictionary
    c. function
    d. list
15. In which of the following operators are dictionaries enclosed?
    a. `{ }`
    b. `( )`
    c. `[ ]`
    d. `<>`
16. Which of the following represent keys in the dictionary?
    a. function or list
    b. numbers or list
    c. strings or functions
    d. numbers or strings
17. Which operator is used to access the values in dictionary?
    a. `{ }`
    b. `( )`
    c. `[ ]`
    d. `<>`
18. Which of the following statements will not create a dictionary?
    a. `{245:"book", 1234:code}`
    b. `("book":245, "code":1234)`
    c. `{ }`
    d. `{"book":245, "code":1234}`
19. Which of the following forms do dictionaries appear in?
    a. keys and values
    b. only keys
    c. list and keys
    d. only values
20. What are the keys in the following code?

```
dictionary = {"book":245, "code":1234}
```

    a. `245 and 1234`
    b. `"book" and "code"`
    c. `"book", 245, "code" and 1234`
    d. `("book":245, "code":1234)`
21. Which of the following methods is used to remove entire elements of a dictionary?
    a. `remove()`
    b. `remove{}`
    c. `clear()`
    d. `clear{}`
22. What will be the output of the following code?

```
dict = {'name': 'ravi', 'age':35}
"ravi" in dict
```

    a. True
    b. false
    c. error
    d. none
23. Which of the following functions of the dictionary gets all the keys from the dictionary?
    a. `dict.key()`
    b. `dict.keys()`
    c. `allkeys()`
    d. `getkeys()`
24. What will be the output of the following code?

```
dict = {'name','ravi','age':35}
>>>print dic['age']
```

    a. `Age`
    b. 35
    c. `Ravi`
    d. error
25. What will be the output of the following code?

```
dict = {'name':'ravi', 'age':35}
>>>print dict['age']
```

    a. `Age`
    b. `[age]`
    c. 35
    d. error

26. Which of the following functions will be used to get the number of entries in dictionary?
    a. `len(dict)` b. `dict.len`
    c. `size(dict)` d. `dict.size`
27. What will be the output of the following code?
```
dict1 = {'john':25,'Salary':18,000}
dict2 = {'kathy':35,'Salary':28,000}
>>>print dict1 > dict2
```
    a. True b. error
    c. false d. none
28. What will be the output of the following code?
```
dict = {'john':25,'Salary':18,000,'Age':45}
>>>print (len(dict))
```
    a. 6 b. 5
    c. 3 d. none
29. Which of the following functions of the dictionary gets all the values from the dictionary?
    a. `dict.values()` b. `dict.value()`
    c. `getvalues()` d. `getvalue()`
30. Which of the following functions returns a list of the dictionary?
    a. `list.items()` b. `dict.list()`
    c. `list.dict()` d. `dict.items()`
31. What value is returned by the method `dict.has_key(key)`, when the key is in the dictionary?
    a. False b. True
    c. Error d. None

Short Questions

1. What is tuple in Python? Compare tuple and list.
2. What will be the output of the given code?
```
>>>tuple = (4, 6, 8, 10)
>>>tuple.append((12, 14, 20, 24))
>>> print len(tuple)
```
3. What will be the output of the given code? Justify your answer.
```
>>>tuple = ('computer', 456, 'book')
>>>print(tuple * 2)
```
4. What will be the output of the given code? Justify your answer.
```
>>>tuple = ('computer', 456, 'book')
>>>print(list)
```
5. What are the built-in tuple functions in Python?
6. What will be the output of the given codes?
   a)
```
>>> tuple = ('computer', 456, 'book')
>>>print(len(tuple))
```
   b)
```
>>> tuple1 = (2400, 456, 33.7, 500)
>>> tuple2 = (33400, 4569, 6687, 4008)
>>>print ('Maximum value in:",tuple2,"is" max(tuple2))
>>>print ('Minimum value in:",tuple1,"is" min(tuple1))
```

c)
```
>>> list = ['computer', 456, 'book']
>>>print ("tuple:", tuple(list))
```

7. What is dictionary? Explain with example.
8. What are the properties of dictionary keys?
9. What will be the output of the following code?

```
>>>dict = {'Name':'john','Age':25,'Salary':28,000}
>>>print(dict)
>>>del dict{'Salary'}
>>>print("dictionary after deletion:",dict)
>>>dict.clear()
>>>print(dict)
```

10. What will be the output of the following code?

```
>>>dict = {'Name':'john','Age':25,'Salary':28,000}
>>>print(list(dict.keys()))
```

11. What will be the output of the following code?

```
>>>dict = {'Name':'john','Age':25,'Salary':28,000}
>>>print(dict)
>>>dict['age'] = 30
>>>print("dictionary after update:", dict)
>>>dict['height'] = 120
>>>print("dictionary after update:", dict)
```

12. What will be the output of the following code?

a)
```
>>>dict = {'Name':'john','Age':25,'Salary':28,000}
>>>print(dict)
>>>print("dict.has_key(key):",dict.has_key('salary'))
>>>print("dict.has_key(key):",dict.has_key('employee code'))
```

b)
```
>>>dict = {'Name':'john','Age':25,'Salary':28,000}
>>>print(dict)
>>>print("representation of dictionary=",str(dict))
```

c)
```
>>>dict = {'Name':'john','Age':25,'Salary':28,000}
>>>print(dict)
>>>print("type(variable)=",type(dict))
>>>str="wxyz"
>>>print("type(variable)=",type(str))
>>>list = [5, 'w',34, 'ravi']
>>>print("type(variable)=",type(list))
```

13. What are the built-in dictionary functions?
14. What will be the output of the following code?

a)
```
>>>dict = {'Name':'john','Age':25,'Salary':28,000}
>>>print(dict)
>>>dict.clear()
>>>print dict
```

b)
```
>>>dict1 = {'Name':'john','Age':25,'Salary':28,000}
>>>print(dict)
>>>dict2=dict1.copy()
>>>print(dict2)
```

c)
```
>>>dict = {'Name':'john','Age':25,'Salary':28,000}
>>>print(dict)
>>>print("keys in dictionary:",dict.keys())
```
d)
```
>>>dict = {'Name':'john','Age':25,'Salary':28,000}
>>>print(dict)
>>>print("values in dictionary:",dict.values())
```
e)
```
>>>dict = {'Name':'john','Age':25,'Salary':28,000}
>>>print(dict)
>>>print("items in dictionary:",dict.items())
```

15. What are the built-in dictionary methods? Explain some of the built-in methods.
16. Write a program to update the dictionary key-value pair.
17. What will be the output of the following code?

a)
```
>>>dict = {'Name':'john','Age':25,'Salary':28,000}
>>>print(dict)
>>>print("dict.get('Age'):",dict.get('Age'))
>>>print("dict.get('Code'):",dict.get('Code',0))
```
b)
```
>>>dict1 = {'Name':'john','Age':25,'Salary':28,000}
>>>print(dict)
>>>print("dict.setdefault('Age'):",dict.setdefault('Age'))
>>>print("dict.setdefault('Code'):",dict.setdefault('Code'))
```
c)
```
>>>list = ['Name','Age'Salary']
>>>dict=dict.fromkeys(list)
>>>print("new dictionary:",dict)
```

Answers to Multiple Choice Questions

1. b	**2.** d	**3.** c	**4.** a	**5.** b	**6.** c	**7.** a	**8.** d	**9.** c	**10.** b
11. a	**12.** d	**13.** c	**14.** b	**15.** a	**16.** d	**17.** c	**18.** b	**19.** a	**20.** b
21. c	**22.** a	**23.** b	**24.** d	**25.** c	**26.** a	**27.** b	**28.** c	**29.** a	**30.** d
31. b									

7 FILES AND EXCEPTIONS

7.1 TEXT FILES

A file in a computer is a location for storing some related data. It holds a specific name for itself. The files are used to store data permanently on a non-volatile memory, such as hard disks. RAM is a volatile memory type because the data it holds is lost, when we turn off the computer. Hence, files are used for storing useful information or data for future reference.

Handling files in Python is quite easy. Generally, files are divided into two categories, text files and binary files. Text files are simple texts in human readable format whereas binary files have binary data which is understood by the computer.

Programs maintain their data by simply reading and writing the text files. In this chapter, we will learn about the programs that read from and write to a text file.

When there is a need to read from or write to a file, we have to open it first. Once reading or writing is done, we have to close it in order to release the resources. The order of the file operations in Python is as follows:

1. Opening a file
2. Perform operations (Read or write)
3. Close the file

7.1.1 Opening a File

Until now, we have been reading from or writing to the standard input and output. Now, we will learn how to manipulate actual data files. Python provides some basic functions and methods that are necessary to manipulate files. Python introduces the `file` object in order to perform some file operations.

Python has a built-in `open()` function to open files from the directory. Two arguments that are mainly needed by the `open()` function are: `file name or file path` and `mode` in which the file is opened.

The syntax for opening a file is:

Syntax

```
file_object = open(file_name [, access_mode])
```

- **`file_name`:** File name contains a string type value containing the name of the file which we want to access.
- **`access_mode`:** The value of `access_mode` specifies the mode in which we want to open the file, i.e., read, write, append, etc. A list of different `access_mode` is given in Table 7.1. The default `access_mode` is `r(reading)`.

Example

```
>>>f = open("test.txt")        # opening file in current directory
>>>f = open("C:/Python27/README.txt")    # specifying full path    # Output
>>>f
<open file 'C:/Python27/README.txt', mode 'r' at 0x02BC5128>       # Output
```

In the given example, we have looked at how to open a file with default access_mode `r`. When we type the name of the file object, Python interpreter gives us the information about the opened file.

TABLE 7.1 List of the different modes of opening the file

Modes	Description
r	It opens a file in reading mode. The file pointer is placed at the starting of the file. It is the default mode.
rb	It opens a file in reading only mode in binary format. The file pointer is placed at the starting of the file.
r+	It opens the file in both reading and writing mode. The file pointer is placed at the starting of the file.
rb+	It opens the file in both reading and writing mode in binary format. The file pointer is placed at the starting of the file.
W	It opens the file in writing only mode. If a file exists, it overwrites the existing file; otherwise, it creates a new file.
Wb	It opens the file in writing only mode in binary format. If a file exists, it overwrites the existing file; otherwise, it creates a new file.
w+	It opens the file in booth reading and writing mode. If a file exists, it overwrites the existing file; otherwise, it creates a new file.
wb+	It opens the file in booth reading and writing mode in binary format. If a file exists, it overwrites the existing file; otherwise, it creates a new file.
a	It opens a file for appending. The file pointer is placed at the end of the file. If the file does not exist in the directory, it creates a new file for writing.
ab	It opens a file for appending in binary format. The file pointer is placed at the end of the file. If the file does not exist in the directory, it creates a new file for writing.
a+	It opens a file for appending and reading. The file pointer is placed at the end of the file. If the file does not exist in the directory, it creates a new file for writing.
ab+	It opens a file for appending and reading in binary format. The file pointer is placed at the end of the file. If the file does not exist in the directory, it creates a new file for writing.

We can always specify the access mode in which a file should be opened for us. The different access modes available in Python are given in Table 7.1. We can also specify whether a file should be opened in the text mode or the binary mode. The default is reading in text mode. The binary mode deals with bytes while we get strings when reading from a text file. The binary mode is used when we deal with non-text files, such as image files, etc.

Examples

```
>>>f = open("test.txt") # opens in r mode(reading only)
>>>f = open("test.txt",'w')  # opens in w mode(writing only)
>>>f = open("image.bmp",'rb+')  # read and write in binary mode
```

TIP

There is an access mode x in Python which opens a file for exclusive creation. If the file already exists, then this operation fails rather than overwriting it.

Check Your Understanding

1. **What are text files? How are they useful?**

Ans. A file in a computer is a location for storing some related data. It has a specific name. The files are used to store data permanently on to a non-volatile memory (such as hard disks). As we know, the Random Access Memory (RAM) is a volatile memory type because the data in it is lost when we turn off the computer. Hence, we use files for storing of useful information or data for future reference.

2. **What is the syntax for opening a file in Python?**

Ans. Syntax

```
file object = open(file_name [, access_mode])
```

- **file_name:** File name contains a string type value containing the name of the file which we want to access.
- **access_mode:** The value of `access_mode` specifies that in which mode we want to open the file, that is, read, write, append, etc. The default `access_mode` is `r(read only)`.

7.1.2 Closing a File

When the operations that are to be performed on an opened file are finished, we have to close the file in order to release the resources. Although Python comes with a garbage collector responsible for cleaning up the unreferenced objects from the memory, we must not rely on it to close a file. Proper closing of a file frees up the resources held with the file. The closing of file is done with a built-in function `close()`.

Syntax

```
fileObject.close()
```

Example

```
# open a file
>>>f = open("test.txt","wb")
# perform file operations
>>>f.close()   # close the file
```

Most recommended way of using file is along with `'with'` keyword. Because, once the `'with'` block exits, file is automatically closed and `file_object` is destroyed.

Example

```
>>> with open("test.txt") as f:
    print f.read()
Hello Python---This is in File.   # Output
```

Note *Although the closing method will close the file instantly, it is not safe. When we are performing some operations on a file and an exception occurs, the code exits without closing the file. Hence, we should use* `try...finally` *block. We will learn about the exceptions in more detail later in this chapter.*

Example

```
>>>try:
... f = open("test.txt")
    # perform operations
... finally:
... f.close()
```

7.1.3 The File Object Attributes

Once a file is opened and a file object created, various pieces of information about that file can be gathered by using some predefined attributes.

There are basically four types of attributes as shown in Table 7.2.

Table 7.2 Types of Attributes

Attribute	Description
`file.closed`	It will return *True* if the file is closed; it will otherwise return *False*.
`file.mode`	It will return the access mode with which the file is opened.
`file.name`	It will return the name of the file.
`file.softspace`	It will return *False* if space explicitly required with print; otherwise it will return *True*.

Example

```
# open a file
>>>f = open("C:/Python27/test.txt","wb")
>>>print f.name
C:/Python27/test.txt          # Output
>>> print f.closed
False              # Output
>>>print f.mode
Wb          # Output
>>>print f.softspace
0           # Output
>>>f.close()              # Close the opened file
>>> print f.closed
True        # Output
```

7.1.4 Writing to a File

After opening a file, we have to perform some operations on the file. Here, we will perform the write operation. In order to write into a file, we have to open it with `w` mode, or `a` mode, or any writing-enabling mode. We should be careful when using the `w` mode because in this mode overwriting persists in case the file already exists.

Note *The `write()` method enables us to write any string to an opened file.*

Syntax

```
fileobject.write(string)
```

The content that we want to write to a file is passed as parameter to the above syntax.

Example

```
# open the file with w mode
>>>f = open("C:/Python27/test.txt","w")
# perform write operation
>>>f.write('writing to the file line 1\n')
>>>f.write('writing to the file line 2\n')
>>>f.write('writing to the file line 3\n')
>>>f.write('writing to the file line 4')
# close the file after writing
>>>f.close()
```

The given example creates a file named `test.txt` if it does not exist, and overwrites into it if it exists. If you open the file, you will find the following content in it.

Output:

```
Writing to the file line 1
Writing to the file line 2
Writing to the file line 3
Writing to the file line 4
```

Note *Python strings can have binary data, not just text.*

7.1.5 Reading from a File

In order to read from a file, we must open the file in the reading mode (`r` mode). There are a number of methods available for reading. We can use `read(size)` method to read the data specified by `size`. If no `size` is provided, it will end up reading to the end of the file.

Reading from any file is done with the method `read()`. The `read()` method enables us to read the strings from an opened file.

Syntax

```
fileobject.read([size])
```

The count parameter gives the **number of bytes** to be read from an opened file. It starts reading from the beginning of the file until the `size` given. If no `size` is provided, it ends up reading until the end of the file.

Example

```
# open the file
>>>f = open("C:/Python27/test.txt", "r")
>>>f.read(7)        # read from starting 7 bytes of data
'writing'           # Output
>>>f.read(6)      # read next 6 bytes of data
'to the'            # Output
>>>f.read()         # read rest of the file
' file line 1\nwriting to the file line 2\nwriting to the file line 3\
nwriting to the file line 4\n'        # Output
>>>f.read()
''  # Output
```

Here we are using the file `'test.txt'` created earlier for reading. `f.read(7)` reads the first 7 bytes of data. After this, `f.read(6)` reads the next 6 bytes and then `f.read()` reads the rest of the file._When we try to read the file after fully reading it, we get an empty string. This is because we have ended up reading the whole file and no string is left to read in the file.

TIP

`readline()` is a method of reading a file line by line. Whenever we write `fileobject.readline()`, it prints one line from that file and continues in this way until the end of the file.

Example

```
#open a file
>>> f=open("C:/Python27/test.txt", "r")
>>>f.readline()                        # reading 1st line
'writing to the file line 1\n'              # Output
>>>f.readline()                        # reading 2nd line
'writing to the file line 2\n'              # Output
>>>f.readline()                        # reading 3rd line
'writing to the file line 3\n'              # Output
>>>f.readline()                        # reading 4th line
'writing to the file line 4\n'              # Output
>>>f.readline()                        # no line to read
''          # Output
# close the file
>>>f.close()
```

Check Your Understanding

1. What is the syntax for closing a file? Give one example.

Ans. Syntax

```
fileObject.close()
```

Example

```
# open a file
>>> f = open("example.txt","r")
# perform reading operation
>>>f.close()    # close the file
```

2. Give the syntax for reading from a file. What is the work of the `readline()` function?

Ans. Syntax

```
fileobject.read([size])
```

The count parameter size gives the **number of bytes** to be read from an opened file. It starts reading from the beginning of the file until the `size` given. If no `size` is provided, it ends up reading until the end of the file.

`readline()`

`readline()` is a method of reading a file line by line. Whenever we write `fileobject.readline()`, it prints one line from that file and continues in this way until the end of the file.

File Positions

We have seen in the previous section that when we read a line or some data from a file, the pointer points to the next line or data, and that when we end up reading whole file, it returns the empty string. In this section, we will learn to check the current position of the pointer and to change the position of the pointer.

In Python, the `tell()` method tells us about the current position of the pointer. The current position tells us where reading will start from at present.

We can also change the position of the pointer with the help of `seek()` method. A number of bytes are passed to be moved by the pointer as arguments to the `seek()` method.

> **Note** *The value 0 indicates that the position of pointer should be set to the beginning of the file; the value 1 indicates that it should be set to the current position; the value 2 indicates that it should be set to the end of the file.*

Example

```
# open the file
>>>f=open("C:/Python27/test.txt", "r")
# read 28 bytes of data
>>>f.read(28)
'writing to the file line 1'         # Output
# check the current position
>>>f.tell()
28L        # Output
# change the position to beginning
>>>f.seek(0)
# again read 28 bytes
>>>f.read(28)
'writing to the file line 1'         # Output
```

7.1.6 Renaming a File

Renaming a file in Python is done with the help of the `rename()` method. The `rename()` method is passed with two arguments, the current filename and the new filename.

Syntax

```
os.rename(current_filename, new_filename)
```

Example

```
# import os
>>>import os
# renaming the file
>>>os.rename("C:/Python27/test.txt","C:/Python27/test1.txt")
```

Here, the `test.txt` file in `C:/Python27` directory is renamed `test1.txt`.

7.1.7 Deleting a File

Deleting a file in Python is done with the help of the `remove()` method. It takes the filename as an argument to be deleted.

Syntax

```
os.remove(filename)
```

Example

```
# import os
>>>import os
# deleting the file
>>>os.remove("C:/Python27/test1.txt")
```

7.1.8 Files Related Methods

The `file` object in Python provides various methods to manipulate files which are listed in the Table 7.3.

Table 7.3 Methods to Manipulate Files

Sr. No.	Methods with Description
1.	`file.close()` After performing operation, it closes the file.
2.	`file.flush()` It flushes the internal buffer memory.
3.	`file.fileno()` It returns the integer file descriptor.
4.	`file.isatty()` It returns `True` if file is connected with `tty(-like)` device, `False` otherwise.
5.	`file.next()` It returns the next line from the file.

6.	`file.read([size])` Reads the size bytes from a file.
7.	`file.readline([size])` It reads the entire one line from a file.
8.	`file.readlines([sizehint])` It reads until the end of the file using `readline`. It returns the list of lines read.
9.	`file.seek([offset])` It changes the current position.
10.	`file.tell()` It returns the file's current position.
11.	`file.truncate([size])` It truncates the file.
12.	`file.write(str)` It writes the `str` string to the file.
13.	`file.writelines(sequence)` It writes the sequence of strings into a file. If each string in the sequence should go into separate lines in file, the string should end with a new line character, `'\n'`.

Check Your Understanding

1. What are the various file positions methods?

Ans. In Python, the `tell()` method tells us about the current position of the pointer. The current position tells us where reading will start from at present.

We can also change the position of the pointer with the help of the `seek()` method. We pass the number of bytes to be moved by the pointer as arguments to the `seek()` method.

2. How are renaming and deleting performed on a file? Give the syntax for each.

Ans. Renaming a file

Renaming a file in Python is done with the help of the `rename()` method. The `rename()` method is passed with two arguments, the current filename and the new filename.

Syntax

```
os.rename(current_filename, new_filename)
```

Deleting a File

Deleting a file in Python is done with the help of the `remove()` method. The `remove()` method takes the filename as an argument to be deleted.

Syntax

```
os.remove(filename)
```

7.2 DIRECTORIES

Directories help us make things more manageable. If there is a large number of files, then related files are placed in different directories. Hence, a directory can be said to be a collection of files and sub directories. The module `os` in Python enables us to use various methods to work with directories.

7.2.1 `mkdir()` Method

The `mkdir()` method in Python is used to make new directories in the current directory. It takes the name of the new directory to be created as an argument.

Syntax

```
os.mkdir("newdir")
```

Example

```
# importos
>>>import os
# create a new directorytestdir
>>>os.makedir("testdir")
```

7.2.2 `chdir()` Method

The `chdir()` method in Python's `os` module is used to change the current directory. It takes the name of the directory that you want to make the current directory as an argument.

Syntax

```
os.chdir("dir_name")
```

Example

```
# importos
>>>import os
# change the current directory to "/home/testdir"
>>>os.chdir("/home/testdir")
```

7.2.3 `getcwd()` Method

The **`getcwd()`** method displays the current directory in which we are working.

Syntax

```
os.getcwd()
```

Example

```
# importos
>>>import os
>>>os.getcwd()    # This will give the address of the current directory
'C:\\Python27'          # Output
```

7.2.4 `rmdir()` Method

The `rmdir()` method in Python is used to remove directories in the current directory. It takes the name of the directory to be deleted as an argument.

TIP

It is required to provide the full location of the directory; otherwise, the directory will be searched in the current directory.

Syntax

```
os.rmdir('directory_name')
```

Example

```
# importos
>>>import os
>>>os.rmdir("/tmp/test")
# it will remove the "/tmp/test" directory        # Output
```

Note *All the contents in a directory should be deleted before removing that directory.*

Check Your Understanding

1. **What are directories? What are the basic methods performed on Directories?**

Ans. Directories help us make things more manageable. If there is a large number of files, then related files are placed in different directories. Hence, a directory can be said to be a collection of files and sub directories. The module `os` in Python enables us to use various methods to work with directories.

Following are the four basic methods that are performed on directories:

- `mkdir()` method (Creating a directory)
- `chdir()` method (Changing the current directory)
- `getcwd()` method (Displaying the current directory)
- `rmdir()` method (Deleting the directory)

2. Give the syntax for each of basic directory methods.

Ans. `mkdir()` method:

Syntax

```
os.mkdir("newdir")
```

`chdir()` method:

Syntax

```
os.chdir("dir_name")
```

`getcwd()` method:

Syntax

```
os.getcwd()
```

`rmdir()` method:

Syntax

```
os.rmdir('directory_name')
```

7.3 EXCEPTIONS

While writing a program, we often end up making some errors. There are many types of errors that can occur in a program. The error caused by writing an improper syntax is termed *syntax error* or *parsing error*; these are also called *compile time errors*.

Errors can also occur at *runtime* and these runtime errors are known as *exceptions*. There are various types of runtime errors in Python. Let us look at a few examples. When a file we try to open does not exist, we get a *FileNotFoundError*. When a division by zero happens, we get a *ZeroDivisionError*. When the module we are trying to import does not exist, we get an *ImportError*. Python creates an exception object for every occurrence of these run-time errors. The user must write a piece of code that can handle the error. If it is not capable of handling the error, the program prints a trace back to that error along with the details of why the error has occurred.

Example

Compile time error (Syntax error)

```
>>>a = 3
>>>if (a < 4)                    # Semicolon is not included
SyntaxError: invalid syntax           # Output
```

The error shown above is a syntax error because there is a problem with the syntax; the `if` statement starts with semicolon.

ZeroDivisionError

```
>>>5/0
```

Output:

```
Traceback (most recent call last):
  File "<pyshell#71>", line 1, in <module>
    5/0
ZeroDivisionError: integer division or modulo by zero
```

Here, we tried to divide 5 by 0. As a result, the interpreter prints `ZeroDivisionError`.

Note *Python provides a very important feature **(Exception Handling)** for handling any unexpected error in our Python programs, and it also adds debug capabilities to them.*

7.3.1 Built-in Exceptions

Any error prone statement can raise exception. There are various built-in exceptions in Python that can be raised when the corresponding errors occur.

Table 7.4 gives the full list of built-in exceptions in Python.

TABLE 7.4 List of Built-in Exceptions in Python

Exception	Cause of Error
`AssertionError`	Raised when `assert` statement fails.
`AttributeError`	Raised when attribute assignment or reference fails.
`EOFError`	Raised when the `input()` functions hit end-of-file condition.
`FloatingPointError`	Raised when a floating point operation fails.
`GeneratorExit`	Raised when a generator's `close()` method is called.
`ImportError`	Raised when the imported module does not exist.
`IndexError`	Raised when an index of a sequence is out of range or not found.
`KeyError`	Raised when a key does not exist in a dictionary.

KeyboardInterrupt	Raised when a user hits interrupt key (ctrl+c).
MemoryError	Raised when an operation runs out of memory.
NameError	Raised when a variable is not found in local or global space.
NotImplementedError	Raised by abstract method.
OSError	Raised when system operation causes system related error.
ReferenceError	Raised when a weak reference proxy is used to access a garbage-collected referent.
RuntimeError	Raised when an error doesn't fall in any other category.
StopIteration	Raised when there is no next item to be iterated by iterator.
SyntaxError	Raised by parser on a syntax error.
IndentationError	Raised when there is an incorrect indentation.
TabError	Raised when indentation is composed of inconsistent tabs and spaces.
SystemError	Raised when an internal error occurred.
SystemExit	Raised by `sys.exit()` function.
TypeError	Raised when a function or operation is applied to an object of incorrect type.
UnboundLocalError	Raised when a reference is made to a local variable in a function or method, but no value has been bound to that function.
UnicodeError	Raised when a Unicode related encoding or decoding occurs.
UnicodeEncodeError	Raised when a Unicode related error occurs during encoding.
UnicodeTranslateError	Raised when a Unicode related error occurs during translating.
ValueError	Raised when a function is passed with an argument of correct type but improper value.
ZeroDivisionError	Raised when a number is divided by zero.

7.3.2 Handling Exceptions

Whenever an exception occurs in Python, it stops the current process and passes it to the calling process until it is handled. If there is no piece of code in your program that can handle the exception, then the program will crash.

For example, assume that a function X calls the function Y, which in turn calls the function Z, and an exception occurs in Z. If this exception is not handled in Z itself, then the exception is passed to Y and then to X. If this exception is not handled, then an error message will be displayed and our program will suddenly halt.

1. `try...except` Python provides a `try` statement for handling exceptions. An operation in the program that can cause the exception is placed in the `try` clause while the block of code that handles the exception is placed in the `except` clause. The block of code for handling the exception is written by the user and it is for him to decide which operation he wants to perform after the exception has been identified.

Syntax

```
try:
the operation which can cause exception here,
.........................
```

```
except Exception1:
if there is exception1, execute this.
except Exception2:
if there is exception2, execute this.
........................
else:
if no exception occurs, execute this.
```

> ***Note*** *A* `try` *block can have multiple* `except` *clauses associated with it. It can be useful to have the* `try` *block include statements that can cause different types of exceptions.*

TIP

After `except` *clause, we can add an* `else` *statement. The statements in the* `else` *block will execute only when the statements in* `try` *block do not raise any exception.*

Example

```
>>>try:
...      file = open("C:/Python27/test.txt","w")
...      file.write("hello python")
...   exceptIOError:
...      print "Error: cannot find file or read data"
...   else:
...      print "content written successfully"
>>>file.close()
```

In the given example, we are trying to open a file `test.txt` with write access mode, and want to write to that file. We have added `try` and `except` blocks.

If the required file is not found or we do not have the permission to write to the file, an exception is raised. The exception is handled by the `except` block and the following statement printed:

```
Error: cannot find file or read data
```

On the other hand, if the data is written to the file then the `else` block will be executed and it will print the following.

Output:

```
content written successfully
```

2. `except` with No Exception We can also write our `try-except` clause with no exception. All types of exceptions that occur are caught by the `try-except` statement. However, because it catches all exceptions, the programmer cannot identify the root cause of a problem that may occur. Hence, this type of programming approach is not considered good.

Syntax

```
try:
    The statements that can cause exceptions
    ........................................
except:
    If Exception occurs, execute this
    ........................................
else:
    If no exception occurs, execute this
```

Example

```
>>>while True:
...         try:
...                 a = int(raw_input("Enter an integer: "))
...                 div = 10/a
...                 break
...         except:
...                 print "Error Occured"
...                 print "Please Enter Valid Value"
...                 print()
... print "Division is",div
```

The output of the program in different scenarios will be:

```
Enter an integer: c
Error Occurred
Please Enter Valid Value

Enter an integer: 0
Error Occurred
Please Enter Valid Value

Enter an integer: 10.2
Error Occurred
Please Enter Valid Value

Enter an integer: 5
Division is 2
```

In the above example, `break` statement is used instead of `else` statement because the `else` statement only executes when there is no exception.

3. `except` with Multiple Exceptions In Python, we can also use the same except statement for handling multiple exceptions in one statement.

Syntax

```
try:
the operation which can cause exception here,
 .........................
except (Exception1 [,Exception2 [,...ExceptionN]]]):
if any of the exception occurs from the above list
execute this,
  ........................................
else:
if no exception occurs, execute this.
```

Example Pseudo Code

```
try:
    # The exception raising block here
    PASS
except (TypeError, ZeroDivisionError, ValueError):
    # Handle multiple exceptions
    #TypeError, ZeroDivisionError, ValueError
    PASS
else:
    # if no exception, then excute this.
```

4. `try....finally` The `try` statement in Python has an optional `finally` clause that can be associated with it. The statements written in `finally` clause will always be executed by the interpreter, whether the `try` statement raises an exception or not.

> **Note** *With the `try` clause, we can use either `except` or `finally`, but not both.*

> **TIP**
>
> *We cannot use the `else` clause along with a `finally` clause.*

Syntax

```
try:
the operation which can cause exception here,
    .........................
    This may be skipped due to exception
finally ():
    This will always execute, no matter what
    ...............................
```

Example

```
>>> try:
...         file = open("testfile","w")
...         try:
...                file.write("Write this to the file")
...         finally:
...                print "Closing file"
...                file.close()
... exceptIOError:
...         print "Error Occurred"
```

In the given example, when an exception is raised by the statements of `try` block, the execution is immediately passed to the `finally` block. After all the statements inside the `finally` block are executed, the exception is raised again and is handled by the `except` block that is associated with the next higher layer `try` block.

In the above example, a nested try block is used, which means a try block inside another try block. The nested try blocks are allowed in python programming language. Although it is not considered as good programming practice but it may be useful sometimes.

7.4 EXCEPTION WITH ARGUMENTS

The `except` clause in Python can also have an argument. Arguments give additional information about the problem due to which the exception has occurred. We can accept the exception's argument by passing a variable in the `except` clause. The contents of arguments may vary from exception to exception.

Syntax

```
try:
    the operation which can cause exception here,
.........................
exceptExceptionType, Argument:
Print the argument value here.
```

If we are writing a code to handle the exceptions, we can define a variable after the name of exception in the `except` statement. If we are defining multiple exceptions, we can define a variable after the tuple of exceptions.

Example

```
# Define a function
>>>def integer(a):
... try:
```

```
...         returnint(a)
... exceptValueError, Argument:
...         print "The Value does not contain Numbers\n", Argument

# calling the function
>>>integer("hello")
The Value does not contain Numbers.          # Output
invalid literal for int() with base 10: 'hello'    # Output
>>>integer(10)
10    # Output
```

7.5 USER-DEFINED EXCEPTIONS

Python allows users to define their own exceptions by creating a new class. The exception class is to be derived, directly or indirectly from Exception class.

Defining of exceptions is pretty easy in Python.

Example

```
>>>class CustomError(Exception)
... pass
...
```

Here, we have created a class with `CustomError` that is derived from the `Exception` class. Now, we can simply call the `CustomError` by using the `raise` keyword.

Example

```
>>>raise CustomError
```

Output:

```
Traceback (most recent call last):
  File "<pyshell#144>", line 1, in <module>
raiseCustomError
CustomError

>>>raise CustomError("An error occurred")
```

Output:

```
Traceback (most recent call last):
  File "<pyshell#145>", line 1, in <module>
raiseCustomError("An error occurred")
CustomError: An error occurred
```

Check Your Understanding

1. What are exceptions?

Ans. While writing a program, we often end up making some errors. There are many types of errors that can occur in a program. The error caused by writing an improper syntax is termed **syntax error** or **parsing error**; these are also called **compile time errors**.

Errors can also be **runtime** and these runtime errors are known as exceptions. There are various types of runtime errors in Python. Let us look at a few examples. When a file we try to open does not exist, we get a **FileNotFoundError**. When a division by zero happens, we get a **ZeroDivisionError**. When the module we are trying to import does not exist, we get an **ImportError**.

2. Give syntax for `try...except` and `try...finally`.

Ans. `try...except:`

Syntax

```
try:
     the operation which can cause exception here,
     .........................
except Exception1:
     if there is exception1, execute this.
except Exception2:
     if there is exception2, execute this.
     .........................
else:
if no exception occurs, execute this.
```

`try....finally:`

Syntax

```
try:
     the operation which can cause exception here,
     .........................
     This may be skipped due to exception
finally ():
     This will always execute, no matter what
     .................................
```

3. What are User-defined Exceptions? Give one example.

Ans. User-defined Exceptions

Python allows users to define their own exceptions by creating a new class. The exception class is to be derived, directly or indirectly from exception class.

Defining of exceptions is pretty easy in Python.

Example

```
>>>class Error(Exception)
... pass
...
```

We have created a class with `Error` that is derived from the exception class.

ALWAYS REMEMBER

- Tuples are the sequence of different types of values.
- To create a tuple, elements are separated by commas inside the parentheses and assigned to a variable.
- Tuples can be created with or without parentheses.
- Nested tuples can also be created.
- A final comma must be added after the element in order to complete the assignment of the tuple.
- In order to access the values in a tuple, it is necessary to use the index number enclosed within square brackets along with the name of the tuple.
- Slicing can be used in order to print the continuous values in a tuple.
- Tuples are immutable and thus the elements or values cannot be modified.
- Tuple assignment allows assignment of values to a tuple of variables on the left side of assignment from the tuple of values on the right side of the assignment.
- A function returns only one value but by returning tuple, a function can return more than one value.
- Asterisk `(*)` is used before the arguments at the time of function definition, which means it collects all the calling function arguments into a tuple and when it is used at the time of calling, it scatters the values of the tuple.
- A dictionary is said to be a mapping between some set of keys and values. Each key is associated to a value. The mapping of a key and value is called as a key-value pair and together they are called one item or element.
- The values in a dictionary can be duplicated, i.e., it is not unique, but the keys in the dictionary are unique.
- The value of the key enclosed within square brackets is used to access the elements from a dictionary. The `get()` method is an alternative method of accessing the elements used with the key.
- The difference between both the accessing methods of dictionary is that when the key is not found in dictionary, it returns `none` instead of `KeyError`.
- Dictionaries are mutable and thus the elements or values can be modified.
- Four methods are used to delete the elements from the dictionary:
  1. `pop()`
  2. `popitem()`
  3. `clear()`
  4. `del`

KEY TERMS

- ✓ **CONCATENATION:** This operator works in tuples in the same way as it does in lists. This operator concatenates two tuples. This is done by the + operator in Python.
- ✓ **DICTIONARY:** A Python dictionary is an unordered collection of items or elements. The dictionary has a key: value pair.
- ✓ **IMMUTABLE:** It is the type in which elements cannot be modified. Tuples are immutable.
- ✓ **`in` OPERATOR:** This operator tells the user whether a given element exists in the tuple or not. It gives a Boolean output, that is, `True` or `False`.
- ✓ **ITERATION:** Iteration can be done in tuples using `for` loop. It helps in traversing through the tuple.
  1. **`len(tuple)`**:It returns the length of the tuple.
  2. **`cmp(tuple1, tuple2)`:** It compares the items of two tuples.
  3. **`max(tuple)`:** It returns the largest value among the elements in a tuple.
  4. **`min(tuple)`:** It returns the smallest value among the elements in a tuple.
  5. **`tuple(seq)`:** It converts a list into a tuple.
  6. **`zip(tuple1, tuple2)`:** It 'zips' elements from two tuples into a list of tuples.
- ✓ **KEY:** It is used to get the value in the dictionary.
- ✓ **KEY-VALUE:** This pair represents the items in the dictionary.
  1. **`dict()`:** Python provides this function to create a dictionary.
  2. **`get()`:** This method is used with the key to access the value in a dictionary.
  3. **`pop()`:** This method removes the item from the dictionary and returns the value of the item.
  4. **`popitem()`:** This method is used to delete and return an arbitrary item from the dictionary.
  5. **`clear()`:** This method removes all the items from the dictionary.
  6. **`del`:** It is used to delete the dictionary itself.
- ✓ **MUTABLE:** It is the type in which elements are modified. Dictionaries are mutable.
  1. **`len(dict)`:** It returns the number of items (length) in the dictionary.
  2. **`cmp(dict1,dict2)`:** It compares the items of two dictionaries.
  3. **`sorted(dict)`:** It returns the sorted list of keys.
  4. **`str(dict)`:** It produces a printable string representation of dictionary.
- ✓ **REPETITION:** This operator repeats the tuples for a given number of times. Repetition is performed by the `*` operator.
- ✓ **TUPLE:** Tuples, just like lists, are the sequence or series of different types of values separated by commas (,).
- ✓ **TUPLE ASSIGNMENT:** It allows the assignment of values to a tuple of variables on the left side of assignment from the tuple of values on the right side of the assignment.
- ✓ **VARIABLE-LENGTH ARGUMENT TUPLES:** Variable number of arguments can also be passed to a function. A variable name which is preceded by an asterisk `(*)` collects the arguments into a tuple.

REVIEW EXERCISES

PROGRAMS

1. Write a function to print the resolution of an image file in Python.

Solution.

```
def imgres(file_name):
    with open(file_name, 'r') as img:
          img.seek(163)
          x = img.read(2)
          h = (x[0] << 8) + x[1]
          x = img.read(2)
          w = (x[0] << 8) + x[1]
          print("Resolution = ",w,"x",h)

>>>imgres("C:\Python27\1.jpg")
Resolution= 320 X 280          #Output
```

2. Write a function to print the hash of any given file in python. (Hint: Use SHA-1 algorithm).

Solution.

```
>>>def hash_of_file(file_name):
    o = hashlib.sha1()
    with open(file_name,'rb') as hash_file:
          pointer = 0
          while pointer != b'':
                pointer = file.read(1024)
                o.update(pointer)
    return o.hexdigest()

>>>code = hash_of_file("C:\Python27\1.mp3")
>>>print(code)

799d7356947cca543c50b76a1852f92427f4csa8     #Output
```

3. Write a program to catch on Divide by zero Exception. Add a finally block too.

Solution.

```
>>>try:
      9/0
    except ZeroDivisionError:
      print "Divide by Zero"
    except Exception, e:
      print "Error Occurred"
    finally:
      print "This always executes"

Divide by Zero          #Output
This always executes
```

4. Write a program to write data in a file for both write and append modes.

Solution.

```
# In write mode
>>>fi = open('note.txt', 'w')
>>>fi.write('123\n456')
>>>fi.close()

# In append mode
>>>fi = open('note.txt', 'a')
>>>fi.write('789\n101112')
>>>fi.close()
```

5. Write a custom exception that could be raised when the text entered by a user consists of less than 6 characters.

Solution.

```
>>>class CustExcp(Exception):
    pass

>>>try:
      i = input("Enter the text: ")
      if len(i) < 6:
            raise CustExcp()
   except CustExcp as ce:
      print("CustomException: Expected length at least 6")

Enter the text: 'abc'
CustomException: Expected length at least 6        #Output
```

6. Write a python program to demonstrate the file and file I/O operations

Solution.

```
# python program to demonstrate files and file I/O operations
# reading the input from the user using raw_input
import os
str = raw_input("Enter your input: ");
print "Received input is : ", str
# To open or create a file
print "opening a new file in writing in binary format mode"
newfl = open("sample1.txt", "wb")
print "File name: ", newfl.name
print "Is the file closed : ", newfl.closed
print "Mode of the file opening : ", newfl.mode
print " File Softspace flag for expicit : ", newfl.softspace
print "closing the file"
# Closing the file
newfl.close()
print "Is the file closed : ", newfl.closed
print "writing into the file"
newf2 = open("sample2.txt", "wb")
newf2.write( "This is my first file to enter data in the python.\nIt is simple
and easy\n");
```

```
print "reading the file sample1.txt"
newf2= open("sample2.txt", "r+")
str1 = newf2.read(18);
print "Read String is : ", str1
# Check current position
position = newf2.tell();
print "Current file position : ", position
# Reposition the pointer in a file
print "seek function on a file"
pos = newf2.seek(0, 0);
str2 = newf2.read(18);
print "reread the same file the output is : ", str2
print "rename the existing file"
os.rename( "sample2.txt", "sample3.txt" )
print "remove the file"
os.remove("sample3.txt")
print "create a new directory"
os.mkdir("FIRST")
print "change the directory"
os.chdir("/home/bin/first")
print "get the current working directory"
os.getcwd()
print "remove directory"
os.rmdir( "/bin/first"  )
print "flush operation on file"
newf2.flush()
print "fileno () and isatty()"
newf2 = open("sample2.txt", "wb")
print "file name is: ", newf2.name
fileid = newf2.fileno()
print "Descriptor of the file: ", fileid
rtrn = newf2.isatty()
print "Return value is: ", rtrn
print "next function on file"
newf3 = open("sample2.txt", "rw+")
for inx in range(3):
   ln = newf3.next()
   print "Line Number %d - %s" % (inx, ln)
print "current position of the file"
posi = newf3.tell()
print "present Position: %d" % (posi)
print "truncate the file"
ln = newf3.readline()
print "Read-Line: %s" % (ln)
newf3.truncate()
print "After truncate"
print "readline() on files"
lne = newf3.readline()
print "Read-Line: %s" % (lne)
sequ = ["This is another way to embed the file \n", "This is last line"]
print" sequence of lines"
```

```
newf3.seek(0, 2)
lin = newf3.writelines( sequ )
newf3.seek(0,0)
for indx in range(7):
   ln = newf3.next()
   print "Line Number %d - %s" % (indx, ln)
```

Output:

```
Enter your input: Welcome to python
Received input is :  Welcome to python
opening a new file in writing in binary format mode
File name:  sample1.txt
Is the file closed :  False
Mode of the file opening :  wb
 File Softspace flag for expicit :  0
closing the file
Is the file closed :  True
writing into the file
reading the file sample1.txt
Read String is :  This is my first f
Current file position :  18
seek function on a file
reread the same file the output is :  This is my first f
rename the existing file
remove the file
create a new directory
change the directory
/home/sample
Opening a new file in writing in binary format mode
reading the file sample1.txt
flush operation on file
fileno () and isatty()
file name is:  sample2.txt
Descriptor of the file:  5
Return value is:  False
next function on file
Traceback (most recent call last):
StopIteration
```

> **Note** *There are prone to be errors when we use the directory functions and the next() using the files.*

7. Write a python program to demonstrate exception handling

Solution.

```
#python program to demonstrate exception handling
# Defining a function.
print"functions that handle exception"
```

```
def tmp_ftoc(var):
   try:
      return int(var)
   except ValueError, Arg:
      print "The argument does not contain numbers\n", Arg
# Function call.
tmp_ftoc("abc");
print "exception on files"
try:
   fs = open("sample1", "r")
   fs.write("I am using this program for exception handling!")
except IOError:
   print "Error: File not found or file not read sucessfully"
else:
   print "File read operation on the file sucessfull"
print "file I/O operation exception"
try:
   fs1 = open("sample2", "w")
   fs1.write("this is my second file for exception handling!")
finally:
   print "Error: File not found or file not read"
print "file exception in closing the file"
try:
   fs2 = open("sample3", "w")
   try:
      fs2.write("Here I am using this file for exception handling!")
   finally:
      print "the file is being closed"
      fs2.close()
except IOError:
   print "Error: File not found or file not read I/O exception"
fs2.close()
print "user defined exception"
class Ntwrkerr(RuntimeError):
   def __innt1__(self1, arg1):
      self1.args = arg1
try:
   raise Ntwrkerr("Hostname is bad")
except Ntwrkerr,e1:
   print e1.args
```

Output:

```
functions that handle exception
The argument does not contain numbers
invalid literal for int() with base 10: 'abc'
exception on files
Error: File not found or file not read sucessfully
file I/O operation exception
Error: File not found or file not read
file exception in closing the file
```

```
the file is being closed
user defined exception
('Hostname is bad',)
```

Multiple Choice Questions

1. Which of the following functions is used to open a file in Python?
   a. `open{}` b. `open()`
   c. `open[]` d. `Open()`
2. What is a file object also known as?
   a. Object source b. File
   c. Object file d. Handle
3. Which of the following is the default mode while opening a file?
   a. Binary b. Number
   c. Text d. None
4. What are the two modes that are used to open a file?
   a. Text or Binary b. Number or Text
   c. Number or Binary d. Text or Number
5. Which of the following is incorrect when we use the binary mode?
   a. Image Files b. Text Files
   c. exe Files d. Non-Text Files
6. What is the default file access mode?
   a. `write (w)` b. `append`
   c. `read (r)` d. None
7. What is the syntax for opening a file in current directory?
   a. `f = open("xyz.txt",'r')` b. `f = open("xyz.txt,'w')`
   c. `f = open("xyz.txt,'a')` d. `f = open("xyz.txt")`
8. What will be used to open a file C:/xyz.txt for reading?
   a. `f = open("C:/xyz.txt")` b. `f = open("C:\xyz.txt",'r')`
   c. `f = open("C://xyz.txt",'r')` d. `f = open("C:/xyz.txt",'r')`
9. Which of the following statements is correct while using `r+` mode for opening a file?
   a. Opens a file for reading only
   b. Opens a file for reading in binary format
   c. Opens a file for both reading and writing
   d. Opens a file for writing only
10. At what position will the file pointer be placed whenever we open a file for reading or writing?
    a. Middle b. Beginning
    c. Second line d. End
11. Which of the following statements is not correct?
    a. When a file is opened for reading, if the file does not exist, an empty file will be opened.
    b. When a file is opened for writing, overwrites the file if the file exists.
    c. When a file is opened for writing, if the file does not exist, creates a new file for writing.
    d. When a file is opened for reading, if the file does not exist, an error occurs.
12. Whenever we open a file for appending, at what position will the file pointer be placed?
    a. Middle b. Beginning
    c. Second line d. End

13. Which of the following statements is correct while using 'a+' mode for opening a file?
    a. Opens a file for appending only
    b. Opens a file for writing only
    c. Opens a file for both appending and reading
    d. Opens a file for both appending and writing
14. Which of the following statements is correct while using 'x' mode?
    a. Open a file for reading
    b. Open a file for exclusive creation
    c. Open a file for appending
    d. Does not open a file
15. In disk, the files are stored in?
    a. Bytes
    b. Bit
    c. Kilobits
    d. Gigabytes
16. What is the syntax to close a file?
    a. `file.close()`
    b. `close()`
    c. `close();`
    d. `fileObject.close()`
17. The `write()` method does not add a newline character ('\n') at which position of the string?
    a. Beginning
    b. Middle
    c. End
    d. None of the above
18. What is the syntax of the `write()` method?
    a. `FileObject.write()`
    b. `fileObject.write(string)`
    c. `file.object.write()`
    d. `file.write()`
19. What is the syntax for reading from a file?
    a. `fileObject.read([size])`
    b. `fileObject.read(size)`
    c. `file.read()`
    d. `file.read(size)`
20. Which module does Python provide to perform operations like renaming and deleting files?
    a. `Is`
    b. `os`
    c. `op`
    d. `ip`
21. Which of the following methods is used to create directories in the current directory?
    a. `chdir()`
    b. `rmdir()`
    c. `mkdir()`
    d. `mcdir()`
22. Which of the following methods is used to change the current directory?
    a. `chdir()`
    b. `rmdir()`
    c. `mkdir()`
    d. `mcdir()`
23. Which of the following methods is used to display the current working directory?
    a. `mkcwd()`
    b. `getcwd()`
    c. `chcwd()`
    d. `setcwd()`
24. Which of the following methods is used to delete the directory?
    a. `chdir()`
    b. `mkdir()`
    c. `mrdir()`
    d. `rmdir()`
25. Which of the following is not an attribute of a file in Python?
    a. Mode
    b. Name
    c. Delete
    d. Closed
26. Which of the following is a condition that is caused by a runtime error in the program?
    a. Exception
    b. Assertion
    c. Attribute
    d. Error

27. How many except statements can a try-except block have?
    a. One
    b. More than zero
    c. Zero
    d. None
28. Which keyword is used to prepare a block of code that throws an exception?
    a. `except`
    b. `import`
    c. `try`
    d. None
29. Which of the following is defined to catch the exception thrown by the try block?
    a. `except`
    b. `import`
    c. `index`
    d. None
30. Which block will the statements be executed in after the try block if no exception is raised inside a try block?
    a. `Try`
    b. `Except`
    c. `Finally`
    d. `else`
31. Check whether the following code is correct or not.

```
try:
        # Do something
except:
        # Do something
finally:
        #Do something
```

    a. Yes
    b. No, `finally` cannot be used with `except`
    c. No, `finally` can be used after `try` block
    d. None of the above
32. Check whether the following code is correct or not?

```
try:
        # Do something
except:
        # Do something
else:
        #Do something
```

    a. Yes
    b. No, `else` cannot be used with `except`
    c. No, `else` can be used after `try` block
    d. None of the above

Short Questions

1. What is a file in Python and why is it used?
2. How to open a file? What are the modes for opening a file?
3. What are the various attributes of the file object?
4. What will be the output of the code below? Justify your answer.

```
>>>fileObject = open("xyz.txt", "w")
>>>print("name of the file:", fo.name)
>>>print("closed or not:", fo.closed)
>>>print("opening mode:", fo.mode)
>>>print("softspace flag:", fo.softspace)
```

5. What will be the output of the given code?
```
>>>fileObject = open("xyz.txt", "wb")
>>>print("name of the file:", fileObject.name)
>>>fileObject.close()
>>>print("file closed")
```
6. How will you rename a file in Python?
7. How will you delete a file in Python?
8. What are the various directories in Python? Explain with examples.
9. What is an exception? Explain with examples.
10. What is exception handling?
11. What will be the output of the given code?
```
>>>try:
x=int(input("first number:")
y=int(input("second number:")
result=x/y
print"result=",result
exceptZeroDivisionError:
print "division by zero"
else:
print "successful division"
```
12. What is `finally` block? What is the syntax for `try...finally` block?

Answers to Multiple Choice Questions

1. b	**2.** d	**3.** c	**4.** a	**5.** b	**6.** c	**7.** a	**8.** d	**9.** c	**10.** b
11. a	**12.** d	**13.** c	**14.** b	**15.** a	**16.** d	**17.** c	**18.** b	**19.** a	**20.** b
21. c	**22.** a	**23.** b	**24.** d	**25.** c	**26.** a	**27.** b	**28.** c	**29.** a	**30.** d
31. b	**32.** a								

8 CLASSES AND OBJECTS

8.1 OVERVIEW OF OOP (OBJECT-ORIENTED PROGRAMMING)

As we know, Python is an object-oriented programming (OOP) language and provides all the features required to support object-oriented programming. OOP mainly focuses on the objects and classes while procedural programming focuses on the functions and methods.

OOP is based on the implementation of real world objects in programming. Such a concept of programming contains objects that contain the data in the form of attributes and classes that contains methods. In this approach, a problem is considered in terms of objects that can be involved in finding the solution to the problem instead of procedures. Hence, through this approach, a person can relate a problem to the real world objects and can work towards its solution with relative ease.

Object is an instance of a class. A class is a collection of data (variables) and methods (functions). A class is the basic structure of an object and is a set of attributes, which can be data members and method members.

Let us understand the concept with an example. We can relate class to a sketch or model of a building. That sketch contains all the information about the structure of the building, such as floors, doorways, exits, rooms, etc. Now, according to our example, the building is an object. Just as various buildings can be based on one model, so too can a class have many objects associated with it.

Some important terms in OOP are as follows:

- **Class:** Classes are defined by the user; the class provides the basic structure for an object. It consists of data members and method members that are used by the instances (objects) of the class.
- **Data Member:** A variable defined in either a class or an object; it holds the data associated with the class or object.
- **Instance Variable:** A variable that is defined in a method; its scope is only within the object that defines it.
- **Class Variable:** A variable that is defined in the class and can be used by all the instances of that class.
- **Instance:** An object is an instance of the class.
- **Instantiation:** The process of creation of an object of a class.
- **Method:** Methods are the functions that are defined in the definition of class and are used by various instances of the class.
- **Function Overloading:** A function defined more than one time with different behaviours is known as function overloading. The operations performed by these functions are different.

- **Inheritance:** A class 'A' that can use the characteristics of another class 'B' is said to be a derived class, i.e., a class inherited from 'B'. The process is called inheritance.

8.1.1 Data Encapsulation

In OOP, restrictions can be imposed on the access to methods and variables. Such restrictions can be used to avoid accidental modification in the data and are known as Encapsulation. Encapsulation is an important feature in OOP.

In fact, we can say that OOP relies strictly on Data Encapsulation.

Most of us are already familiar with the term abstraction. Abstraction means data-hiding. Encapsulation and abstraction can be used as synonyms since both of them relate to the data-hiding concept.

Generally, in the context of programming, we can restrict the access to some of the object's components, ensuring that these components cannot be accessed from outside the object but from inside the object only. For accessing these types of data, some special methods are used.

These methods are known as `getters()` and `setters()`.

8.1.2 Polymorphism

The word 'Poly' means 'many'. Therefore, the term 'polymorphism' means that the object of a class can have many different forms to respond in different ways to any message or action.

In other words, polymorphism is the capability for a message or data to be processed in one or more ways.

Let us look at an example:

If a base class is mammals, then horse, human, and cat are its subclasses. All the mammals can see in the daytime. Therefore, if the message 'see in the daytime' is passed to mammals, all the mammals including the human, the horse and the cat will respond to it. Whereas, if the message 'see during the night time' is passed to the mammals, then only the cat will respond to the message as it can see during the night as well as in the daytime. Hence, the cat, which is a mammal, can behave differently from the other mammals.

This is called polymorphism and is illustrated in Fig. 8.1.

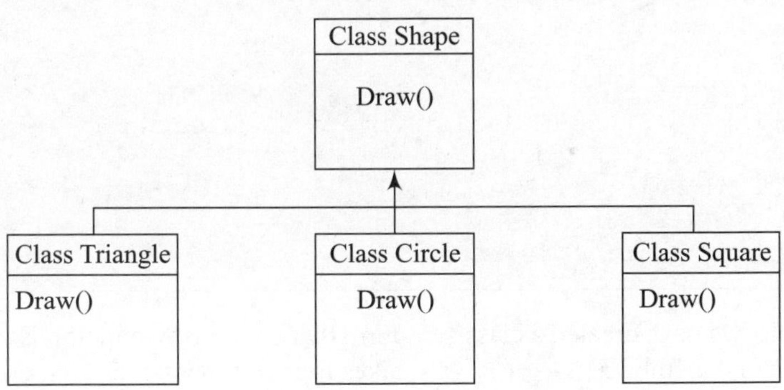

Figure 8.1 Polymorphism

8.2 CLASS DEFINITION

A class can be defined as a blue print or a previously defined structure from which objects are made. It can also be defined as a group of objects that share similar attributes and relationships with each other.

For example:

- Fruit is a class, and apple, mango and banana are its objects. The attributes of these objects can be color, taste, etc.
- Vehicle is a class and car, scooter, bus, truck, etc., can be its objects. The attributes of these objects can be speed, brake, power of engine, etc.

In Python, a class is defined by using a keyword `class`. After that, the first statement can be a docstring (optional) that contains the information about the class. Now, in the body of class, the attributes are defined. These attributes can be data members or method members.

In Python, as soon as we define a class, the interpreter instantly creates an object that has the same name as the class name. Although, we can create more objects of the same class. With the help of objects, we can access the attributes defined in the class.

Syntax

```
class class_name:
     'This is docstring which is optional'
     class_suite
```

A new local new space is created by a Class, where all its attributes (data or function) are defined. Special attributes with double underscores (_)are also present, for example- _doc_ gives the docstring of that class. As soon as the class is defined, a new class object is created with same name, which allows access to the different attributes, also to instantiate new object of that class.

Example

```
>>>class Student:
... 'student details'
... def fill_details(self,name,branch,year):
...         self.name = name
...         self.branch = branch
...         self.year = year
...         print("A Student detail object is created")
... def print_details(self):
...         print('Name: ', self.name)
...         print('Branch: ',self.branch)
...         print('Year: ',self.year)
```

In the given example, we have created a class `Student` that contains two methods: `fill_details` and `print_details`. The first method `fill_details` takes four arguments: `self`, `name`, `branch` and `year`. The second method `print_details` takes exactly one argument: `self`.

In the next section, we will find out how these class and methods are used.

Note *The methods in the classes are defined in the same way as the functions are defined in the preceding sections. The only difference is that the every method will have self as its first argument.*

TIP

At the time of calling the method, we do not need to add self as an argument. The Python interpreter does it for us.

Check Your Understanding

1. What is Object-Oriented Programming?

Ans. The Object-Oriented programming approach mainly focuses on the objects and classes while procedural programming focuses on the functions and methods.

The object is an instance of class. It is a collection of data (variables) and methods (functions). A class can also be called the basic structure of object. Class is a set of attributes, which can be data members and method members.

2. Define class, method, instance and function overloading.

Ans. **Class:** Classes are defined by the user; the class provides the basic structure for an object. It consists of data members and method members that are used by the instances (objects) of the class.

Method: Methods are the functions defined in the definition of class and are used by various instances of the class.

Instance: An object is an instance of the class.

Function Overloading: A function that can be defined more than one time with different behaviours is known as function overloading. The operations performed by these functions are different.

3. Give the syntax for class definition.

Ans. **Syntax**

```
class class_name:
        'This is docstring which is optional'
    class_suite
```

8.3 CREATING OBJECTS

An object is an instance of a class that has some attributes and behaviour. The object behaves according to the class of which it is an object.

Objects can be used to access the attributes of the class. The syntax of creating an object in Python is similar to that for calling a function.

Syntax

```
obj_name = class_name()
```

Example

```
s1 = Student()
```

The above statement creates an object `s1` of the class `Student` which we defined earlier.

Now, we can access the methods (attributes) which are defined in the class `Student`. We can use a method from the class `Student` with the `object name` followed by a `dot`, which is then followed by the `method name` with valid arguments.

Example

```
# creating an object of Student class
>>> s1 = Student()
# creating another object of Student class
>>>s2 = Student()
# using the method fill_details with proper attributes
>>> s1.fill_details('John','CSE','2002')
A Student detail object is created
>>>s2.fill_details('Jack','ECE','2004')
A Student detail object is created
# using the print_detail method with proper attributes

>>>s1.print_details()
Name: John          # Output
Branch: CSE         # Output
Year: 2002          # Output

>>>s2.print_details()
Name: Jack          # Output
Branch: ECE         # Output
Year: 2004          # Output
```

In this example, we create two objects (instances) `s1` and `s2` of class `Student`. Then afterwards, we use the `fill_details` method of class with the object names as prefix and passed the valid arguments. The details of the students are stored in the objects. Now, the second method `print_details` is called with the same convention. The method `print_details` prints the details of all stored students.

8.3.1 Objects are Mutable

Objects are mutable— this statement tells us that the state of an object can be changed at any point of time by making changes to its attributes.

For example, consider the class `Student` which was defined earlier. We created an object `s1` and filled the details of the student using `fill_details` method. If, at any point of time, it is required to change the value of branch from `ECE` to `CSE`, it can be done in the same object by reassigning it a new value.

Example

```
# Create an instance of class Student
>>>s1 = Student()
# Fill details in that object
>>>s1.fill_details('John','ECE',2004)
A Student detail object is created
# Printing details of the object s1
>>>s1.print_details()
```

Output:

```
Name: John
Branch: ECE
Year: 2004
```

Now, what if it is required to change the value of `branch` of object `s1` to `CSE`? Will we create a new object? Definitely not. We can change the value in the same object by simply reassigning the value to it.

```
#Change the value of branch from ECE to CSE
>>>s1.fill_details('John','CSE',2004)
A Student detail object is created
# The branch is changed from ECE to CSE
>>>s1.print_details()
```

Output:

```
Name: John
Branch: CSE
Year: 2004
```

Now, the state of object `s1` has been permanently changed.

Note *Objects can be passed as an argument to a function and a function can also return an object.*

Check Your Understanding

1. How are the objects created in Python? Give an example.

Ans. Creating Objects

Objects can be used to access the attributes of the class. The syntax for creating an object in Python is similar to that for calling a function.

Syntax

```
obj_name = class_name()
```

Example

```
# define a class
>>>class A:
    def print_det(self):
          print 'This is a class'

# create object of class A
>>> object = A()
>>>object.print_det()
This is a class          # Output
```

2. What do you understand by "Objects are mutable"?

Ans. Objects are mutable means that the state of an object can be changed at any point in time by making changes to its attributes.

8.4 OBJECTS AS ARGUMENTS

The instance of a class can be passed as an argument to a function in Python.

Let us say, we have a class Triangle. We make an instance of this class and define the attributes that are sides of this triangle. Then, that object or instance of Triangle can be passed to a function which calculates the perimeter of the triangle.

Example

First of all, we will create a class `Triangle` with no statements.

```
>>>class Triangle:
    pass
```

Now, we create an object `t1` of the class `Triangle` and assign the value of sides `a, b, c` of the triangles here.

```
>>>t1 = Triangle()
>>>t1.a = 10
>>>t1.b = 18
>>>t1.c = 23
```

Now, we define a function `perimeter`, which calculates the perimeter of a triangle. This function takes an object or instance of a class as an argument.

```
>>>def perimeter(obj):
    per = t1.a + t1.b + t1.c
    print("Perimeter of triangle: ", per)
```

Now, we pass the object `t1` to the function `perimeter`, which calculates the perimeter of the triangle that is in this object.

```
>>>perimeter(t1)                      # Passing object as argument
Perimeter of triangle: 51             # Output
```

8.5 OBJECTS AS RETURN VALUES

The instances of a class can also be returned by a function, i.e., a function can return instances or objects.

Let us say, we are creating an object of `Triangle` class and a function `size_double` that doubles the size of the triangle. Now, when the object of `Triangle` class is passed to this function, it doubles the size of the triangle in that object and returns the Double sized triangle that is in the form of object.

Example

Create a class `triangle` and define two methods: one is `create_triangle,` which will create the triangle, and the other is `print_sides,` which will print the sides of the triangle.

```
>>>class Triangle:
    defcreate_triangle(self,a,b,c):
          self.a = a
          self.b = b
          self.c = c
          print("The triangle is created")
    defprint_sides(self):
          print('Side a: ', self.a)
          print('Side b: ', self.b)
          print('Side c: ', self.c)
```

Create an object `t1` of the `Triangle` class and create a triangle in it.

```
>>>t1 = Triangle()
>>>t1.create_triangle(10,20,30)
The triangle is created          # Output
```

Define a function `size_double` that will take an object as an argument and return a triangle in the form of an object that is double in size.

```
>>>defsize_double(obj):
    t2 = Triangle()
    t2.a = t1.a *2
    t2.b = t1.b *2
    t2.c = t1.c *2
    return t2                 # Returning object
>>>t2 = size_double(t1)     # Passing object as argument
>>>t2.print_sides()
```

Output:

```
Side a: 20
Side b: 40
Side c: 60
```

Hence, we got a triangle that is double in size with the triangle that was passed as an argument.

> ***Note*** *The purpose of the dot notation is to identify the variable you are referring to unambiguously.*

TIP

Class definitions can appear anywhere in the program, but they usually appear near the beginning.

8.6 BUILT-IN CLASS ATTRIBUTES

In Python, every class contains various built-in attributes. They can be accessed with a dot operator just as in the case of user-defined attributes we have come across earlier.

The built-in class attributes in Python are as follows:

1. `__dict__`: It displays the dictionary in which the class's namespace is stored.
2. `__name__`: It displays the name of the class.
3. `__bases__`: It displays the tuple that contains the base classes, possibly empty. It displays them in the order in which they occur in the base class list.
4. `__doc__`: It displays the documentation string of the class. It displays none if the docstring isn't given.
5. `__module__`: It displays the name of the module in which the class is defined. Generally, the value of this attribute is "`__main__`" in interactive mode.

Example

```
# Create the class Student
>>>class Student:
    'student details'

    # Add method member fill_details
    deffill_details(self,name,branch,year):
            self.name = name
            self.branch = branch
            self.year = year
            print("A Student detail object is created")

    # Add method member print_details
    defprint_details(self):
            print('Name: ', self.name)
            print('Branch: ',self.branch)
            print('Year: ',self.year)

>>>print "Student.__doc__: ",Student.__doc__
Student.__doc__:  student details

>>>print "Student.__name__: ",Student.__name__
```

```
Student.__name__:  Student

>>>print "Student.__module__: ",Student.__module__
Student.__module__:  __main__

>>>print "Student.__bases__: ",Student.__bases__
Student.__bases__:  ()

>>>print "Student.__dict__: ", Student.__dict__
Student.__dict__:   {'__module__': '__main__', 'fill_details': <function
fill_details at 0x02CDAC30>, '__doc__': 'student details', 'print_details':
<function print_details at 0x02CDACB0>}
```

Check Your Understanding

1. **What do you understand by arguments "Instances as return values"?**

Ans. **Instances as return values**

The instances of a class can also be returned by a function i.e. a function can return the instances or objects.

2. **Define __dict__, __bases__, __name__ built-in class attributes. Give Example.**

Ans. **`__dict__`**: It displays the dictionary in which the class's namespace is stored.

`__name__`: It displays the name of the class.

`__bases__`: It displays the tuple that contains the base classes, possibly empty. It displays them in the order in which they occur in the base class list.

Example

```
>>>print "__name__: ",PrintStatement.__name__
__name__:  PrintStatement

>>>print "__bases__: ",PrintStatement.__bases__
__bases__:  ()

>>>print "PrintStatement.__dict__: ",PrintStatement.__dict__
PrintStatement.__dict__:  {'__module__': '__main__', '__doc__':
None, 'print_method': <function print_method at 0x02CE3130>}
```

8.7 INHERITANCE

Inheritance is a very important concept in OOP. Inheritance, generally, means to acquire the features of something. In OOP, it means the reusability of code. It is the capability of a class to derive the properties of another class that has already been created.

Let us look at an example illustrated in Fig. 8.2.

- Vehicle is a class that is further divided into two subclasses, automobiles (driven by motors) and pulled vehicles (driven by men). Therefore, vehicle is the base class and automobiles and pulled vehicles are its subclasses. These subclasses inherit some of the properties of the base class vehicle.
- Truck and car are the subclasses of the class automobile that is the base class for them. They inherit some of the properties of base class automobiles. Similarly, the rickshaw and bullock cart are the subclasses of pulled vehicles that serves as the base class for them.

The main advantage of inheritance in the context of programming is that the code can be written once in the base class and then reused repeatedly in the subclasses.

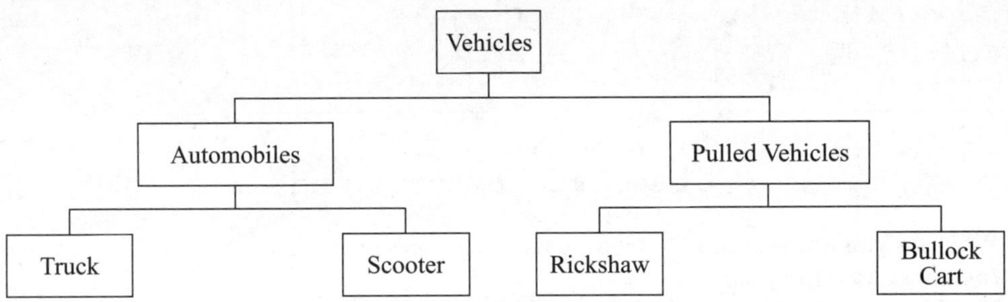

Figure 8.2 Example of Inheritance

Inheritance generally involves acquiring the features of a predecessor. With the help of inheritance, we can inherit a class from another class. If a class A is inherited from another class B, then class A can use all the features (like variables and methods) of class B.

The class which inherits the features of another class is known as subclass. If we want to inherit a class, we use the class name with the name of the class that is to be inherited in the parentheses.

Syntax

```
class sub_classname(Parent_classname):
     'Optional Docstring'
     Class_suite
```

Example

Define a parent class `Person`

```
>>>class Person(object):
     'returns a Person object with given name'
     defget_name(self,name):
            self.name = name
     defget_details(self):
            'returns a string containing name of person'
            return self.name

Define a subclass Student
>>>class Student(Person):
     'return a Student object, takes 3 arguments'
```

```
    deffill_details(self, name, branch, year):
        Person.get_name(self,name)
        self.branch = branch
        self.year = year
    defget_details(self):
        'returns student details'
        print("Name: ", self.name)
        print("Branch: ", self.branch)
        print("Year: ", self.year)
```

Define a subclass `Teacher`

```
>>>class Teacher(Person):
    'returns a Teacher object, takes 2 arguments'
    deffill_details(self, name, branch):
        Person.get_name(self,name)
        self.branch = branch
    defget_details(self):
        print("Name: ", self.name)
        print("Branch: ", self.branch)
```

Define one object for each class

```
>>>person1 = Person()
>>>student1 = Student()
>>>teacher1 = Teacher()
```

Fill details in the objects

```
>>> person1.get_name('John')
>>> student1.fill_details('Jinnie', 'CSE', 2005)
>>> teacher1.fill_details('Jack', 'ECE')
```

Print the details using parent class function

```
>>>print(person1.get_details())
John        # Output
>>>print(student1.get_details())
Name: Jinnie            # Output
Branch: CSE             # Output
Year: 2005        # Output
>>>print(teacher1.get_details())
Name: Jack        # Output
Branch: ECE             # Output
```

In the example illustrated above, we have defined a parent class `Person` that has two methods: `get_name()` and `get_details()`.

Now, we have defined two subclasses: the `student` class, which has two methods: `fill_details()` and `get_details()`, and `teacher` class, which also has two methods: `fill_details()` and `get_details()`.

We have used the parent class method `get_details()` in the subclasses `student` and `teacher` to get the names of students and teachers respectively. This is called inheritance.

8.7.1 Multiple Inheritance

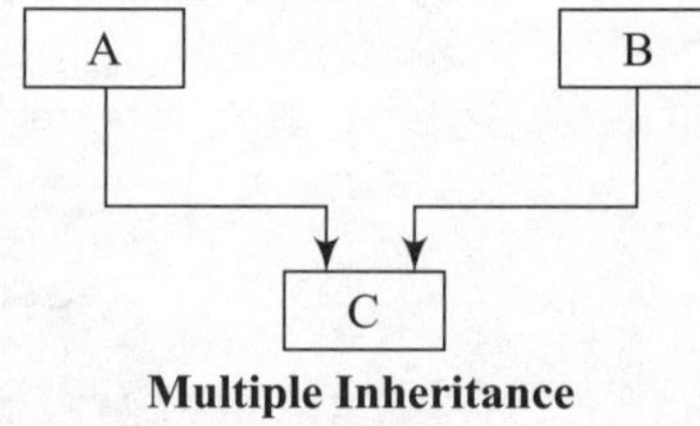

Figure 8.3 Multiple Inheritance

In multiple inheritance, a subclass is derived from more than one base classes. The subclass inherits the properties of all the base classes. In Fig. 8.3, subclass C inherits the properties of two base classes A and B.

Let us look at an example:

There are three classes, Water animal (fish, octopus, etc.), Land animal (Tigers, lions, etc.) and Amphibian (frog, crocodiles, etc.).

Here, Amphibian is the subclass that derives the properties of the base classes, water animal and land animal. Therefore, its animals (objects) frog and crocodile live both on land and water.

We can also define multiple inheritance in Python. When a class inherits the features of more than one class this is known as multiple inheritance. It is defined in the same way as inheritance.

Syntax

```
# Define your first parent class
class A
........class_suite.........

# Define your second parent class
class B
.......Class_suite.........

# Define the subclass inheriting both A and B
class C(A,B)
.........class_suite..........
```

Example

```
>>> class A:                          #Defining class A
    def x(self):
          print("method of A")

>>> class B:                          #Defining Class B
    def x(self):
          print("method of B")

>>> class C(A,B):                     #Defining class C
    pass

>>> y = C()
>>> B.x(y)
method of B                     #Output
>>> A.x(y)
method of A                     #Output
```

In the above example, two classes `A` and `B` are defined and then another class `C` is defined which inherits the two classes `A` and `B`. Now, an object of class `C` is created, through which the methods of classes `A` and `B` are accessed.

8.8 METHOD OVERRIDING

Method overriding is allowed in Python. Method overriding means that the method of parent class can be used in the subclass with different or special functionality.

Example

```
>>>class Parent:
     defovr_method(self):
          print 'This is in Parent Class'

>>>class Child(Parent):
     defovr_method(self):
          print 'This is in Child Class'

>>>c = Child()
>>>c.ovr_method()
This is in Child Class          # Output
```

Note *The `pass` statement has no effect; it is only necessary because a compound statement must have something in its body.*

TIP

The initialization method (`__init__`) is a special method that is invoked when an object is created. It is also known as the constructor method for a class.

8.9 DATA ENCAPSULATION

In Python Programming Language, encapsulation is a process to restrict the access of data members. This means that the internal details of an object may not be visible from outside of the object definition. But Python provides some methods which assist in accessing these sorts of data.

The members in a class can be assigned in three ways i.e., public, protected and private. If the name of a member is preceded by single underscore, it is assigned as a protected member, whereas if the name of a member is preceded by double underscore, it is assigned as a private member and if the name is not preceded by anything then it is a public member.

Let us summarise this concept in the given table below:

Name	Notation	Behaviour
varname	Public	Can be accessed from anywhere
_varname	Protected	They are like the public members but they cannot be directly accessed from outside
__varname	Private	They cannot be seen and accessed from outside the class

Let us understand this concept with the help of an example:

Example

```
>>> class MyClass(object):              # Defining class
    def __init__(self, x, y, z):
            self.var1 = x               # public data member
            self._var2 = y              # protected data member
            self.__var3 = z             # private data member


>>> obj = MyClass(3,4,5)
>>> obj.var1
3                          # Output
>>> obj.var1 = 10
>>> obj.var1
10                         # Output

>>> obj._var2
4                          # Output
>>> obj._var2 = 12
>>> obj._var2
12                         # Output

>>> obj.__var3             # Private member is not accessible

Traceback (most recent call last):
  File "<pyshell#71>", line 1, in <module>
    obj.__var3
AttributeError: 'MyClass' object has no attribute '__var3'
```

Note *The value of a private variable can be set by a Python method called setter method.*

Example (Getters and Setters)

```
>>> class A:
    def __init__(self,p):
            self.__p = p          #Defining private member
    def getP(self):               #Defining getters
            return self.__p
    def setP(self, p):            #Defining Setters
            self.__p = p


>>> a1 = A(22)
>>> a1.getP()                     #Getting value through get function
22
>>> a1.setP(43)                   #Setting value through set function
>>> a1.getP()
43
```

8.10 DATA HIDING

In Python programming, there might be some cases when you intend to hide the attributes of objects outside the class definition. To accomplish this, use double score (__) before the name of the attributes and these attributes will not be visible directly outside the class definition. Let us understand the Python data hiding by a simple example given below:

Example

```
>>> class MyClass:                    # defining class
      __a = 0;
      def sum(self, increment):
              self.__a += increment
              print self.__a


>>> b = MyClass()                     # creating instance of class
>>> b.sum(2)
2
>>> b.sum(5)
7
>>> print b.__a

Traceback (most recent call last):
  File "<pyshell#24>", line 1, in <module>
    print b.__a
AttributeError: MyClass instance has no attribute '__a'
```

As seen in the above example that the variable __a is not accessible as we tried to access it; the Python interpreter generates an error immediately. In such a case, the Python secures the members by internally changing the names to incorporate the name of the class. If you intend to access these attributes then the syntax for accessing the variable is:

```
objectName.__className__attributeName
```

In the above code, if we use the aforementioned syntax to access the attributes, then the following changes are seen in the output:

```
>>> class MyClass:                        # Defining class
      __a = 0;
      def sum(self, increment):
              self.__a += increment
              print self.__a


>>> b = MyClass()                         # creating instance of class
>>> b.sum(2)
2
>>> b.sum(5)
7
>>> print b._MyClass__a                   # Accessing the hidden variable
7
```

Check Your Understanding

1. Define Inheritance and multiple inheritance. Give syntax for both.

Ans. Inheritance

Inheritance generally means to acquire the features of something. The same is the meaning in the context of the classes. With the help of inheritance, we can inherit a class from another class. If a class A is inherited from another class B, then class A can use all the features (like variables and methods) of class B.

Syntax

```
class sub_classname(Parent_classname):
    'Optional Docstring'
    Class_suite
```

Multiple Inheritance

We can also define multiple inheritance in Python. When a class inherits the features of more than one class it is known as multiple inheritance. It is defined in the same way as inheritance.

Syntax

```
# Define your first parent class
class A
........class_suite.........

# Define your second parent class
class B
.......Class_suite.........

# Define the subclass inheriting both A and B
class C(A,B)
.........class_suite..........
```

ALWAYS REMEMBER

- Python provides all the features required to support OOP.
- OOP approach mainly focuses on the objects and classes whereas procedural programming focuses on the functions and methods.
- An object is a collection of data and methods.
- An object is an instance of a class.

- Class is a set of objects that share the same attributes, which can be data member and method member.
- Data member is a variable that is defined either in class or in object and that holds the data associated with the class or object.
- Methods are the functions defined in the definition of class, and are used by various instances of the class.
- When a function is defined more than once with different behaviours, this is known as function overloading.
- In method overloading, the operations performed by the methods are different.
- When a class uses the characteristics of another class, it is said to be a derived class or inherited class and the process is called inheritance.
- When a class inherits the features of more than one class, this is called multiple inheritance.
- Method overriding means that the method of parent class can be used in the subclass with different or special functionality.
- The first argument of every method is `self`.
- Objects can be used to access the attributes of the class.
- The state of an object can be changed at any point of time by making changes to its attributes. Thus, it can be said that the objects are mutable.
- The instance of a class can be passed as an argument to a function in Python.
- The instances of a class can also be returned by a function, i.e., a function can return the instances or objects.
- There are various built-in attributes that can be accessed with a dot operator.

KEY TERMS

✓ **OBJECT:** Object is a real time entity.

✓ **CLASS:** Classes provide the basic structure for an object. It consists of data members and method members that are used by the objects of the class.

✓ **DATA MEMBER:** A variable defined either in a class or in an object, which holds the data that is associated with the class or object.

✓ **INSTANCE VARIABLE:** A variable which is defined in a method and whose scope is only within the object it is defined.

✓ **CLASS VARIABLE:** A variable which is defined in the class and can be used by all the instances of that class.

✓ **INSTANCE:** An object is an instance of the class.

✓ **INSTANTIATION:** The process of creation of an object of a class.

✓ **METHOD:** Methods are the functions which are defined in the definition of class and are used by various instances of the class.

✓ **METHOD OVERLOADING:** A function can be defined more than one time with different behaviours. This is known as function overloading or method overloading. The operations performed by these functions are different.

✓ **INHERITANCE:** A class 'A' that can use the characteristics of another class 'B' is said to be a derived class or inherited from 'B'. The process is called inheritance.

✓ **METHOD OVERRIDING:** When the method of the parent class can be used in a subclass with different or special functionality, it is known as method overriding.

1. **`class`**: This is the keyword used to define a class.
2. **`self`**: It is the first argument of every method.
3. **`__dict__`**: A class attribute that displays the dictionary in which the class's namespace is stored.
4. **`__name__`**: A class attribute that displays the name of the class.
5. **`__bases__`**: A class attribute that displays the tuple containing the base classes, possibly empty.
6. **`__doc__`**: A class attribute which displays the documentation string of the class
7. **`__module__`**: A class attribute which displays the name of the module in which the class is defined.

REVIEW EXERCISES

PROGRAMS

1. Write a program that defines a class with two methods: `inputStr()` that will get the string using console input and `printStr()` that will print the string in upper case. Also, test the class methods with a function.

Solution.

```
>>> class UpperString(object):
        def __init__(self):
                self.o = ""
        def inputStr(self):
                self.o = raw_input()
        def printStr(self):
                print self.o.upper()

>>> a = UpperString()
>>> a.inputStr()
'python'                        #Input from user
>>> a.printStr()
'PYTHON'                        #Output
```

2. Write a program that defines a class named Rectangle that takes the parameters length and breadth. The class Rectangle should also contain a method for computing its perimeter.

Solution.

```
>>> class Rectangle(object):
        def __init__(self,l,b):
                self.length = l
                self.breadth = b
```

```
    def perimeter(self):
            return
            self.length+self.breadth

>>> a = Rectangle(10,15)
>>> print a.perimeter()
25                                  #Output
```

3. Write a function that has a class `Animal` with a method `legs`. Create two subclasses `Tiger` and `Dog`. Now, access the method `leg` explicitly with the class `Dog` and implicitly with the class `Tiger`.

Solution.

```
#for explicitly access, we need to override the method in Dog class.
>>> class Animal(object):
    def legs(self):
            print "legs Animal() method"

>>> class Dog(Animal):
    def legs(self):
            print "legs Dog() method"

>>> class Tiger(Animal):
    pass

>>> a = Animal()
>>> d = Dog()
>>> t = Tiger()
>>> a.legs()
legs Animal() method                #Output
>>> d.legs()                        #Accessing method explicitly (override)
legs Dog() method                   #Output
>>> t.legs()                        #Accessing method implicitly
legs Animal() method                #Output
```

4. Write a program that defines a class named `Employee`. Define two subclasses: `Engineer` and `Manager`. Every class should have a method named `printDesignation()` that prints Engineer for `Engineer` class and Manager for `Manager` class.

Solution.

```
>>> class Employee(object):
    def printDesignation(self):
            return "Not Known"

>>> class Engineer(Employee):
    def printDesignation(self):
            return "Engineer"

>>> class Manager(Employee):
    def printDesignation(self):
            return "Manager"
```

```
>>> e = Engineer()
>>> m = Manager()
>>> print e.printDesignation()
Engineer                #Output
>>> print m.printDesignation()
Manager                 #Output
```

5. Write a Python program to demonstrate classes and their attributes.

Solution.

```
# python program to demonstrate class and their attributes
class Person:
   print "Inside the class"
   pcount = 0

   def __init__(self, name, age, salary):
      self.name = name
      self.age = age
      self.salary = salary
      Person.pcount += 1

   def dispcount(self):
     print "Total number of persons", Person.pcount

   def dispperson(self):
     print "Person Name : ", self.name,  ", age:", self.age, "Salary: ",
self.salary
print "creating objects to the class"
per1 = Person("ruby", 24, 2000)
per2 = Person("Perl", 27, 5000)
per1.dispperson()
per2.dispperson()
print "Total number of person %d" % Person.pcount

print "details of the person class and class attributes"
print "Person.__doc__:", Person.__doc__
print "Person.__name__:", Person.__name__
print "Person.__module__:", Person.__module__
print "Person.__bases__:", Person.__bases__
print "Person.__dict__:", Person.__dict__
# Returns true if 'sex' attribute exists
print hasattr(Person, 'sex')
# Set attribute 'sal' to 3000
setattr(Person, 'salary', 3000)
print  Person.salary
# Delete attribute 'salary'
delattr(Person, 'salary')
print "After deleting the atribute salary", Person.salary
```

```
Output:
Total number of person 2
details of the person class and class attributes
Person.__doc__: None
Person.__name__: Person
Person.__module__: __main__
Person.__bases__: ()
Person.__dict__: {'__module__': '__main__', 'pcount': 2, 'dispcount': <func-
tion dispcount at 0x7fc0ba6e27d0>, 'dispperson': <function dispperson at
0x7fc0ba6e2848>, '__d
oc__': None, '__init__': <function __init__ at 0x7fc0ba6e2758>}
False
3000
After deleting the atribute salary
Traceback (most recent call last):
  File "Person.py", line 37, in <module>
    print "After deleting the atribute salary", Person.salary
AttributeError: class Person has no attribute 'salary'
Note: Save the file name as Person.py. The user can try the "getattr(Person,
age)" which is can be added to the code and check the functionality.
```

6. Write a Python program to demonstrate Inheritance and method overriding

Solution.

```
class Person:         # define Person class
   PersonAttr = 150
   def __init__(self):
      print "Calling Person constructor"

   def PersonMethod(self):
      print 'Calling Person method'

   def setAttr(self, attr):
      Person.PersonAttr = attr

   def getAttr(self):
      print "Person attribute :", Person.PersonAttr

   def myMethod(self):
      print 'Calling Person method'

class Subperson(Person): # define Subperson class
   def __init__(self):
      print "Calling Subperson constructor"

   def SubpersonMethod(self):
      print 'Calling Subperson method'

   def myMethod(self):
      print 'Calling Subperson method'
```

```
c = Subperson()             # instance of Subperson
c.SubpersonMethod()         # Subperson calls its method
c.PersonMethod()            # calls Person's method
c.setAttr(300)              # again call Person's method
c.getAttr()                 # again call Person's method
c = Subperson()             # instance of Subperson
c.myMethod()                # Subperson calls overridden method
```

Output:

```
Calling Subperson constructor
Calling Subperson method
Calling Subperson constructor
Calling Subperson method
Calling Person method
Person attribute : 300
Calling Subperson constructor
Calling Subperson method
Calling Person method
Person attribute : 300
Calling Subperson constructor
Calling Subperson method
```

7. Write a Python program to demonstrate multiple inheritances

Solution.

```
#Python program to demonstrate multiple inheritance
# base class 1

class trans(object):
        def higher(this,that):
                if this.getcapc() > that.getcapc():
                        return this
                return that
        @staticmethod
        def maximumm(collect):
                uptonow = collect[0]
                for tryme in collect:
                        uptonow = uptonow.higher(tryme)
                return uptonow

# base class-2

class label(object):
        def nameset(this,name):
                this.name = name
        def nameget(this):
                return this.name.upper()

# Two classes which both use multiple inheritance

class mulchildclass(trans,label):
        def __init__(current,dest,time,length,pereach):
```

```
                current.time = time
                current.leng = length
                current.pe = pereach
                current.nameset(dest)
        def getcapc(current):
                return current.leng * current.pe

class secmulchild(trans,label):
        def __init__(current,dest,pereach):
                current.pe = pereach
                current.nameset(dest)
        def getcapc(current):
                return current.pe -1

perl = mulchildclass("perl","07:17",2,75)
ruby = mulchildclass("ruby","07:24",1,61)
rhino= secmulchild("rhino",5)
Mystore = mulchildclass("Mystore sales","07:45",7,65)
sara = secmulchild("sara jane",8)

flows = [rhino,perl,sara,Mystore,ruby]

for flow in flows:
        commuters = flow.getcapc()
        destiny = flow.nameget()
        print "To",destiny,"carrying",commuters

print "\nLet's see is perl or ruby has the higher capacity"
toby = perl.higher(sara)
print toby.nameget(),":",toby.getcapc()

print "\nLet's see which has the maximumm capacity of all"
toby = trans.maximumm(flows)
print toby.nameget(),":",toby.getcapc()
```

Output:

```
o RHINO carrying 4
To PERL carrying 150
To SARA JANE carrying 7
To MYSTORE SALES carrying 455
To RUBY carrying 61

Let's see is perl or ruby has the higher capacity
PERL : 150

Let's see which has the maximumm capacity of all
MYSTORE SALES : 455
```

Note *This program is demonstration for multiple inheritance and transfer of funds which is a simple application to find who has made the highest transfer. There are 2 base classes and 2 child classes.*

Multiple Choice Questions

1. Which of the following represents real world entity?
   a. Class b. Object
   c. Method d. Data Field
2. Suppose `p is python`. What is `p.upper()`?
   a. PYTHON b. Python
   c. PyThOn d. python
3. Which keyword is required to define a class?
   a. Def b. class
   c. create d. return
4. Analyse the following code:

```
class A:
  def__init__(self):
         self.p=1
         self._q=1

  defgetq(xyz):
         returnself._q
a=A()
a.p=20
print(a.p)
```

   a. The program has an error because `p` is private
   b. The program has an error because `q` is private
   c. The program prints 1
   d. The program prints 20
5. Analyse the following code:

```
class A:
      def__init__(self,p):
      self.p=p

      def print(self):
             print(p)
a=A("Python")
a.print()
```

   a. The program has an error because `class A` does not have a constructor.
   b. The program has an error because `class A` should have a `print(self,p)` method.
   c. The program has an error because `class A` should have a `print(p)` method.
   d. The program will execute fine if `print(p)` is replaced by `print(self.p)`.
6. Analyse the following code:

```
class A:
     def__init__(self,p="Python"):
     self.p=p

     def print(self):
             print(self.p)
a=A()
a.print()
```

a. The program has an error because `class A` does not have a constructor.
b. The program has an error because `class A` should have a `print(self,p)` method.
c. The program executes fine and prints nothing.
d. The program executes fine and prints Python.

7. Which of the following is used to create an object?
   a. Constructor
   b. Class
   c. Method
   d. Data field

8. Which of the following statements is not correct?
   a. Each object must have unique id.
   b. Same kind objects must have same type.
   c. Same type objects must have same id.
   d. A variable that holds a value is the reference to an object of that value.

9. What is the output of the following code?
```
Print(type(('US','India','Africa')))
```
   a. `<class,'set'>`
   b. `<class,'list'>`
   c. `<class,'dict'>`
   d. `<class,'tuple'>`

10. What is the output of the following code?
```
Print(type(1J))
```
   a. `<class,'int'>`
   b. `<class,'list'>`
   c. `<class,'float'>`
   d. `<class,'command'>`

11.
```
defMyFunction():
"Python is an interesting language"
return 1
print(MyFunction.__doc__[10:12])
```
   What will be the output?
   a. `Is`
   b. `an`
   c. `te`
   d. `er`

12. What is the output of the following code?
```
Class Employee:
        def__init__(self):
        pass
    defgetEmpId(self):
        print(__name__)
s=Employee()
s.getEmpId()
```
   a. `__name__`
   b. `__main__`
   c. `Employee`
   d. Error

13. What is the output of the following code?
```
Print(type(1/5))
```
   a. `<class,'int'>`
   b. `<class,'list'>`
   c. `<class,'float'>`
   d. `<class,'command'>`

14. Which of the following is known as an instance of class?
   a. Object
   b. Program
   c. Data
   d. Method

15. Which of the following is a blueprint that defines objects of the same type?
    a. A class
    b. An object
    c. A method
    d. A program
16. Which of the following is most accurate for the given declaration:
    `x=Square()`
    a. x contains an int value.
    b. x contains an object of square type.
    c. An int value can be assigned to x.
    d. x contains a reference to a square object.
17. Which of the following is the description of a set of objects that share the same attributes, operations, and semantics?
    a. Class
    b. Constructor
    c. Function
    d. Method
18. Which of the following is responsible for initialising the objects of its class?
    a. Constructor
    b. Destructor
    c. Iterator
    d. None of the above

Short Questions

1. What is the OOP concept? Define classes and objects in Python.
2. Explain the OOP principle inheritance in Python.
3. What is docstring in Python?
4. Differentiate between method overloading and method overriding.
5. What is the use of `pass` in Python?
6. What is __init__.py? Give an example.
7. How can we count the number of instances in a program?
8. How can we copy an object in Python?
9. What will be the output of the given code? Explain your answer.

```
classParent (object):
    a=1
class Child1(Parent):
    pass

class Child2(Parent):
    pass

print Parent.a,Child1.a,Child2.a
Child2.a=5
print Parent.a,Child1.a,Child2.a
Parent.a=4
print Parent.a,Child1.a,Child2.a
```

10. Consider the code of dictionary:

```
classSubDict(dict):
    def __missing__(self, key):
        return[]
```

Will the code that follows work? Give reasons.

```
d=SubDict()
d['florp']=127
```

Answers to Multiple Choice Questions

1. d	**2.** a	**3.** b	**4.** d	**5.** d	**6.** d	**7.** a	**8.** c	**9.** d	**10.** d
11. b	**12.** b	**13.** c	**14.** a	**15.** a	**16.** d	**17.** a	**18.** a		

Appendix

A

PRACTICE EXERCISES WITH ALGORITHM AND FLOW CHART

SOLUTIONS AVAILABLE ON OLC

Practice Problem 1 Write a program to determine the Greatest Common Divisor (GCD) of two numbers.

Algorithm

```
Step 1 - Start
Step 2 - Accept the two numbers whose GCD is to be found (num1, num2)
Step 3 - Call function GCD(num1,num2)
Step 4 - Display the value returned by the function call GCD(num1,num2)
Step 5 - Stop

GCD(a,b)
Step 1 - Start
Step 2 - If b > a goto Step 3 else goto Step 4
Step 3 - Return the result of the function call GCD(b,a) to the calling
function
Step 4 - If b = 0 goto Step 5 else goto Step 6
Step 5 - Return the value a to the calling function
Step 6 - Return the result of the function call GCD(b,a mod b) to the calling
function
```

Flow Chart

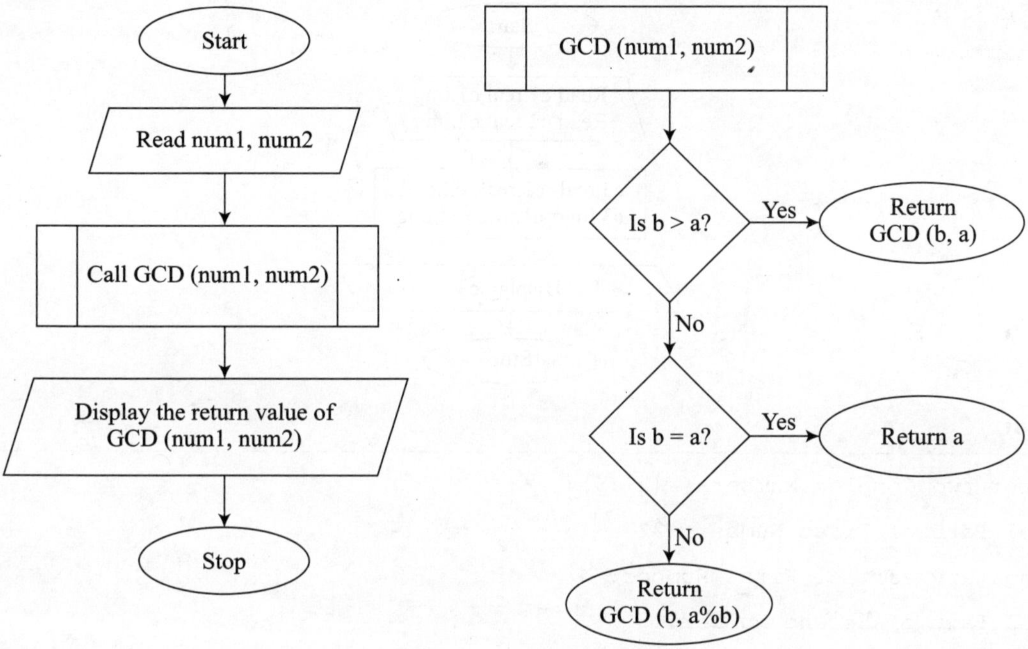

Output

```
Enter the two numbers whose GCD is to be found: 18      12

GCD of 18 and 12 is 6
```

Practice Problem 2 Write a program to accept two complex numbers and find their sum.

Algorithm

```
Step 1 - Start
Step 2 - Define a structure to represent a complex number
          STRUCTURE complex
          REAL real
          REAL img
          END STRUCTURE
          STRUCTURE complex c1, c2
Step 3 - Read the real and imaginary parts of the first complex number
(c1.real, c1.img)
Step 4 - Read the real and imaginary parts of the second complex number
(c2.real, c2.img)
Step 5 - Calculate c3.real=c1.real+c2.real
Step 6 - Calculate c3.img=c1.img+c2.img
Step 7 - Display c3
Step 8 - Stop
```

Flow Chart

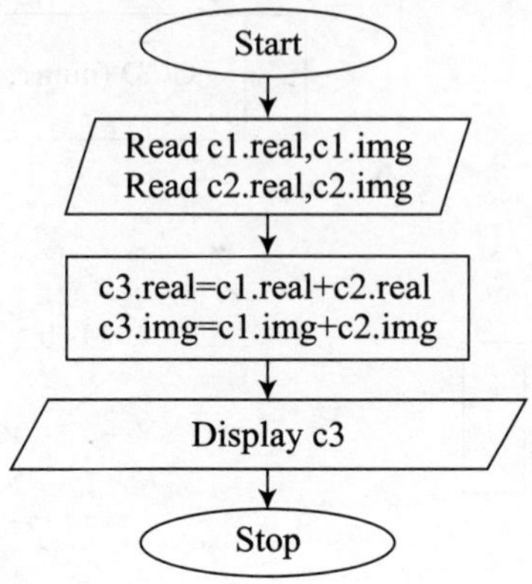

Output

```
Enter two Complex Numbers  (x+iy):
Real Part of First Number: 22
Imaginary Part of First Number: 4
Real Part of Second Number: 5
Imaginary Part of Second Number: 3
22.00+(4.00)i + 5.00+(3.00)i = 27.00+(7.00)i
```

Practice Problem 3 Write a program to simulate a simple calculator for performing basic arithmetic operations.

Algorithm

```
Step 1 - Start
Step 2 - Display a list of operations for the user to choose from
          1. Addition
          2. Subtraction
          3. Multiplication
          4. Division
Step 3 - Read the choice entered by the user (choice)
Step 4 - Read the two operands (num1, num2)
Step 5 - If choice = 1 goto Step 6 else goto Step 7
Step 6 - Calculate num1 + num2, display the result and goto Step 14
Step 7 - If choice = 2 goto Step 8 else goto Step 9
Step 8 - Calculate num1 - num2, display the result and goto Step 14
Step 9 - If choice = 3 goto Step 10 else goto Step 11
Step 10 - Calculate num1 X num2, display the result and goto Step 14
Step 11 - If choice = 4 goto Step 12 else goto Step 13
Step 12 - Calculate num1 / num2, display the result and goto Step 14
Step 13 - Display the message "Invalid Choice"
Step 14 - Stop
```

Flow Chart

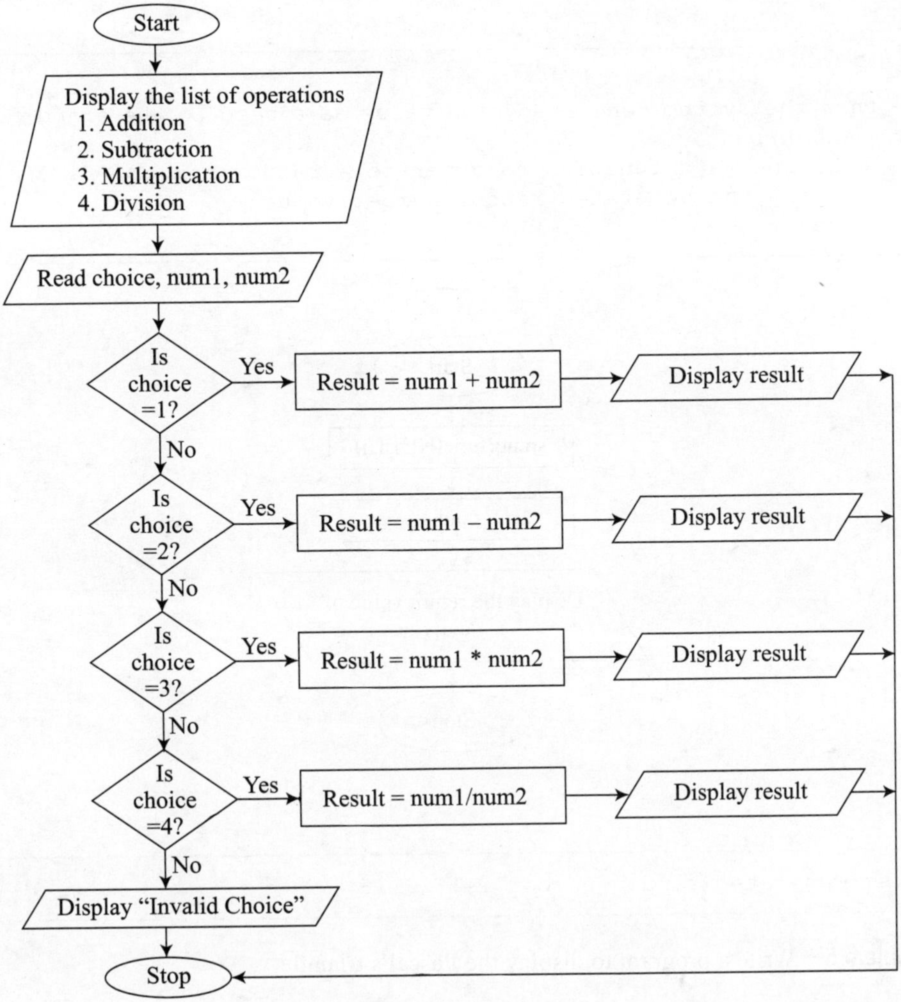

Output

```
**********Simple Calc***********

Choose a type of operation from the following:
        1.    Addition
        2.    Subtraction
        3.    Multiplication
        4.    Division
3

Enter the two operands: 18.25   2.23

18.25 * 2.23 = 40.70
```

Practice Problem 4 Write a program to generate random numbers.

Algorithm

```
Step 1 - Start
Step 2 - Pass the system generated time value as a seed to the srand function,
srand(time(NULL))
Step 3 - Call the rand function to generate a random number, rand()
Step 4 - Display the generated random number value
Step 5 - Stop
```

Flow Chart

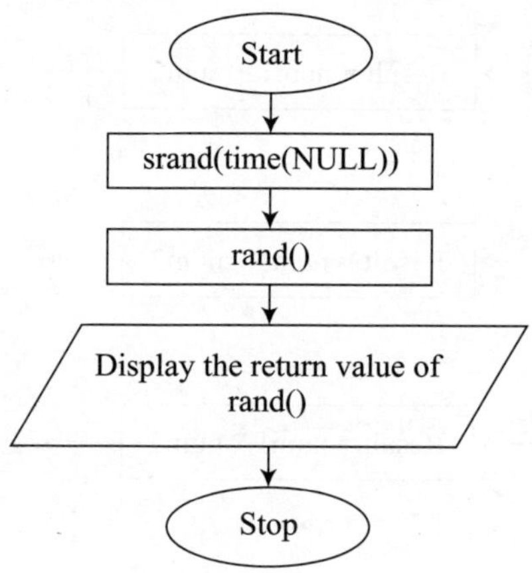

Output

```
The system generated random number is: 23176
```

Practice Problem 5 Write a program to display the Pascal's triangle.

Algorithm

```
Step 1 - Start
Step 2 - Set b = 1 and y = 0
Step 3 - Read the number of rows for the Pascal's triangle (row)
Step 4 - Repeat Steps 5-17 while y < row
Step 5 - Initialise the looping counter x = 40-3*y
Step 6 - Repeat Steps 7-8 while x > 0
Step 7 - Print a blank space on the output screen
Step 8 - x = x - 1
Step 9 - Initialize the looping counter z = 0
Step 10 - Repeat Steps 11-15 while z <= y
Step 11 - If z = 0 OR y = 0 goto Step 12 else goto Step 13
Step 12 - b = 1
```

```
Step 13 - b=(b*(y-z+1))/z
Step 14 - Display the value of b in a field width of 6 characters
Step 15 - z = z + 1
Step 16 - Print a new line character
Step 17 - y = y + 1
Step 18 - Stop
```

Flow Chart

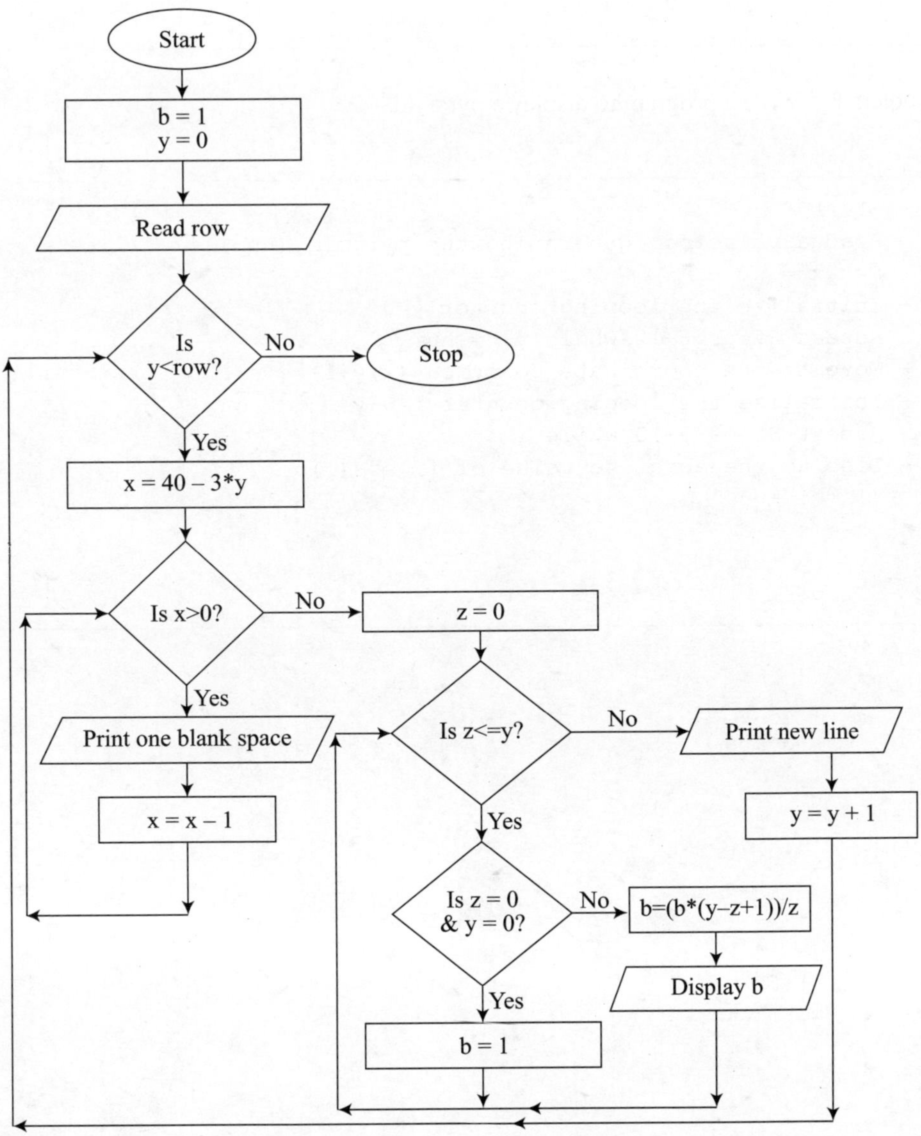

Output

```
Enter the number of rows for the Pascal's triangle:6

******Pascal's Triangle******
                                         1
                                      1     1
                                   1     2     1
                                1     3     3     1
                             1     4     6     4     1
                          1     5    10    10     5     1
```

Practice Problem 6 Write a program to display a pyramid.

Algorithm

```
Step 1 - Start
Step 2 - Read a value for generating the pyramid (num)
Step 3 - Set x = 40
Step 4 - Initialize the looping counter y=0
Step 5 - Repeat Steps 6-12 while y <= num
Step 6 - Move to the coordinate position (x,y+1)
Step 7 - Initialise the looping counter i=0-y
Step 8 - Repeat Steps 9-10 while i <= y
Step 9 - Display the absolute value of i, abs(i)
Step 10 - i = i + 1
Step 11 - x = x - 3
Step 12 - y = y + 1
Step 13 - Stop
```

Flow Chart

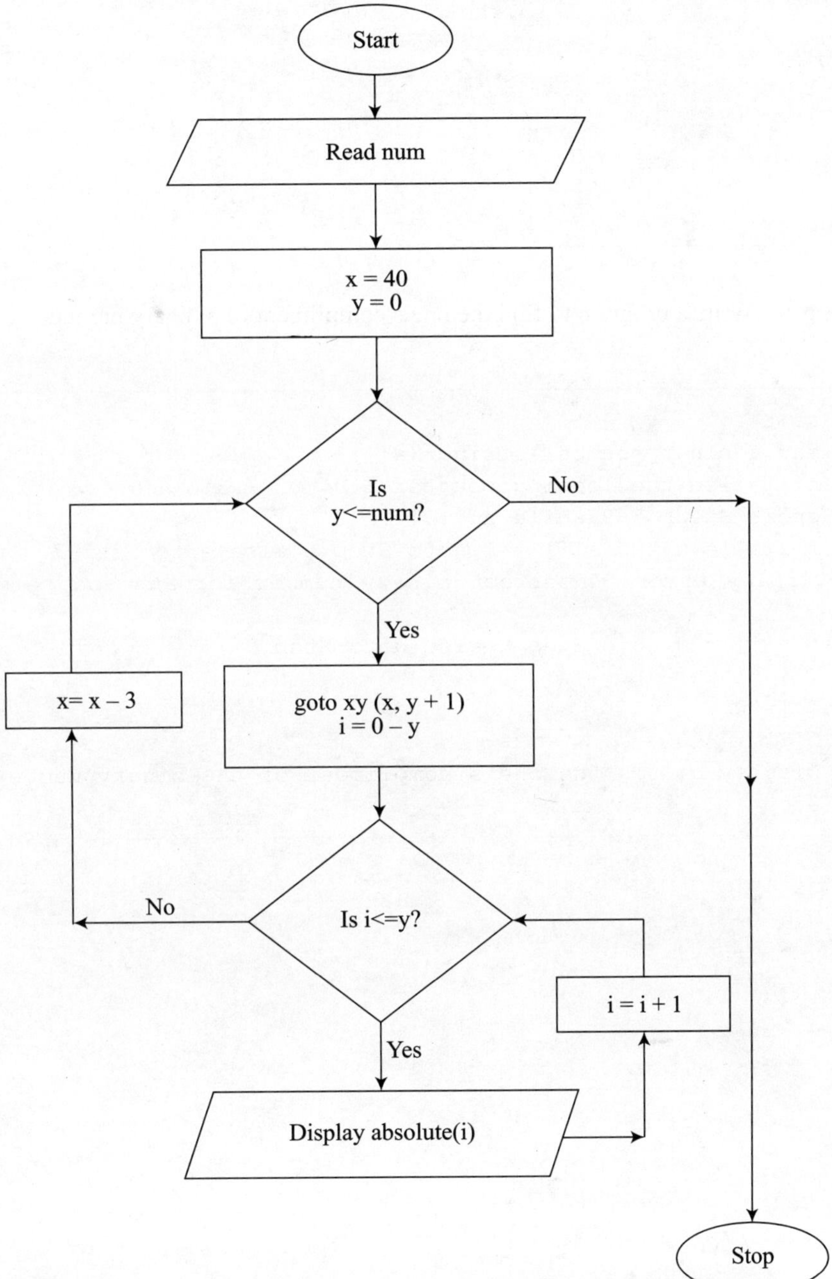
Start
Read num
x = 40
y = 0
Is
y<=num?
No
Yes
x= x – 3
goto xy (x, y + 1)
i = 0 – y
No
Is i<=y?
i = i + 1
Yes
Display absolute(i)
Stop

Output

```
                                        0
Enter a number for                  1   0   1
generating the pyramid:         2   1   0   1   2
7                           3   2   1   0   1   2   3
                        4   3   2   1   0   1   2   3   4
                    5   4   3   2   1   0   1   2   3   4   5
                6   5   4   3   2   1   0   1   2   3   4   5   6
            7   6   5   4   3   2   1   0   1   2   3   4   5   6   7
```

Practice Problem 7 Write a program to find the one's compliment of a binary number.

Algorithm

```
Step 1 - Start
Step 2 - Read a binary number string (a[])
Step 3 - Initialise the looping counter i=0
Step 4 - Repeat Steps 5-9 while a[i] != '\0'
Step 5 - If a[i]!= 0 AND a[i]!= 1 goto Step 6 else goto Step 7
Step 6 - Display error "Incorrect binary number format" and terminate the
program
Step 7 - If a[i] = 0 goto Step 8 else goto Step 9
Step 8 - b[i]='1'
Step 9 - b[i]='0'
Step 10 - b[i] = '\0'
Step 11 - Display b[] as the one's compliment of the binary number a[]
Step 12 - Stop
```

Flow Chart

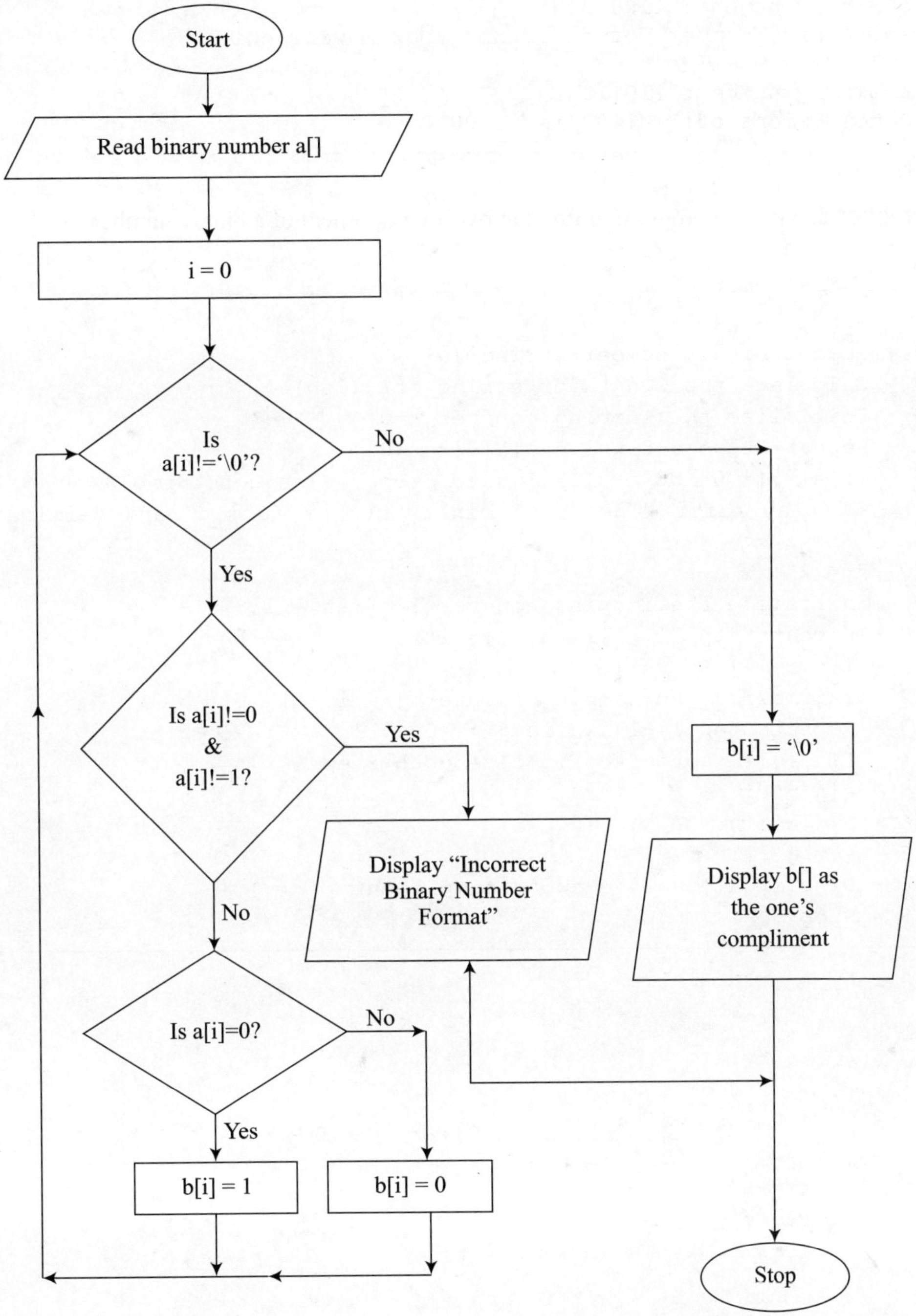
Start
Read binary number a[]
i = 0
Is
a[i]!='\0'?
No
Yes
Is a[i]!=0
&
a[i]!=1?
Yes
No
Display "Incorrect
Binary Number
Format"
Is a[i]=0?
No
Yes
b[i] = 1
b[i] = 0
b[i] = '\0'
Display b[] as
the one's
compliment
Stop

Output

```
Enter a binary number: 11001210
Incorrect binary number format...the program will quit

Enter a binary number: 1101101
The 1's compliment of 1101101 is 0010010
```

Practice Problem 8 Write a program to find the two's compliment of a binary number.

Algorithm

```
Step 1 - Start
Step 2 - Read a binary number string (a[])
Step 3 - Calculate the length of string str (len)
Step 4 - Initialise the looping counter k=0
Step 5 - Repeat Steps 6-8 while a[k] != '\0'
Step 6 - If a[k]!= 0 AND a[k]!= 1 goto Step 7 else goto Step 8
Step 7 - Display error "Incorrect binary number format" and terminate the
program
Step 8 - k = k + 1
Step 9 - Initialise the looping counter i = len - 1
Step 10 - Repeat Step 11 while a[i]!='1'
Step 11 - i = i - 1
Step 12 - Initialise the looping counter j = i - 1
Step 13 - Repeat Step 14-17 while j >= 0
Step 14 - If a[j]=1 goto Step 15 else goto Step 16
Step 15 - a[j]='0'
Step 16 - a[j]='1'
Step 17 - j = j - 1
Step 18 - Display a[] as the two's compliment
Step 19 - Stop
```

Flow Chart

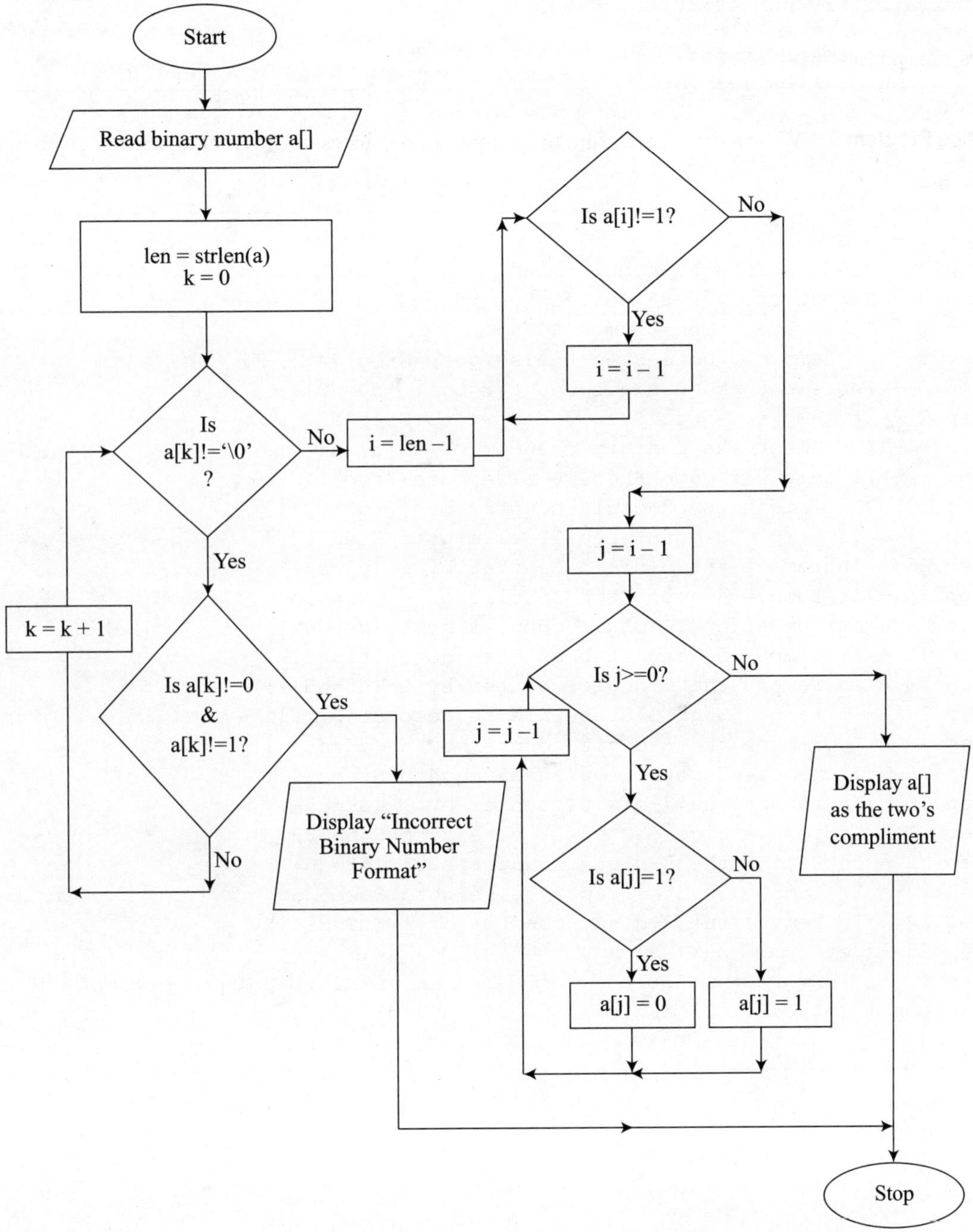
Start
Read binary number a[]
len = strlen(a)
k = 0
Is
a[k]!='\0'
?
No
i = len –1
Is a[i]!=1?
No
Yes
i = i – 1
j = i – 1
Yes
k = k + 1
Is a[k]!=0
&
a[k]!=1?
Yes
No
Display "Incorrect
Binary Number
Format"
Is j>=0?
No
j = j –1
Yes
Display a[]
as the two's
compliment
Is a[j]=1?
No
Yes
a[j] = 0
a[j] = 1
Stop

Output

```
Enter a binary number: 01011001001

2's compliment = 10100110111
```

Practice Problem 9 Write a program to find the number of instances of different digits in a given number.

Algorithm

```
Step 1 - Start
Step 2 - Read an integer number (num)
Step 3 - Repeat steps 4-25 while (num!=0)
Step 4 - Calculate temp = num % 10
Step 5 - If temp = 0 goto Step 6 else goto Step 7
Step 6 - Increment the 0-digit counter by 1 (d0=d0+1)
Step 7 - If temp = 1 goto Step 8 else goto Step 9
Step 8 - Increment the 1-digit counter by 1 (d1=d1+1)
Step 9 - If temp = 2 goto Step 10 else goto Step 11
Step 10 - Increment the 2-digit counter by 1 (d2=d2+1)
Step 11 - If temp = 3 goto Step 12 else goto Step 13
Step 12 - Increment the 3-digit counter by 1 (d3=d3+1)
Step 13 - If temp = 4 goto Step 14 else goto Step 15
Step 14 - Increment the 4-digit counter by 1 (d4=d4+1)
Step 15 - If temp = 5 goto Step 16 else goto Step 17
Step 16 - Increment the 5-digit counter by 1 (d5=d5+1)
Step 17 - If temp = 6 goto Step 18 else goto Step 19
Step 18 - Increment the 6-digit counter by 6 (d6=d6+1)
Step 19 - If temp = 7 goto Step 20 else goto Step 21
Step 20 - Increment the 7-digit counter by 1 (d7=d7+1)
Step 21 - If temp = 8 goto Step 22 else goto Step 23
Step 22 - Increment the 8-digit counter by 1 (d8=d8+1)
Step 23 - If temp = 9 goto Step 24 else goto Step 25
Step 24 - Increment the 9-digit counter by 1 (d9=d9+1)
Step 25 - Set num = num / 10
Step 26 - Display the number of instances of digits (0-9) present in the
number num (d0, d1, d2, d3, d4, d5, d6, d7, d8, d9)
Step 27 - Stop
```

Flow Chart

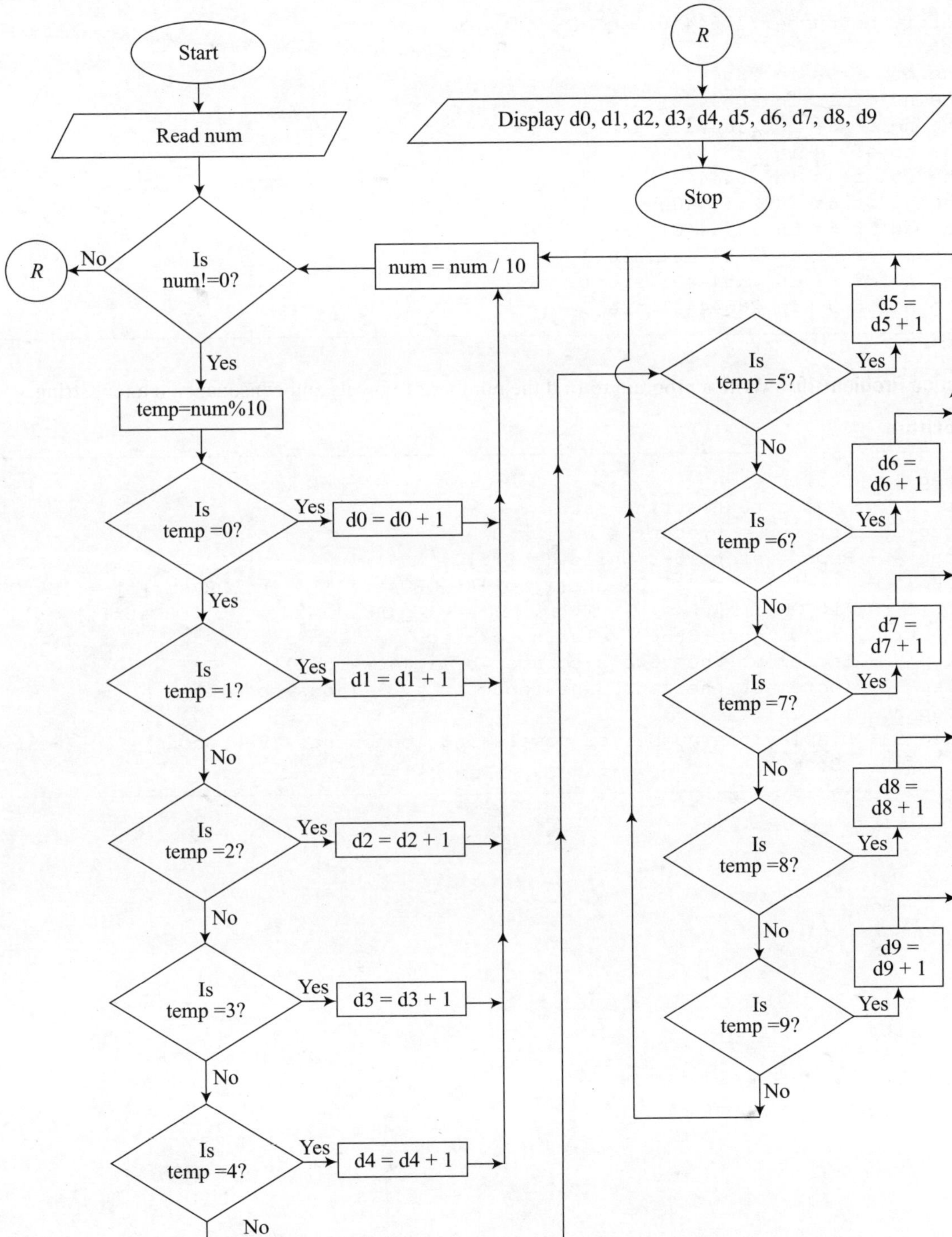
Start
Read num
Is num!=0?
No
R
Yes
temp=num%10
Is temp =0?
Yes
d0 = d0 + 1
Yes
Is temp =1?
Yes
d1 = d1 + 1
No
Is temp =2?
Yes
d2 = d2 + 1
No
Is temp =3?
Yes
d3 = d3 + 1
No
Is temp =4?
Yes
d4 = d4 + 1
No
num = num / 10
R
Display d0, d1, d2, d3, d4, d5, d6, d7, d8, d9
Stop
Is temp =5?
Yes
d5 = d5 + 1
No
Is temp =6?
Yes
d6 = d6 + 1
No
Is temp =7?
Yes
d7 = d7 + 1
No
Is temp =8?
Yes
d8 = d8 + 1
No
Is temp =9?
Yes
d9 = d9 + 1
No

Output

```
Enter the number:28544401

The no of 0s in 28544401 are 1
The no of 1s in 28544401 are 1
The no of 2s in 28544401 are 1
The no of 3s in 28544401 are 0
The no of 4s in 28544401 are 3
The no of 5s in 28544401 are 1
The no of 6s in 28544401 are 0
The no of 7s in 28544401 are 0
The no of 8s in 28544401 are 1
The no of 9s in 28544401 are 0
```

Practice Problem 10 Write a program to find the number of vowels and consonants in a text string.

Algorithm

```
Step 1 - Start
Step 2 - Read a text string (str)
Step 3 - Set vow = 0, cons = 0, i = 0
Step 4 - Repeat steps 5-8 while (str[i]!='\0')
Step 5 - if str[i] = 'a' OR str[i] = 'A' OR str[i] = 'e' OR str[i] = 'E' OR
str[i] = 'i' OR str[i] = 'I' OR str[i] = 'o' OR str[i] = 'O' OR str[i] = 'u'
OR str[i] = 'U' goto Step 6 else goto Step 7
Step 6 - Increment the vowels counter by 1 (vow=vow+1)
Step 7 - Increment the consonants counter by 1 (cons=cons+1)
Step 8 - i = i + 1
Step 9 - Display the number of vowels and consonants (vow, cons)
Step 10 - Stop
```

Flow Chart

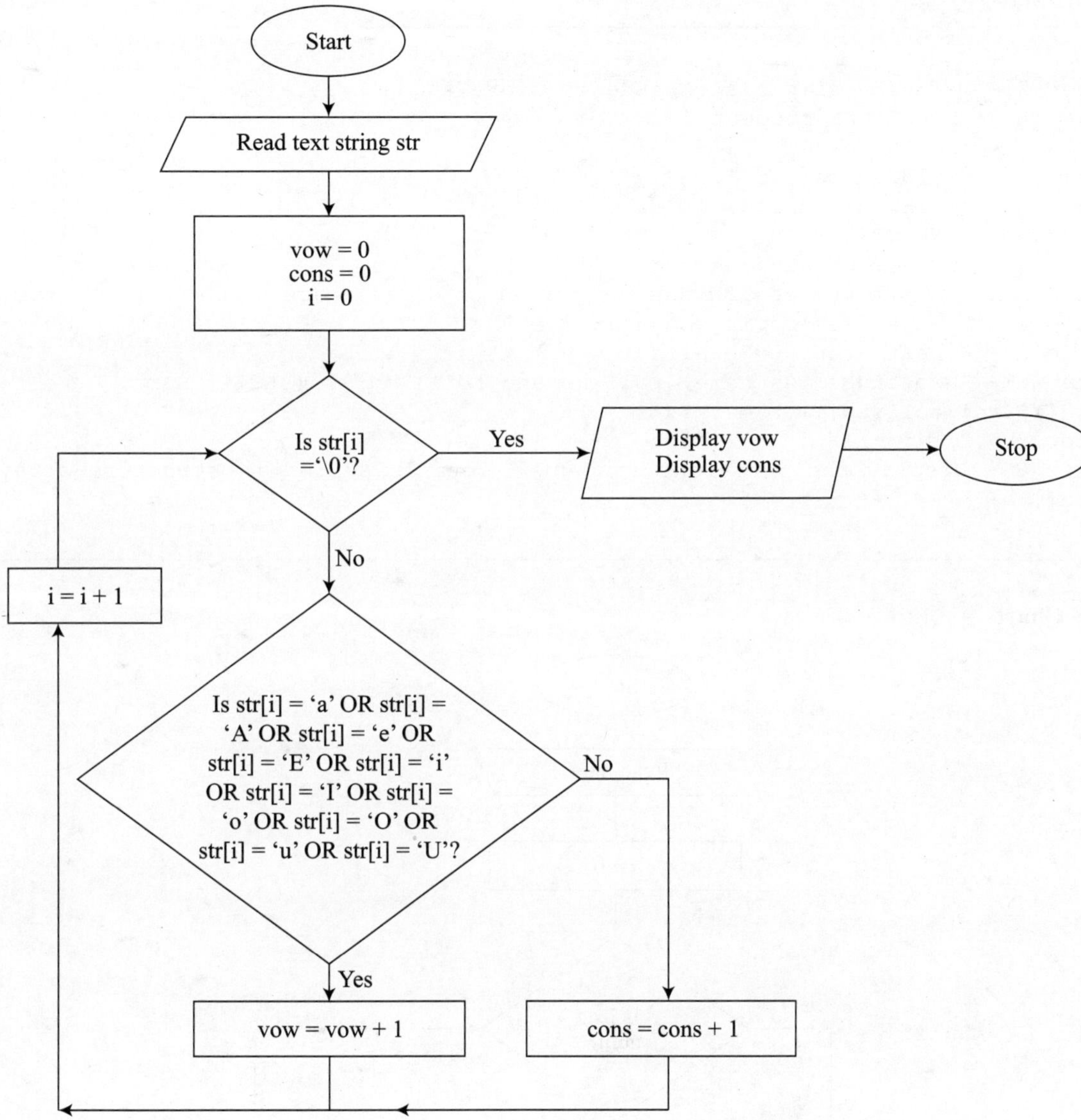

Output

```
Enter a string: Chennai

Number of Vowels = 3
Number of Consonants = 4
```

Practice Problem 11 Write a program that uses a simple structure for storing different students' details.

Algorithm

```
Step 1 - Start
Step 2 - Define a simple structure to store student details
          STRUCTURE student
          STRING name
          INTEGER rollno
          INTEGER t_marks
          END STRUCTURE
          STRUCTURE student std[]
Step 3 – Read the number of students for which details are to be entered (num)
Step 4 – Initialise looping counter i = 0
Step 5 – Repeat Steps 6=8 while i < num
Step 6 – Read student's name, roll no and total marks (std[i].name,
std[i].rollno, std[i].t_marks)
Step 7 – i = i + 1
Step 8 – Display the different students' details stored in structure array
std[]
Step 9 - Stop
```

Flow Chart

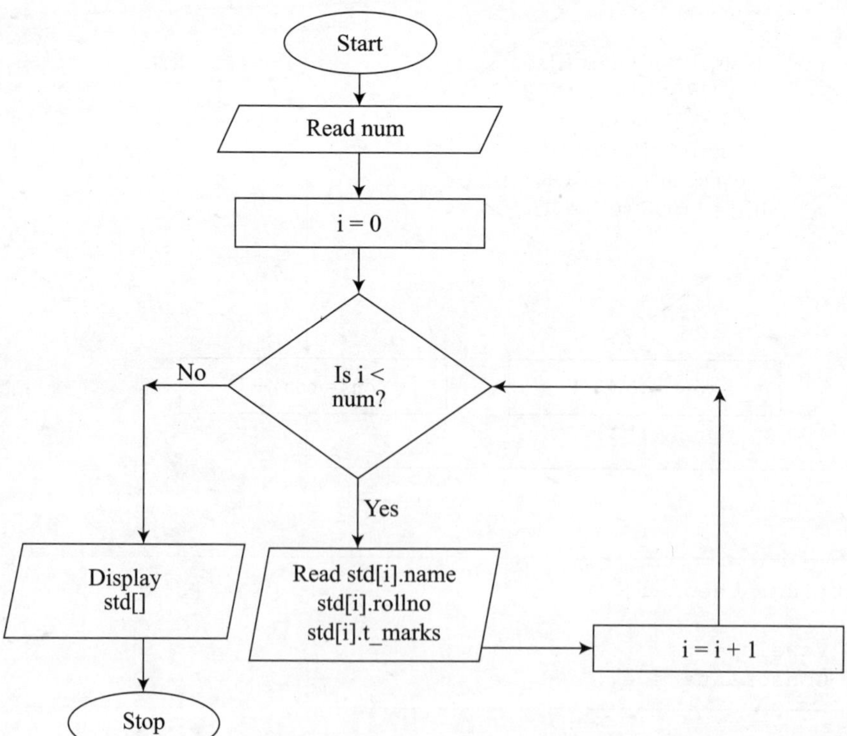

Output

```
Enter the number of students: 3

Enter the details for 1 student

 Name Arjun

 Roll No. 1

 Total Marks 399

Enter the details for 2 student

 Name Binoy

 Roll No. 2

 Total Marks 432

Enter the details for 3 student

 Name Chitra

 Roll No. 3

 Total Marks 402

 Press any key to display the student details!
student 1
 Name Arjun
 Roll No. 1
 Total Marks 399

student 2
 Name Binoy
 Roll No. 2
 Total Marks 432

student 3
 Name Chitra
 Roll No. 3
 Total Marks 402
```

Practice Problem 12 Write a program to find the sum of the following series:

$1 + x + x^2 + x^3 + \ldots\ldots + x^n$

Algorithm

```
Step 1 - Start
Step 2 - Read the values of x and n
Step 3 - If n <= 0 OR x <=0 goto Step 4 else goto Step 5
Step 4 - Display error "Invalid values" and terminate the program
Step 5 - Set sum = 1
Step 6 - Initialise the looping counter i = 1
Step 7 - Repeat Steps 8-9 while i<=n
Step 8 - sum = sum + POWER(x,i)
Step 9 - i = i + 1
Step 10 - Display sum as the resultant sum of the series
Step 11 - Stop
```

Flow Chart

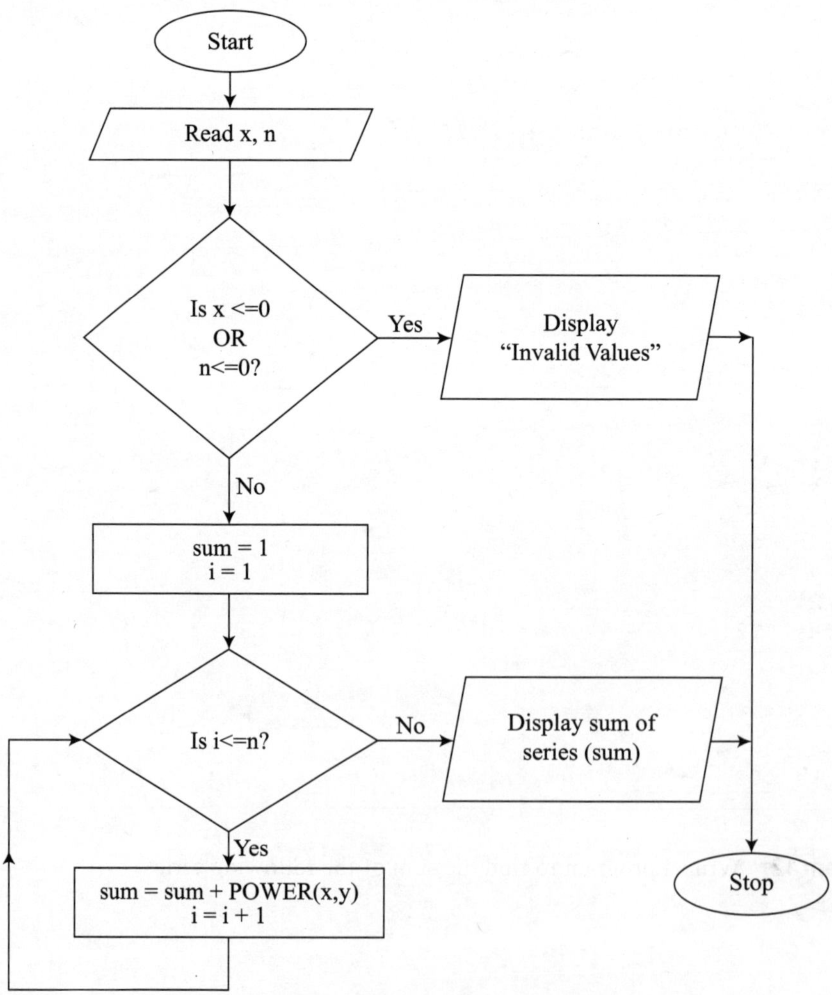

Output

```
Enter the values of x and n:2
5
Sum of series=63
```

Practice Problem 13 Write a program to find the sum of the following series:

1 + 2 + 3 + ...+ n

Algorithm

```
Step 1 - Start
Step 2 - Read n
Step 3 - Set sum = 0
Step 4 - Initialise the looping counter i = 1
Step 5 - Repeat Steps 6-8 while i<=n
Step 6 - sum = sum + i
Step 7 - i = i + 1
Step 8 - Display sum as the resultant sum of the series
Step 9 - Stop
```

Flow Chart

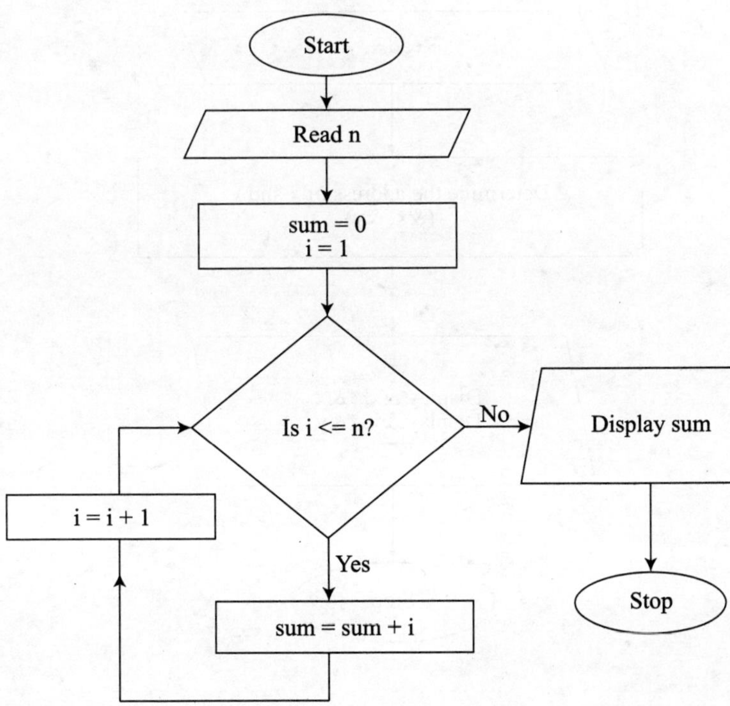

Output

```
Enter the value of n 6

The Sum of the series 1 + 2 + .... + n (for n = 6) is 21
```

Practice Problem 14 Write a program to print the value and address of variables.

Algorithm

```
Step 1 - Start
Step 2 - Read the values of x and y
Step 3 - Determine the addresses of x and y using ampersand (&) operator (&x, &y)
Step 4 - Print the address and value of x (&x, *&x)
Step 5 - Print the address and value of y (&y, *&y)
Step 6 - Stop
```

Flow Chart

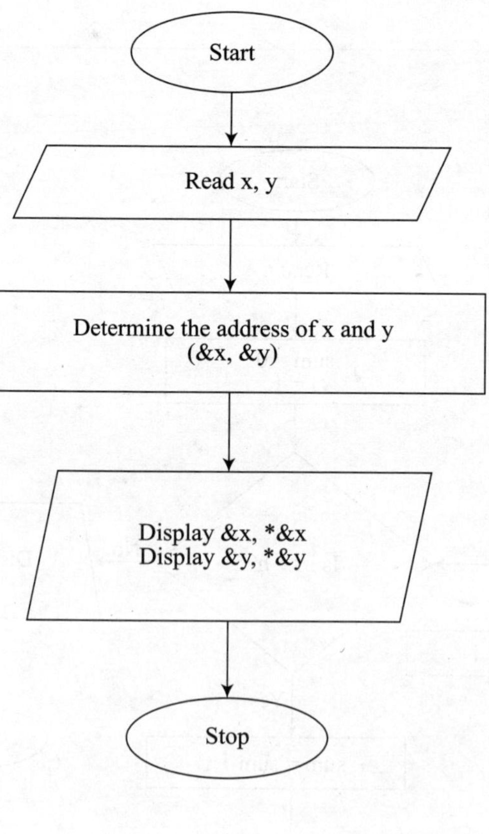

Output

```
Enter the values of x and y 22
44
Address of x is 65524
Value of x is 22
Address of y is 65522
Value of y is 44
```

Practice Problem 15 Write a program to copy the contents of one file into another.

Algorithm

```
Step 1 - Start
Step 2 - Read the command line arguments (argc, argv)
Step 3 - If argc !=3 goto Step 4 else goto Step 5
Step 4 - Display "Invalid number of arguments" and terminate the program
Step 5 - Open the source file specified by argv[1] in read mode and assign
its starting location to file pointer fs (fs = fopen(argv[1],"r"))
Step 6 - If fs=NULL goto Step 7 else goto Step 8
Step 7 - Display "Source file cannot be opened" and terminate the program
Step 8 - Open the target file specified by argv[2] in write mode and assign
its starting location to file pointer ft (ft = fopen(argv[2],"w"))
Step 9 - If ft=NULL goto Step 10 else goto Step 11
Step 10 - Display "Target file cannot be opened" and terminate the program
Step 11 - Repeat Steps 12-14 indefinitely
Step 12 - Read the first character of the source file (ch)
Step 13 - If ch = EOF goto Step 15 else goto Step 14
Step 14 - Copy character ch into the target file
Step 15 - Close the file pointers fs and ft
Step 16 - Display "Files copied successfully"
Step 17 - Stop
```

Flow Chart

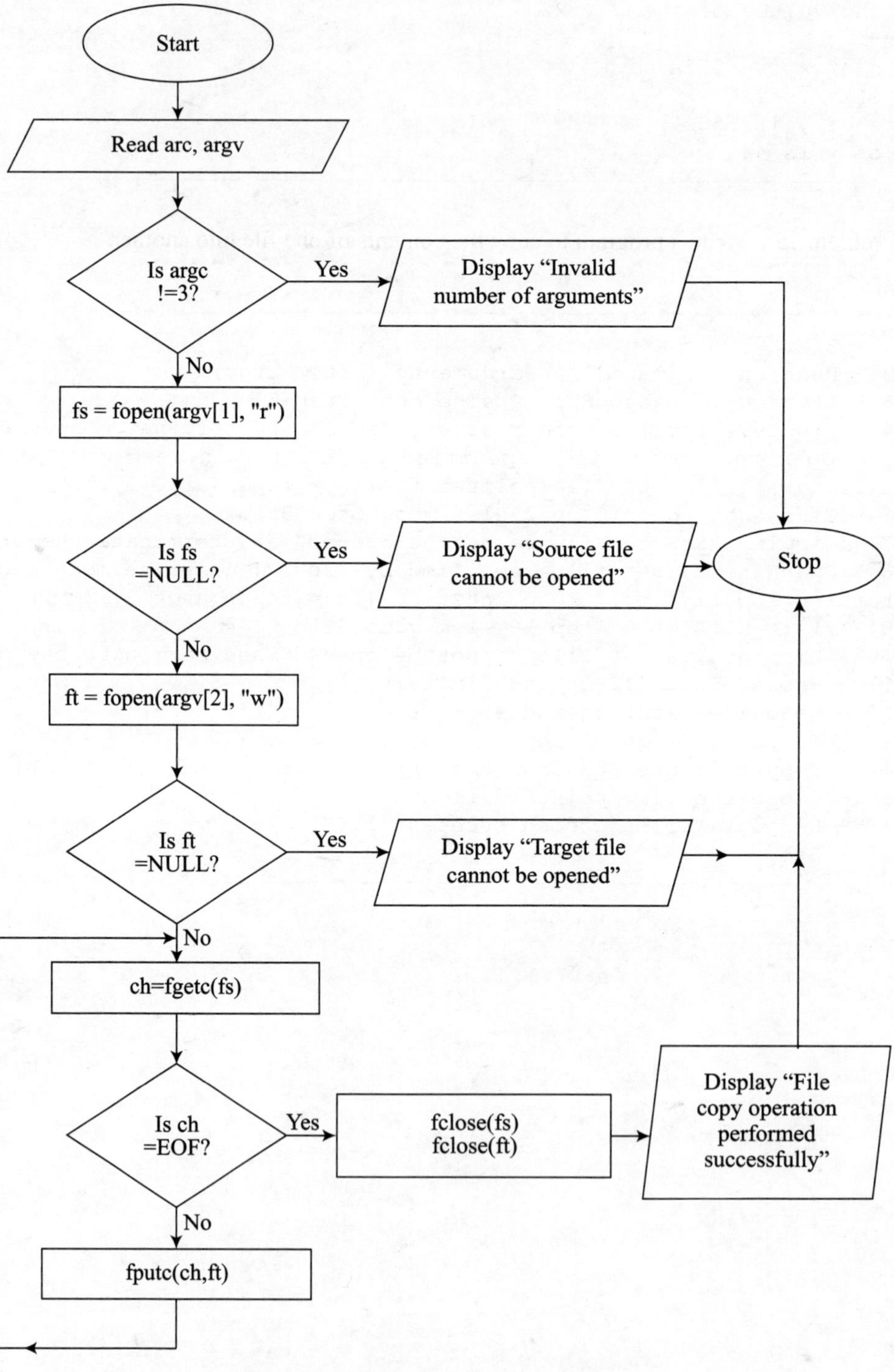
Start
Read arc, argv
Is argc !=3?
Yes
Display "Invalid number of arguments"
No
fs = fopen(argv[1], "r")
Is fs =NULL?
Yes
Display "Source file cannot be opened"
Stop
No
ft = fopen(argv[2], "w")
Is ft =NULL?
Yes
Display "Target file cannot be opened"
No
ch=fgetc(fs)
Is ch =EOF?
Yes
fclose(fs)
fclose(ft)
Display "File copy operation performed successfully"
No
fputc(ch,ft)

Output

```
D:\TC\BIN>15.exe s1.txt t1.txt
File copy operation performed successfully
```

Practice Problem 16 Write a program to count the number of characters in a file.

Algorithm

```
Step 1 - Start
Step 2 - Read the command line arguments (argc, argv)
Step 3 - Initialise count = 0
Step 4 - If argc !=2 goto Step 5 else goto Step 6
Step 5 - Display "Invalid number of arguments" and terminate the program
Step 6 - Open the source file specified by argv[1] in read mode and assign
its starting location to file pointer fs (fs = fopen(argv[1],"r"))
Step 7 - If fs=NULL goto Step 8 else goto Step 9
Step 8 - Display "Source file cannot be opened" and terminate the program
Step 9 - Repeat Steps 10-12 indefinitely
Step 10 - Read the first character of the source file (ch)
Step 11 - If ch = EOF goto Step 13 else goto Step 12
Step 12 - count = count + 1
Step 13 - Close the file pointer fs
Step 14 - Display count as the number characters contained in the source file
Step 15 - Stop
```

Flow Chart

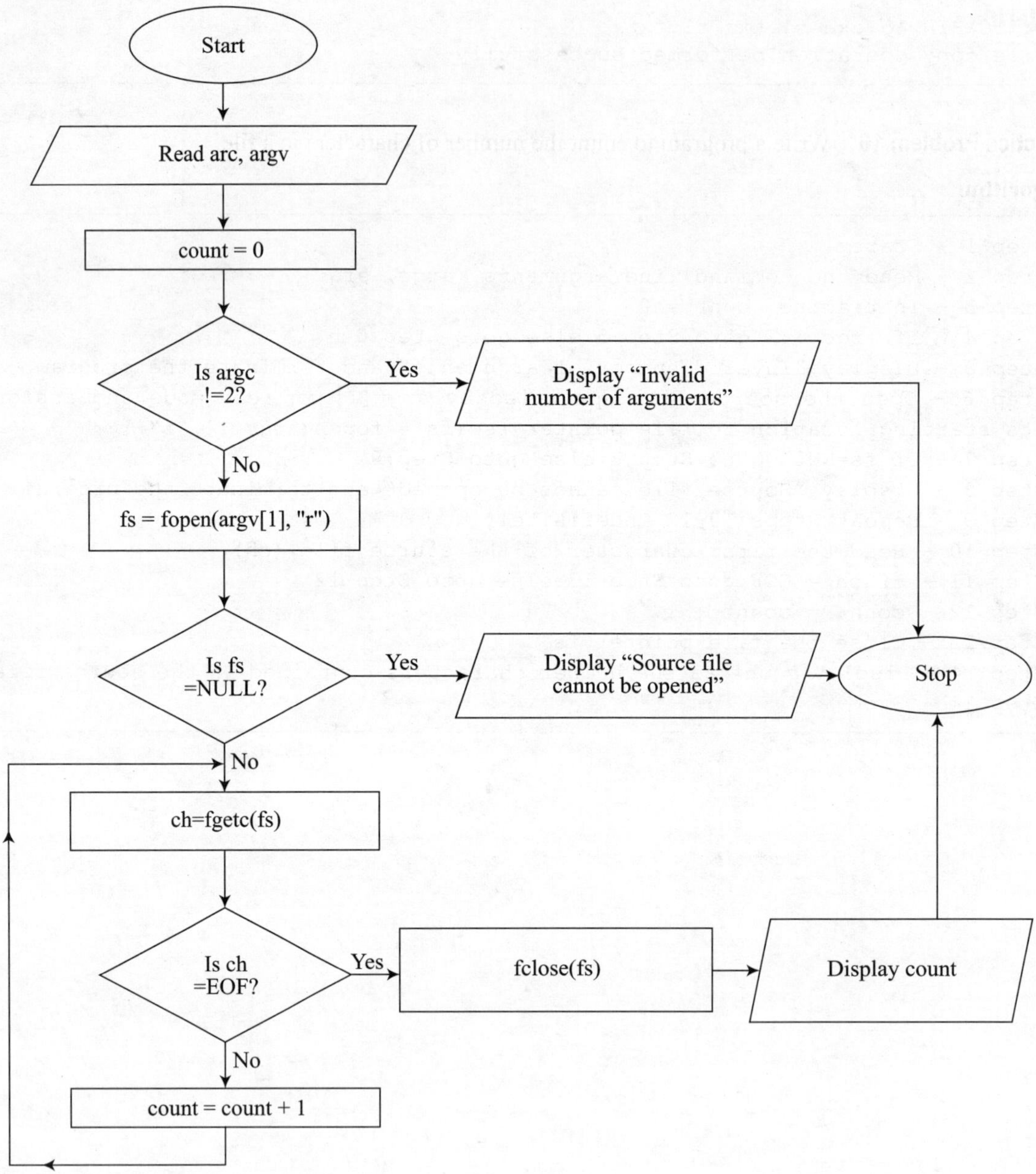

Output

```
D:\TC\BIN>16.exe s1.txt

The number of characters in s1.txt is 15
```

Practice Problem 17 Write a program to find the transpose of a matrix.

Algorithm

```
Step 1 - Start
Step 2 - Read a 3 X 3 matrix (a[3][3])
Step 3 - Initialise the looping counter i = 0
Step 4 - Repeat Steps 5-9 while i<3
Step 5 - Initialize the looping counter j = 0
Step 6 - Repeat Steps 7-8 while j<3
Step 7 - b[i][j]=a[j][i]
Step 8 - j = j + 1
Step 9 - i = i + 1
Step 10 - Display b[][] as the transpose of the matrix a[][]
Step 11 - Stop
```

Flow Chart

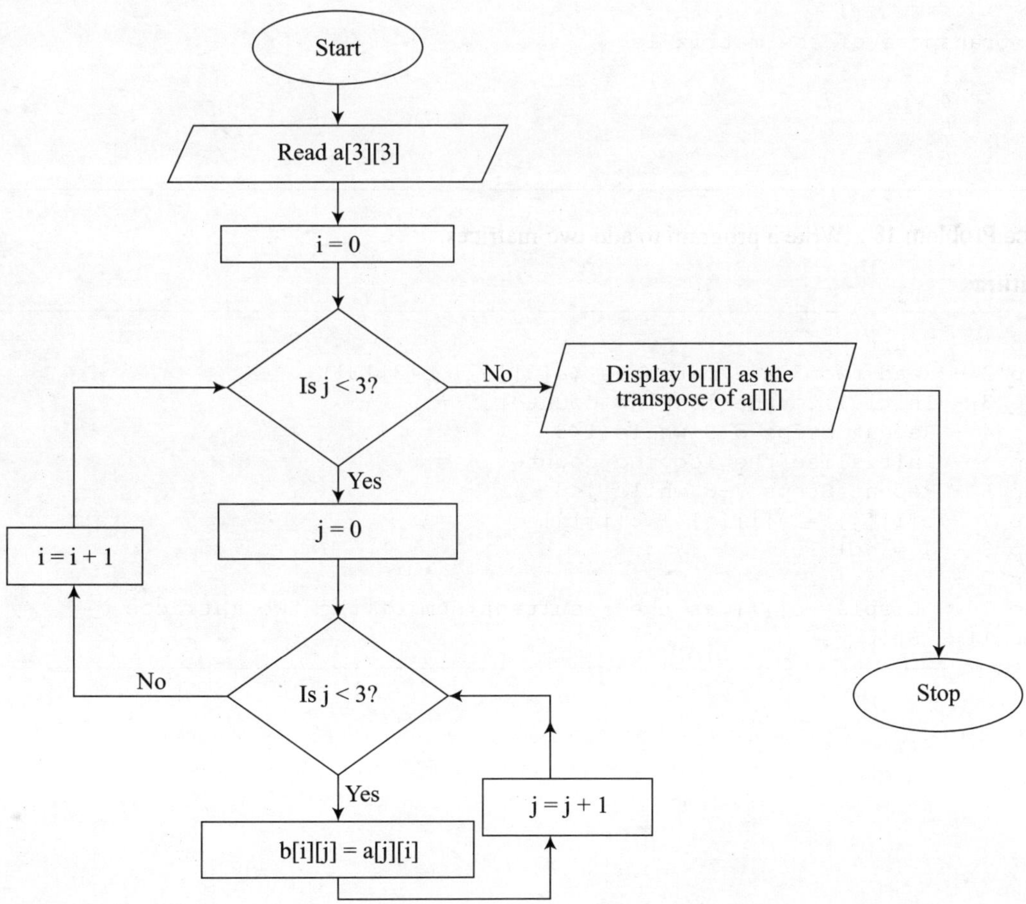

Output

```
Enter a 3 X 3 matrix:
a[0][0] = 1
a[0][1] = 2
a[0][2] = 3
a[1][0] = 4
a[1][1] = 5
a[1][2] = 6
a[2][0] = 7
a[2][1] = 8
a[2][2] = 9

The entered matrix is:

1       2       3
4       5       6
7       8       9

The transpose of the matrix is:

1       4       7
2       5       8
3       6       9
```

Practice Problem 18 Write a program to add two matrices.

Algorithm

```
Step 1 - Start
Step 2 - Read two 3 X 3 matrices (a[3][3], b[3][3])
Step 3 - Initialize the looping counter i = 0
Step 4 - Repeat Steps 5-9 while i<3
Step 5 - Initialise the looping counter j = 0
Step 6 - Repeat Steps 7-8 while j<3
Step 7 - c[i][j] = a[i][j] + b[i][j]
Step 8 - j = j + 1
Step 9 - i = i + 1
Step 10 - Display c[][] as the resultant sum of the two matrices
Step 11 - Stop
```

Flow Chart

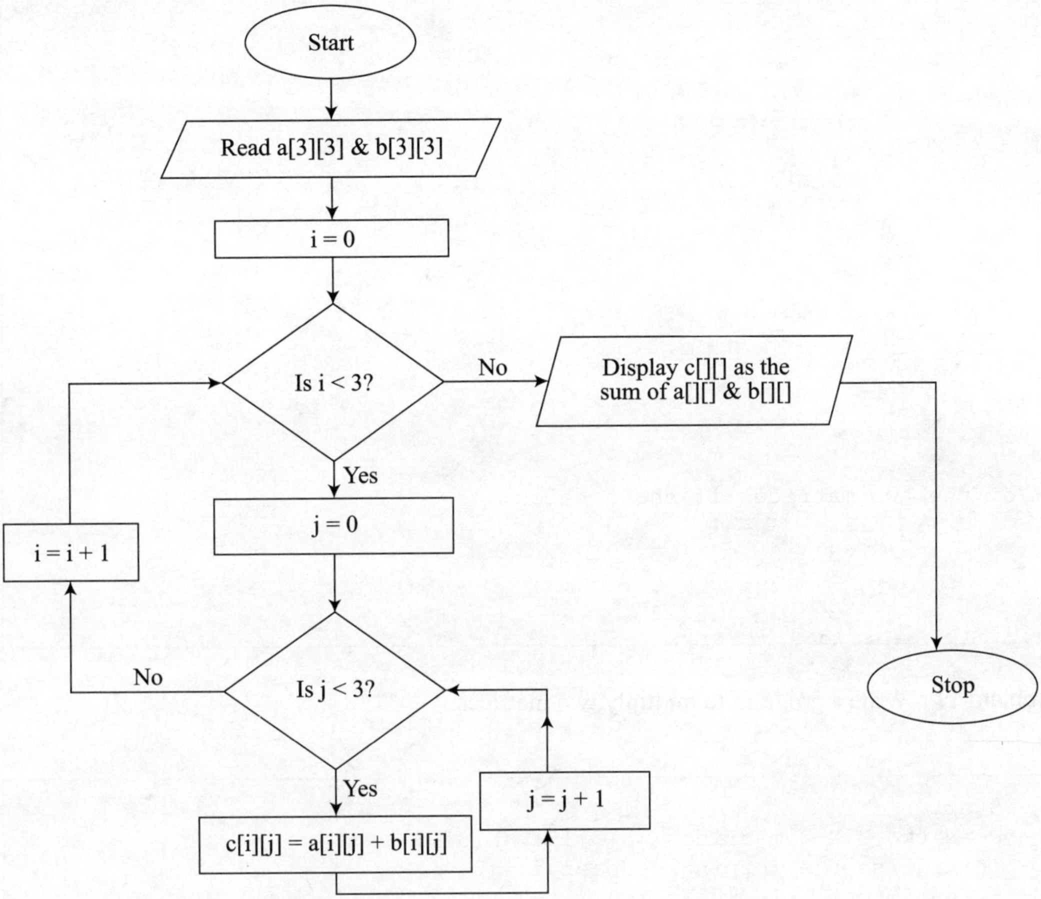

Output

```
Enter the first 3 X 3 matrix:
a[0][0] = 1
a[0][1] = 1
a[0][2] = 1
a[1][0] = 1
a[1][1] = 1
a[1][2] = 1
a[2][0] = 1
a[2][1] = 1
a[2][2] = 1
```

```
Enter the second 3 X 3 matrix:
b[0][0] = 2
b[0][1] = 2
b[0][2] = 2
b[1][0] = 2
b[1][1] = 2
b[1][2] = 2
b[2][0] = 2
b[2][1] = 2
b[2][2] = 2

The entered matrices are:

1       1       1                       2       2       2
1       1       1                       2       2       2
1       1       1                       2       2       2

The sum of the two matrices is shown below:

                    3   3       3
                    3   3       3
                    3   3       3
```

Practice Problem 19 Write a program to multiply two matrices.

Algorithm

```
Step 1 - Start
Step 2 - Read two 3 X 3 matrices (a[3][3], b[3][3])
Step 3 - Initialise the looping counter i = 0
Step 4 - Repeat Steps 5-13 while i<3
Step 5 - Initialise the looping counter j = 0
Step 6 - Repeat Steps 7-12 while j<3
Step 7 - c[i][j]=0
Step 8 - Initialise the looping counter k = 0
Step 9 - Repeat Steps 10-11 while k<3
Step 10 - c[i][j]=c[i][j]+a[i][k]*b[k][j]
Step 11 - k = k + 1
Step 12 - j = j + 1
Step 13 - i = i + 1
Step 14 - Display c[][] as the resultant product of the two matrices
Step 15 - Stop
```

Flow Chart

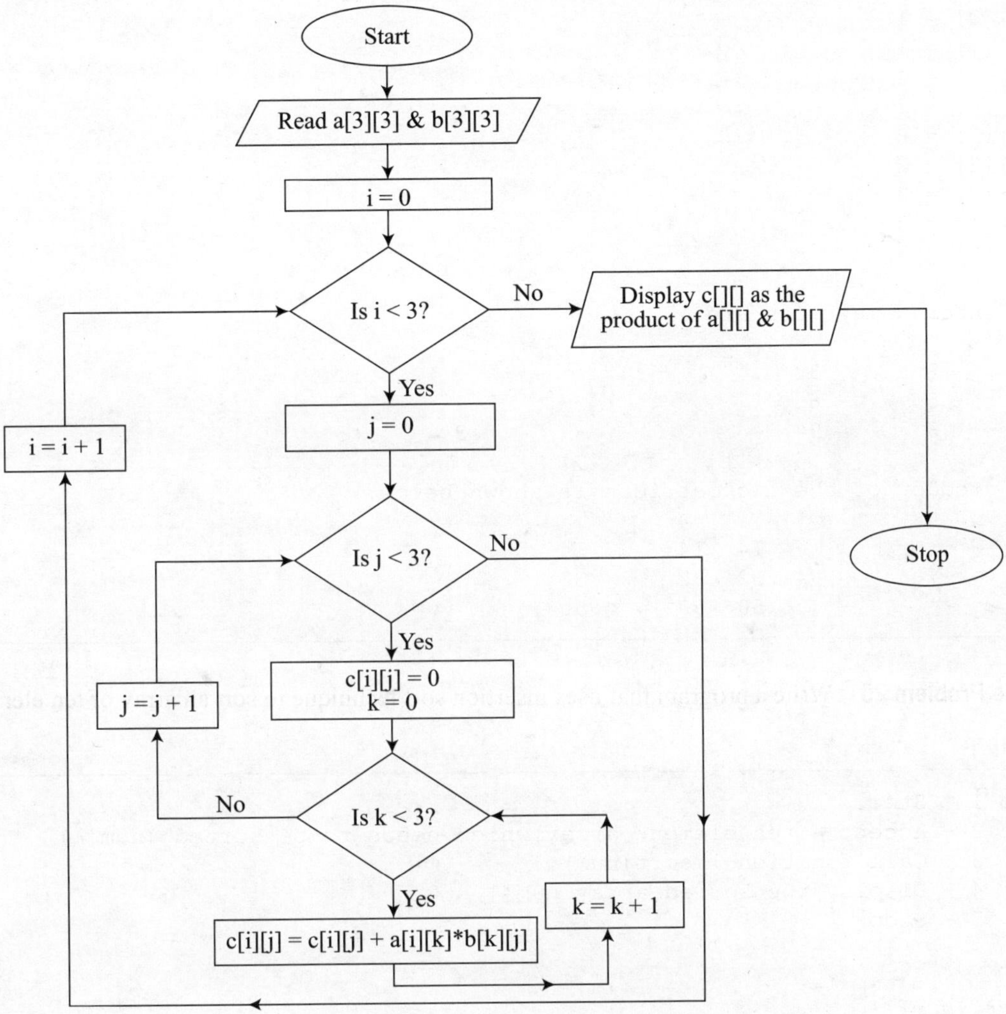

Output

```
Enter the first 3 X 3 matrix:
a[0][0] = 1
a[0][1] = 2
a[0][2] = 3
a[1][0] = 4
a[1][1] = 5
a[1][2] = 6
a[2][0] = 7
a[2][1] = 8
a[2][2] = 9
```

```
Enter the second 3 X 3 matrix:
b[0][0] = 1
b[0][1] = 1
b[0][2] = 1
b[1][0] = 2
b[1][1] = 2
b[1][2] = 2
b[2][0] = 3
b[2][1] = 3
b[2][2] = 3

The entered matrices are:

1       2       3                                 1       1       1
4       5       6                                 2       2       2
7       8       9                                 3       3       3

The product of the two matrices is shown below:

                    14  14      14
                    32  32      32
                    50  50      50
```

Practice Problem 20 Write a program that uses insertion sort technique to sort an array of ten elements.

Algorithm

```
Step 1 - Start
Step 2 - Accept a ten element array which needs to be sorted (num[])
Step 3 - Call function i_sort(num)
Step 4 - Display the sorted array num[]
Step 5 - Stop


i_sort(num[])
Step 1 - Start
Step 2 - Initialise the looping counter j = 1
Step 3 - Repeat Steps 4-10 while j<10
Step 4 - Set temp = num[j]
Step 5 - Initialise the looping counter i = j-1
Step 6 - Repeat Steps 7-8 while i>=0 AND temp<num[i]
Step 7 - num[i+1]=num[i]
Step 8 - i = i - 1
Step 9 - num[i+1]=temp
Step 10 - j = j + 1
Step 11 - Stop
```

Flow Chart

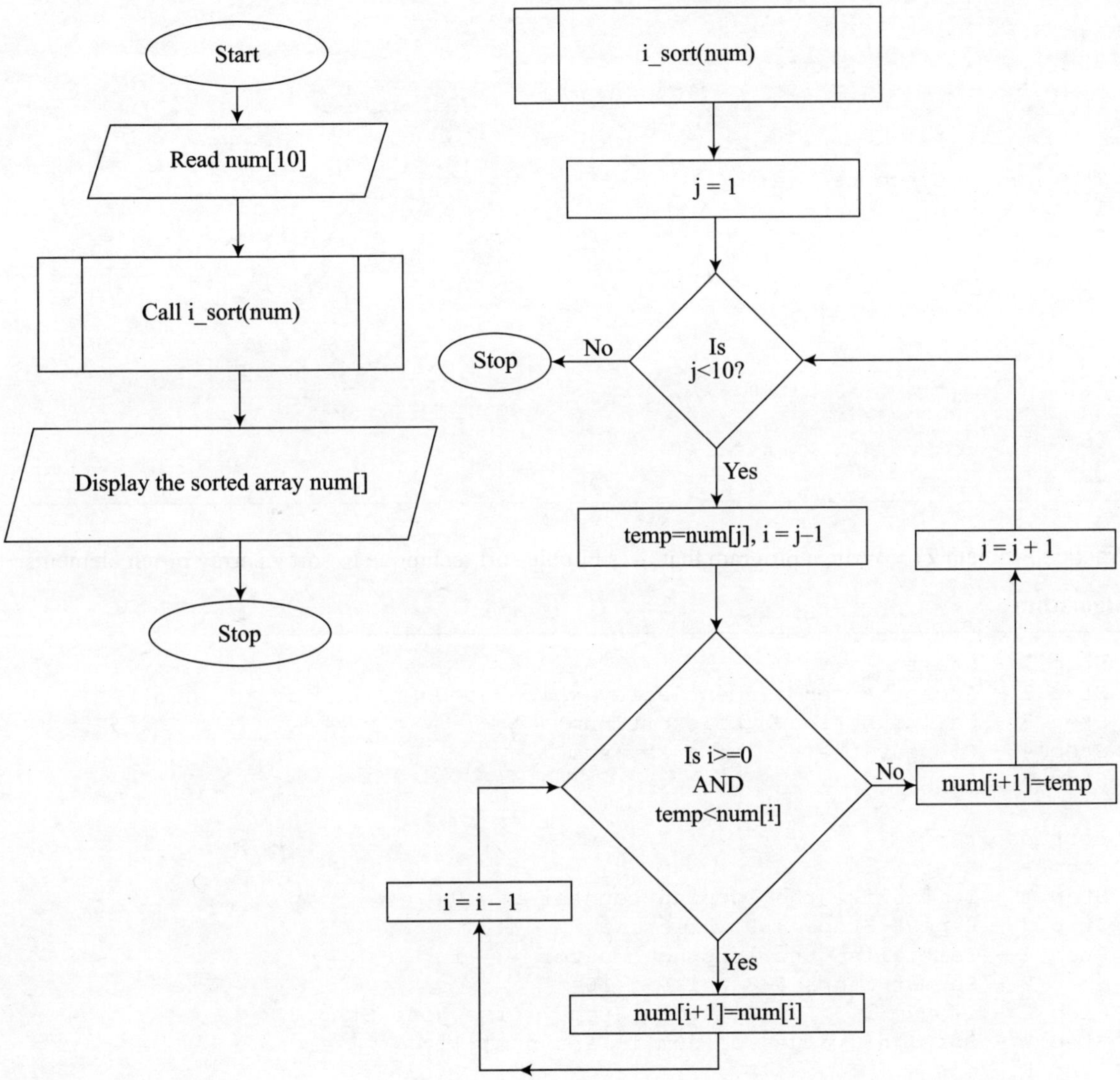

Output

```
Enter the ten elements to sort:
22
33
1
2
65
```

```
18
7
54
78
5


The sorted elements are:
1
2
5
7
18
22
33
54
65
78
```

Practice Problem 21 Write a program that uses bubble sort technique to sort an array of ten elements.

Algorithm

```
Step 1 - Start
Step 2 - Accept a ten element array which needs to be sorted (num[])
Step 3 - Call function bubblesort(num)
Step 4 - Display the sorted array num[]
Step 5 - Stop

bubblesort(num[])
Step 1 - Start
Step 2 - Initialise the looping counter i = 0
Step 3 - Repeat Steps 4-9 while i<9
Step 4 - Initialise the looping counter j = i
Step 5 - Repeat Steps 6-8 while j<10
Step 6 - If num[i] > num[j] goto Step 7 else goto Step 8
Step 7 - Swap the values of num[i] and num[j]
Step 8 - j = j + 1
Step 9 - i = i + 1
Step 10 - Stop
```

Flow Chart

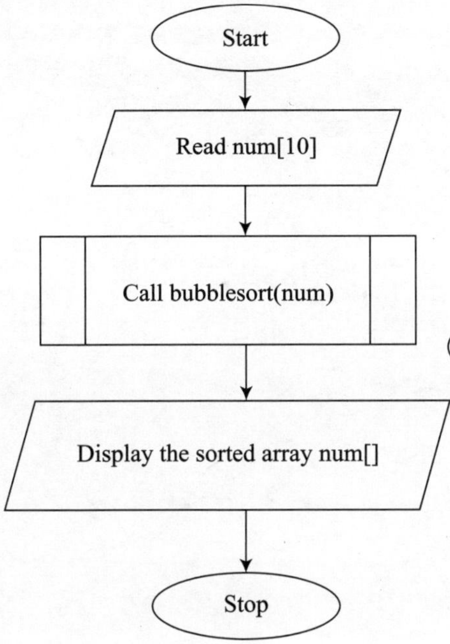
Start
Read num[10]
Call bubblesort(num)
Display the sorted array num[]
Stop

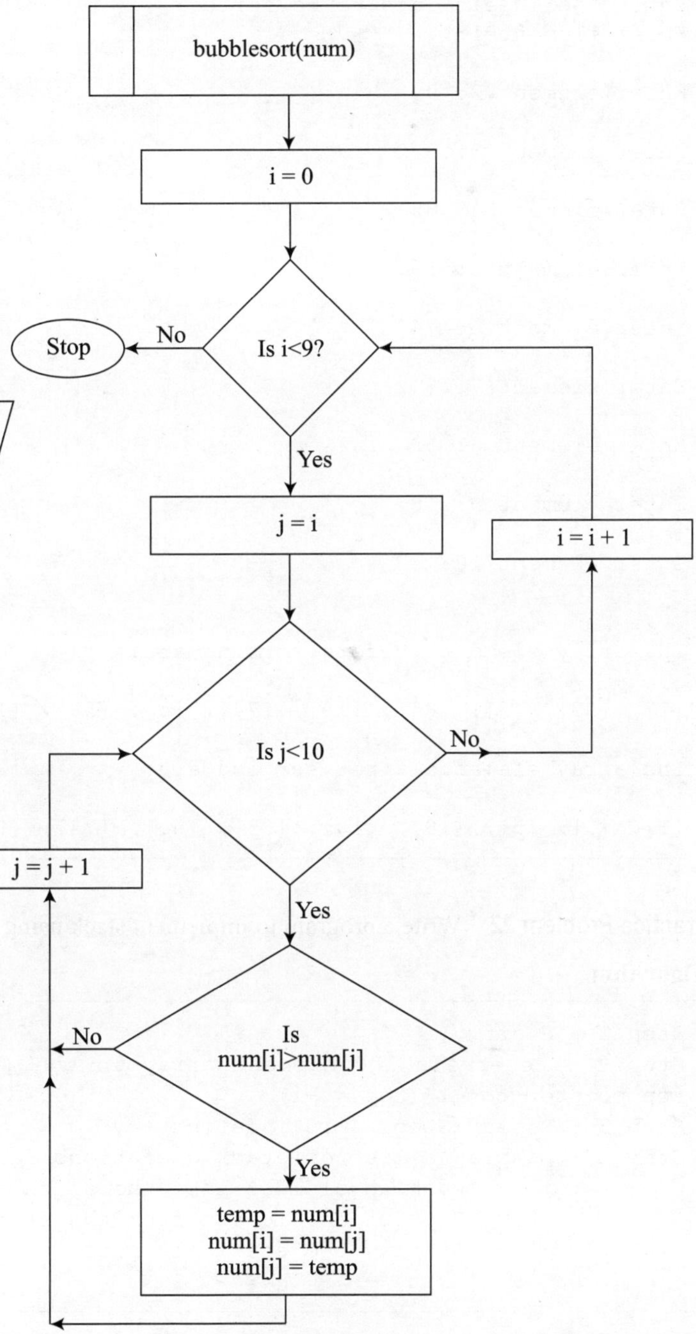
bubblesort(num)
i = 0
Is i<9?
No
Stop
Yes
j = i
i = i + 1
Is j<10
No
Yes
j = j + 1
Is
num[i]>num[j]
No
Yes
temp = num[i]
num[i] = num[j]
num[j] = temp

Output

```
Enter the 10 elements to be sorted:
Enter element 1: 1

Enter element 2: 99

Enter element 3: 3

Enter element 4: 85

Enter element 5: 19

Enter element 6: 74

Enter element 7: 5

Enter element 8: 59

Enter element 9: 18

Enter element 10: 33


The array elements before sorting are:

[1], [99], [3], [85], [19], [74], [5], [59], [18], [33],

The array elements after sorting are:

[1], [3], [5], [18], [19], [33], [59], [74], [85], [99],
```

Practice Problem 22 Write a program to implement stack using arrays.

Algorithm

```
Step 1 - Start
Step 2 - Reserve a 100 element array in the memory stack[100] and set its
top pointer to -1 (top = -1)
Step 3 - Repeat Steps 4-15 indefinitely
Step 4 - Display a list of stack operations for the user to choose from
          1.   Push an element into the stack
          2.   Pop out an element from the stack
          3.   Display the stack elements
          4.   Exit
```

```
Step 5 - Read the choice entered by the user (choice)
Step 6 - If choice = 1 goto Step 7 else goto Step 9
Step 7 - Read the element to be pushed (num1)
Step 8 - Call the push function, push(num1) and goto Step 3
Step 9 - If choice = 2 goto Step 10 else goto Step 12
Step 10 - Call the pop function, pop()
Step 11 - Display the popped element and goto Step 3
Step 12 - If choice = 3 goto Step 13 else goto Step 14
Step 13 - Call the display function, display() and goto Step 3
Step 14 - If choice = 4 goto Step 16 else goto Step 15
Step 15 - Display message "Invalid Choice" and goto Step 3
Step 16 - Stop

push(element)
Step 1 - Start
Step 2 - If top = 99 goto Step 3 else goto Step 4
Step 3 - Display message "Stack Full" and exit
Step 4 - top = top + 1
Step 5 - Stack[top] = element
Step 6 - Stop

pop()
Step 1 - Start
Step 2 - If top = -1 goto Step 3 else goto Step 4
Step 3 - Display message "Stack Empty" and exit
Step 4 - Return stack[top] and set top = top - 1
Step 5 - Stop

display()
Step 1 - Start
Step 2 - Set i = 0
Step 3 - Repeat steps 4-5 while i<=top
Step 4 - Display stack[i]
Step 5 - i = i + 1
Step 6 - Stop
```

Flow Chart

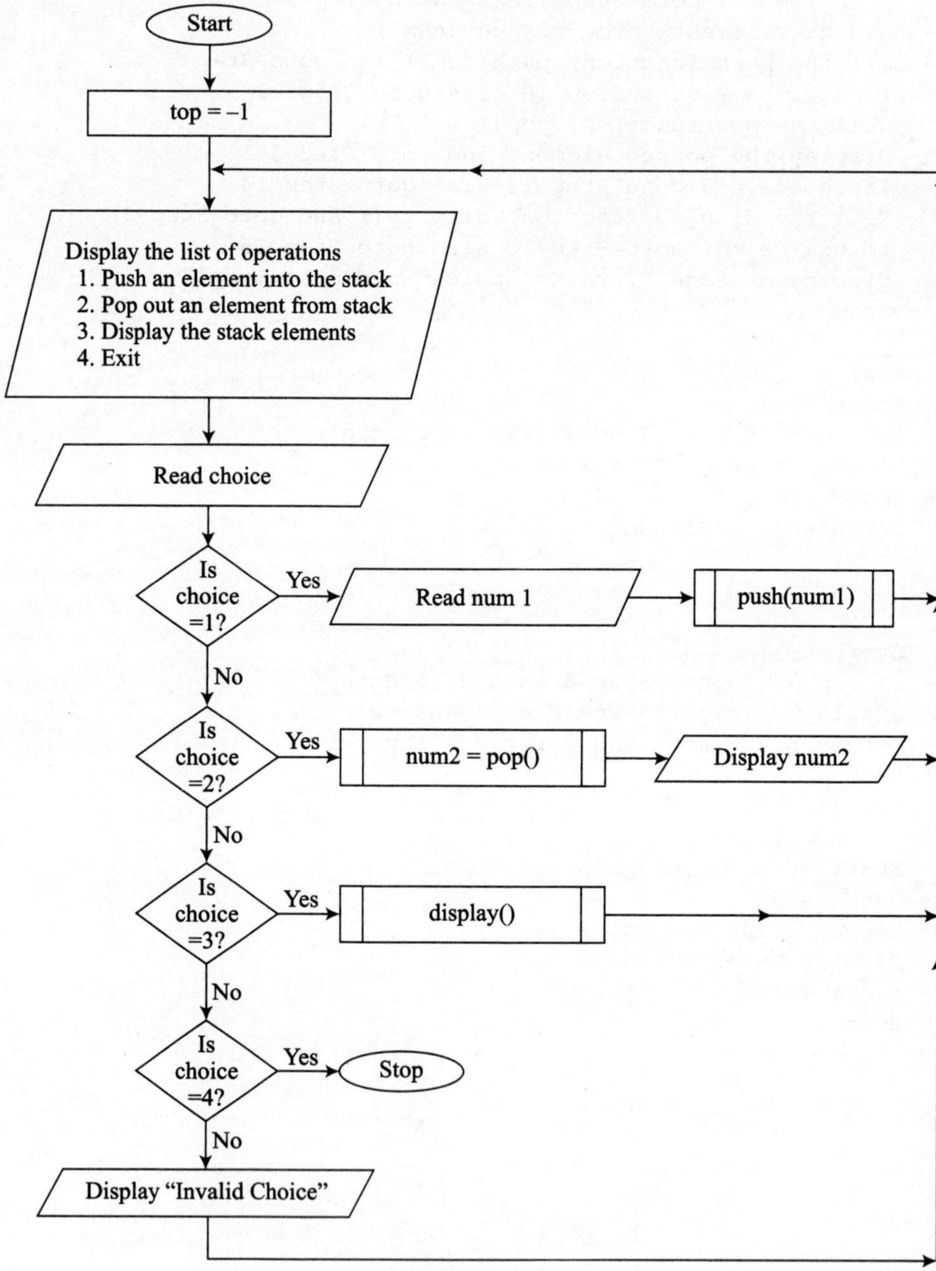
Start
top = –1
Display the list of operations
1. Push an element into the stack
2. Pop out an element from stack
3. Display the stack elements
4. Exit
Read choice
Is choice =1?
Yes
Read num 1
push(num1)
No
Is choice =2?
Yes
num2 = pop()
Display num2
No
Is choice =3?
Yes
display()
No
Is choice =4?
Yes
Stop
No
Display "Invalid Choice"

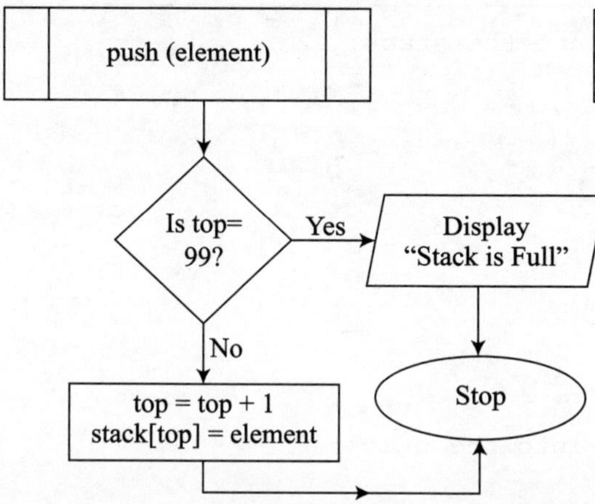

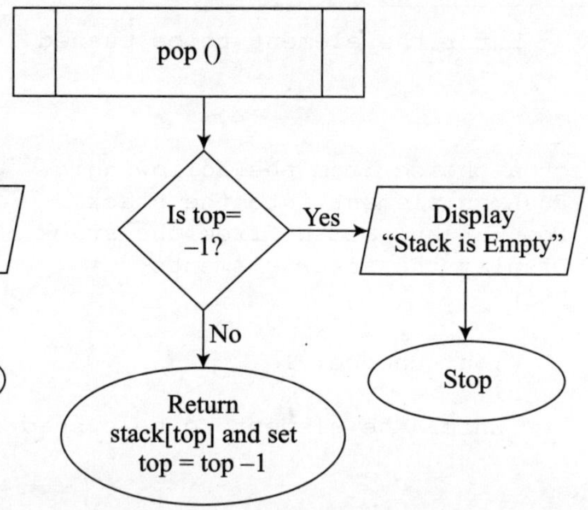

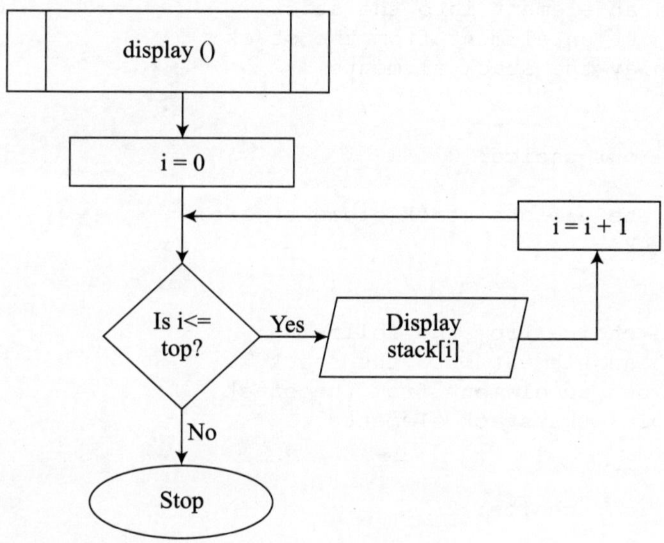

Output

```
Select a choice from the following:
[1] Push an element into the stack
[2] Pop out an element from the stack
[3] Display the stack elements
[4] Exit

     Your choice: 1
```

```
       Enter the element to be pushed into the stack: 42


Select a choice from the following:
[1] Push an element into the stack
[2] Pop out an element from the stack
[3] Display the stack elements
[4] Exit

        Your choice: 1

        Enter the element to be pushed into the stack: 2


Select a choice from the following:
[1] Push an element into the stack
[2] Pop out an element from the stack
[3] Display the stack elements
[4] Exit

        Your choice: 3

        The various stack elements are:
        42      2


Select a choice from the following:
[1] Push an element into the stack
[2] Pop out an element from the stack
[3] Display the stack elements
[4] Exit

        Your choice: 2

        2 element popped out of the stack

Select a choice from the following:
[1] Push an element into the stack
[2] Pop out an element from the stack
[3] Display the stack elements
[4] Exit

        Your choice: 4
```

Practice Problem 23 Write a program to implement stack using pointers.

Algorithm

```
Step 1 - Start
Step 2 - Define a structure to represent a stack
     STRUCTURE stack
     INTEGER element
     STRUCTURE stack *stptr
     END STRUCTURE
     STRUCTURE stack *top
Step 3 - Repeat Steps 4-X indefinitely
Step 4 - Display a list of stack operations for the user to choose from
         1.   Push an element into the stack
         2.   Pop out an element from the stack
         3.   Display the stack elements
         4.   Exit
Step 5 - Read the choice entered by the user (choice)
Step 6 - If choice = 1 goto Step 7 else goto Step 9
Step 7 - Read the element to be pushed (num1)
Step 8 - Call the push function, push(num1) and goto Step 3
Step 9 - If choice = 2 goto Step 10 else goto Step 12
Step 10 - Call the pop function, pop()
Step 11 - Display the popped element and goto Step 3
Step 12 - If choice = 3 goto Step 13 else goto Step 14
Step 13 - Call the display function, display() and goto Step 3
Step 14 - If choice = 4 goto Step 16 else goto Step 15
Step 15 - Display message "Invalid Choice" and goto Step 3
Step 16 - Stop

push(value)
Step 1 - Start
Step 2 - Reserve a block of memory of size stack and assign its address to
pointer ptr, (ptr=(struct stack*)malloc(sizeof(struct stack)))
Step 3 - Set ptr->element = value
Step 4 - Set ptr->stptr=top
Step 5 - top = ptr
Step 6 - Return

pop()
Step 1 - Start
Step 2 - If top = NULL goto Step 3 else goto Step 4
Step 3 - Display message "Stack Empty" and exit
Step 4 - Set temp=top->element
Step 5 - Set top=top->stptr
Step 6 - return (temp)

display()
Step 1 - Start
```

```
Step 2 - Create a pointer (ptr1) of type stack and assign it the value
contained in top, (struct stack *ptr1=top)
Step 3 - Repeat steps 4-5 while ptr1!=NULL
Step 4 - Display ptr1->element
Step 5 - ptr1=ptr1->stptr
Step 6 - Stop
```

Flow Chart

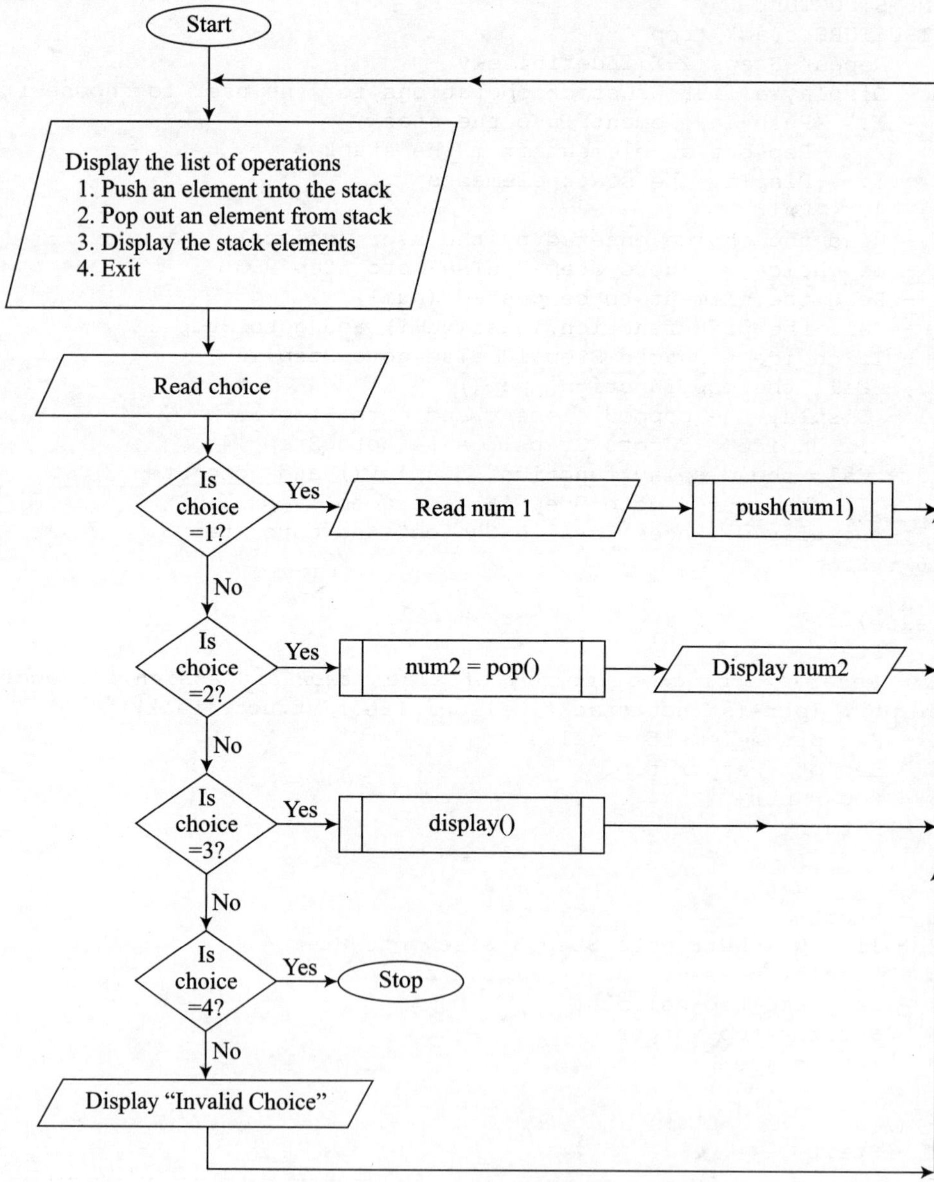

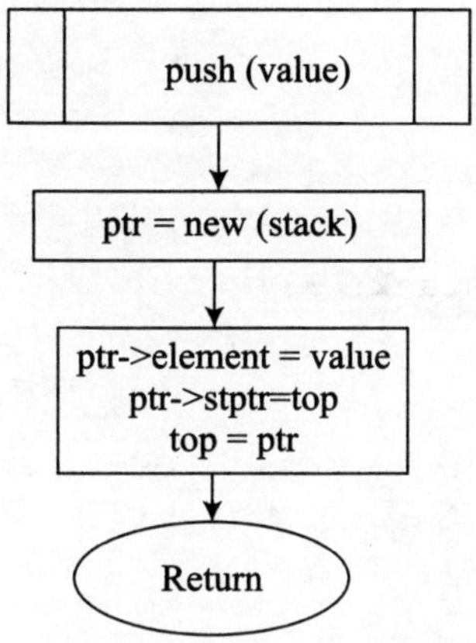

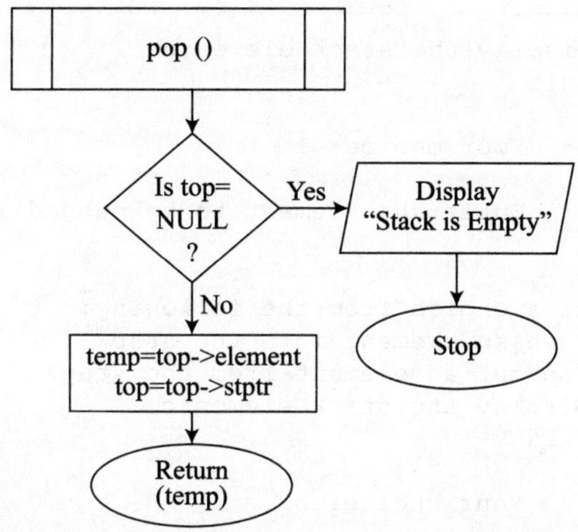

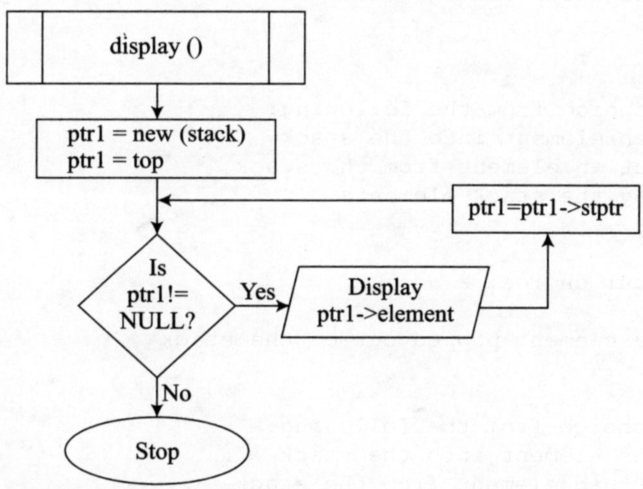

Output

```
Select a choice from the following:
[1] Push an element into the stack
[2] Pop out an element from the stack
[3] Display the stack elements
[4] Exit

        Your choice: 1

        Enter the element to be pushed into the stack: 66

Select a choice from the following:
[1] Push an element into the stack
[2] Pop out an element from the stack
```

```
[3] Display the stack elements
[4] Exit

        Your choice: 1

        Enter the element to be pushed into the stack: 33


Select a choice from the following:
[1] Push an element into the stack
[2] Pop out an element from the stack
[3] Display the stack elements
[4] Exit

        Your choice: 3

The various stack elements are:
33      66


Select a choice from the following:
[1] Push an element into the stack
[2] Pop out an element from the stack
[3] Display the stack elements
[4] Exit

        Your choice: 2

        33 element popped out of the stack


Select a choice from the following:
[1] Push an element into the stack
[2] Pop out an element from the stack
[3] Display the stack elements
[4] Exit

        Your choice: 4
```

Practice Problem 24 Write a program that uses linear search technique to search an element in an array.

Algorithm

```
Step 1 - Start
Step 2 - Read a 10 element array (array[])
Step 3 - Read the element that needs to be searched (element)
Step 4 - Set flag = 0
Step 5 - Initialise the looping counter j = 0
Step 6 - Repeat Steps 7-9 while j<10
Step 7 - If array[j] = element goto Step 8 else goto Step 9
```

```
Step 8 - Display j as the location where element has been found, set flag =
1 and goto Step 10
Step 9 - Set j = j + 1
Step 10 - If flag = 0 goto Step 11 else goto Step 12
Step 11 - Display message "element not found in the array"
Step 12 - Stop
```

Flow Chart

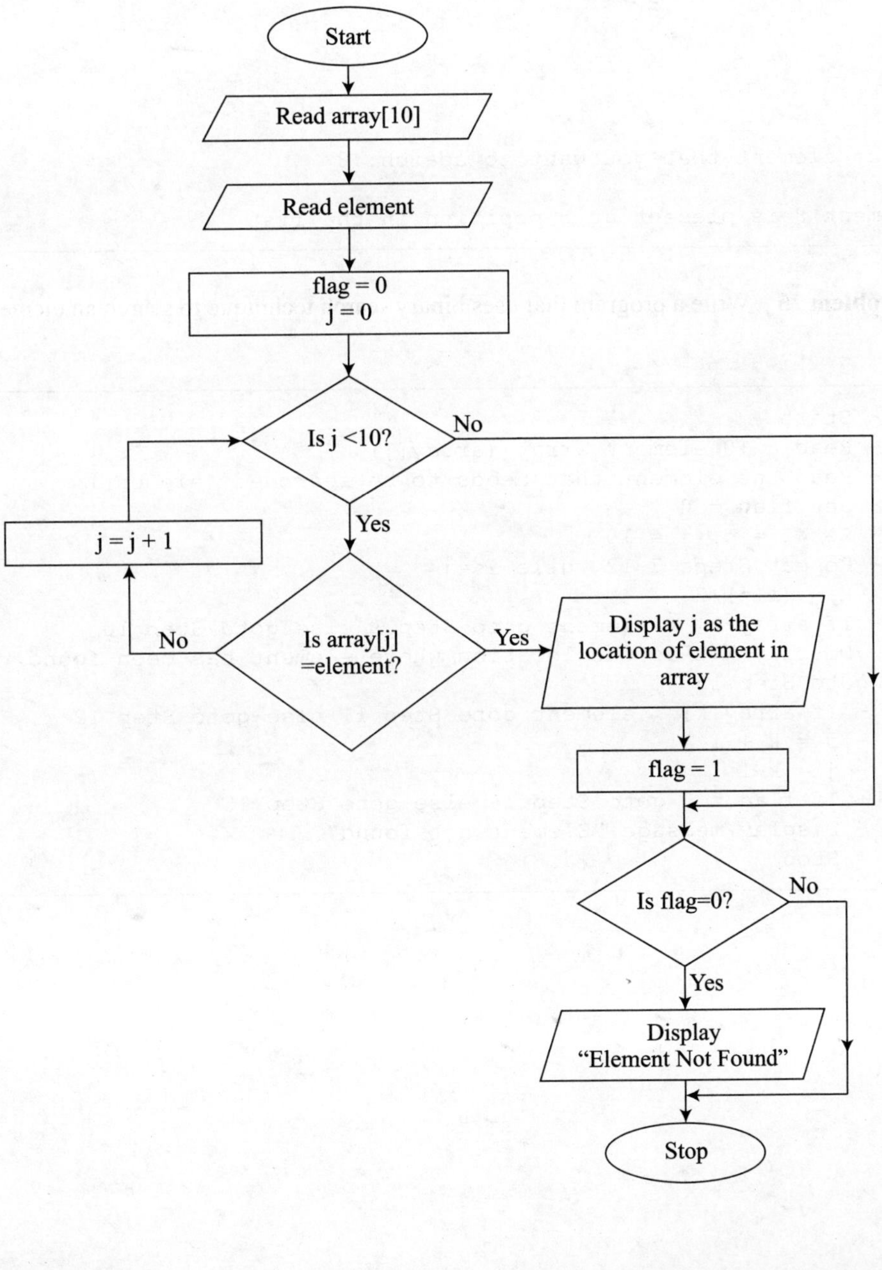

Output

```
Enter the 10 elements of the list:
1
2
3
9
8
7
4
5
6
22


Enter the element that you want to search: 8

The element 8 is present at 5 position in the list
```

Practice Problem 25 Write a program that uses binary search technique to search an element in an array.

Algorithm

```
Step 1 - Start
Step 2 - Read a 10 element array (array[])
Step 3 - Read the element that needs to be searched (element)
Step 4 - Set flag = 0
Step 5 - Set i = o, j = 10
Step 6 - Repeat Steps 7-12 while i<=j
Step 7 - k = (i+j)/2
Step 8 - If array[k] = element goto Step 9 else goto Step 10
Step 9 - Display k+1 as the location where element has been found, set flag
= 1 and goto Step 13
Step 10 - If array[k] < element goto Step 11 else goto Step 12
Step 11 - i = k + 1
Step 12 - j = k-1
Step 13 - If flag = 0 goto Step 14 else goto Step 15
Step 14 - Display message "Element not found"
Step 15 = Stop
```

Flow Chart

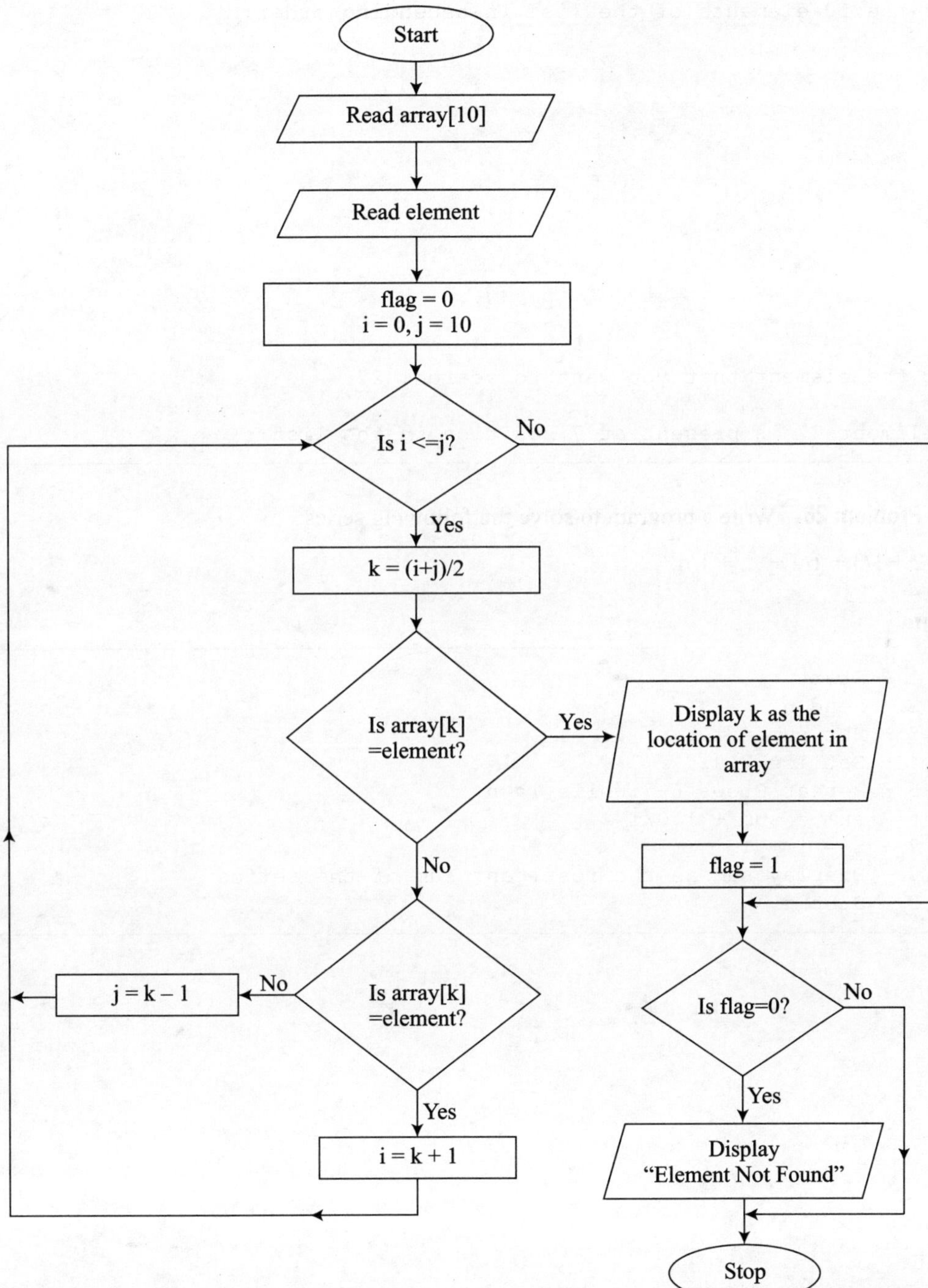
Start
Read array[10]
Read element
flag = 0
i = 0, j = 10
Is i <=j?
No
Yes
k = (i+j)/2
Is array[k]
=element?
Yes
Display k as the
location of element in
array
No
flag = 1
j = k – 1
No
Is array[k]
=element?
Is flag=0?
No
Yes
Yes
i = k + 1
Display
"Element Not Found"
Stop

Output

```
Enter the 10 elements of the list in ascending order:
1
3
5
6
13
19
27
33
99
102


Enter the element that you want to search: 27

The element 27 is present at 7 position in the list
```

Practice Problem 26 Write a program to solve the following series:

1 + 1/2 + 1/3 + 1/4 + … + 1/n

Algorithm

```
Step 1 - Start
Step 2 - Read n
Step 3 - Set sum = 1.0
Step 4 - Set i = 2.0
Step 5 - Repeat Steps 6-7 while i<=n
Step 6 - sum = sum + 1.0/i
Step 7 - i = i + 1
Step 8 - Display sum as the resultant sum of the series
Step 9 - Stop
```

Flow Chart

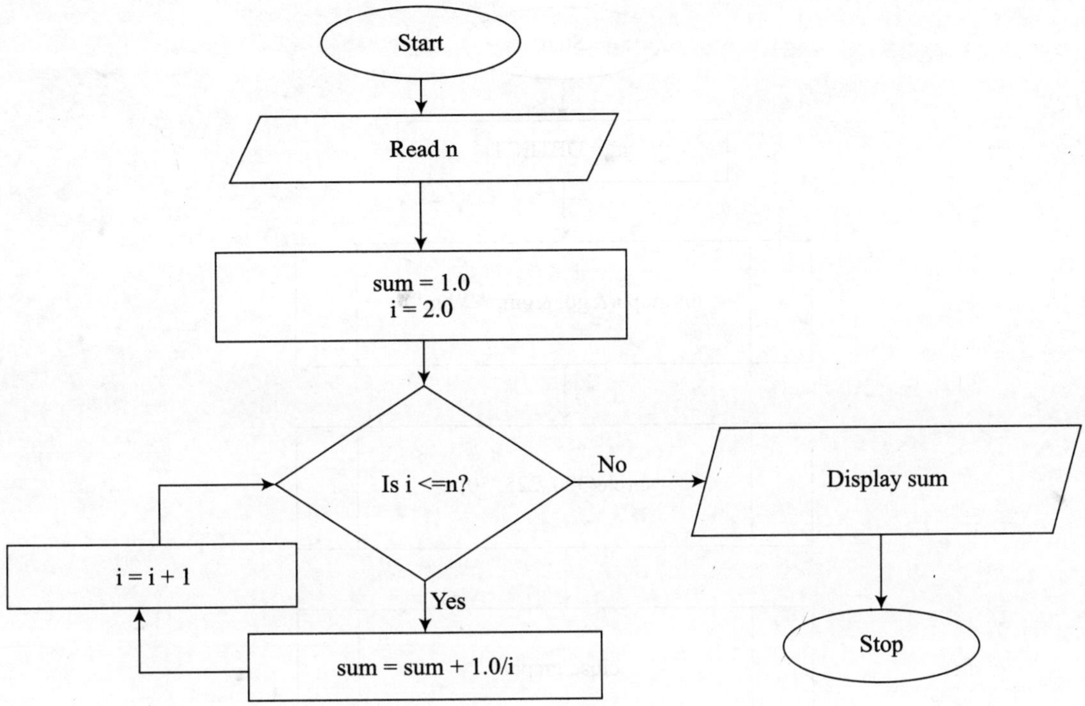

Output

```
Enter the value of n: 11

The sum of the series 1 + 1/2 + 1/3 +....+1/n = 3.01987734
```

Practice Problem 27 Write a program to draw a circle.

Algorithm

```
Step 1 - Start
Step 2 - Set gd = DETECT
Step 3 - Call in-build function, initgraph(&gd, &gm, "..\\bgi")
Step 4 - Call in-built function, circle(320, 225, 50)
Step 5 - closegraph()
Step 6 - Stop
```

Flow Chart

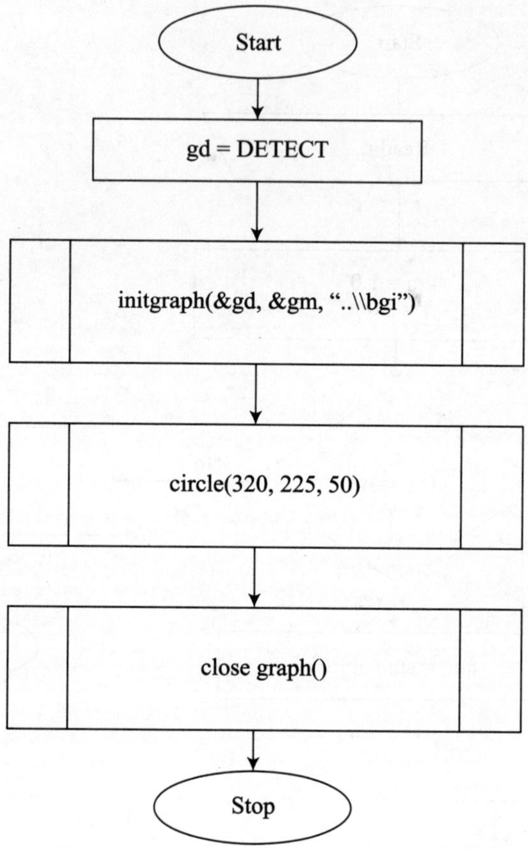

Output

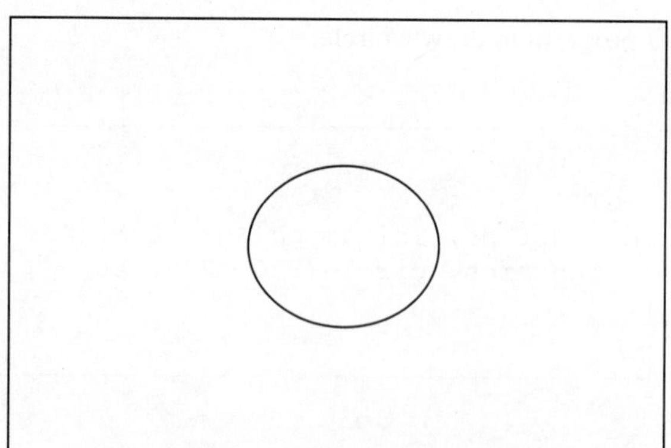

Practice Problem 28 Write a program to draw a rectangle.

Algorithm

```
Step 1 - Start
Step 2 - Set gd = DETECT
Step 3 - Call in-build function, initgraph(&gd, &gm, "..\\bgi")
Step 4 - Call in-built function, rectangle(320, 225, 50,100)
Step 5 - closegraph()
Step 6 - Stop
```

Flow Chart

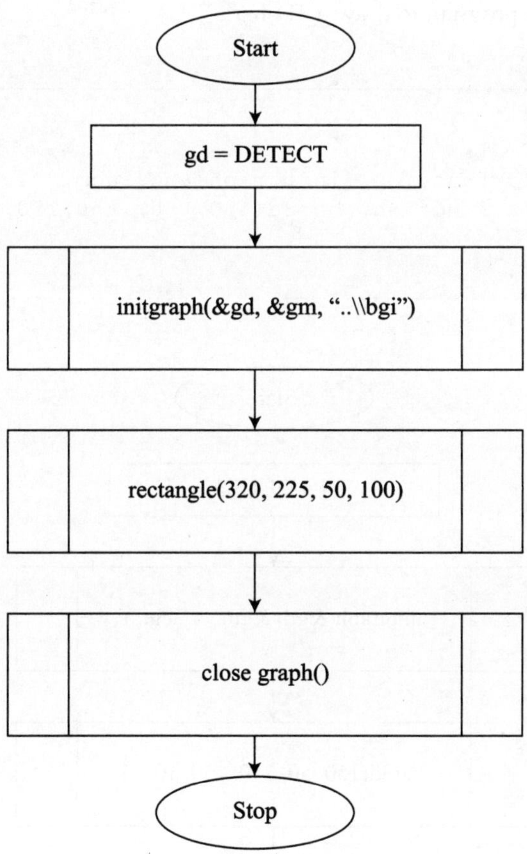

Output

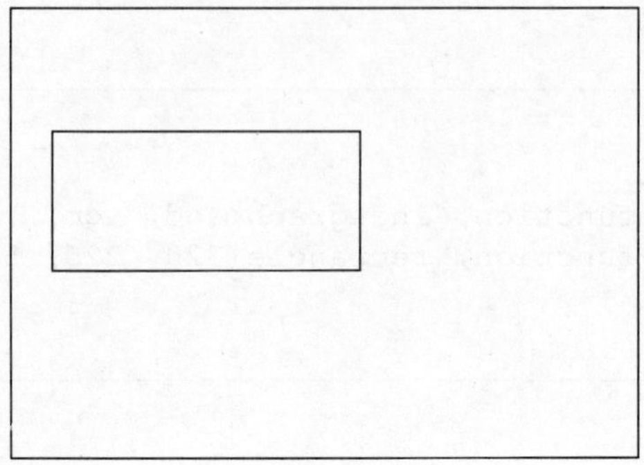

Practice Problem 29 Write a program to draw a 3D-bar.

Algorithm

```
Step 1 - Start
Step 2 - Set gd = DETECT
Step 3 - Call in-build function, initgraph(&gd, &gm, "..\\bgi")
Step 4 - Call in-built function, bar3d(150, 50, 250,150, 10, 1)
Step 5 - closegraph()
Step 6 - Stop
```

Flow Chart

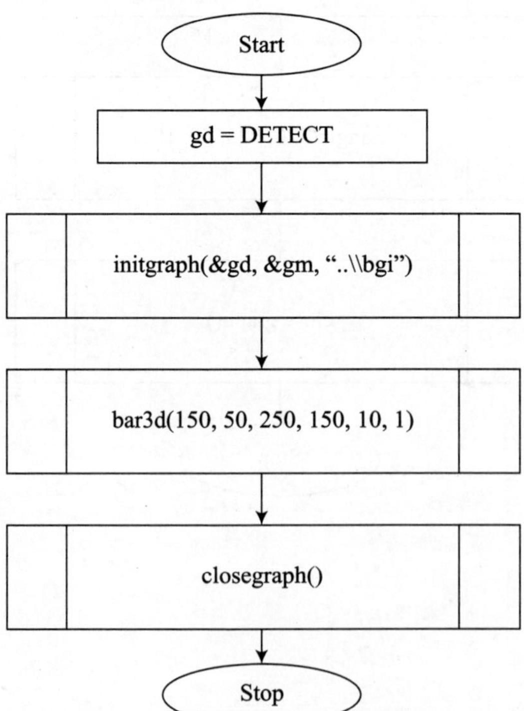

Output

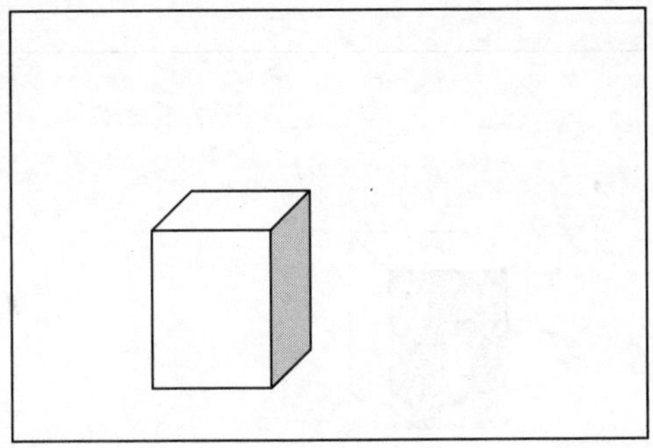

Practice Problem 30 Write a program to draw a shape and fill it with color.

Algorithm

```
Step 1 - Start
Step 2 - Set gd = DETECT
Step 3 - Call in-build function, initgraph(&gd, &gm, "..\\bgi")
Step 4 - Call in-build function, setfillstyle(SOLID_FILL,RED)
Step 4 - Call in-built function, bar3d(150, 50, 250,150, 10, 1)
Step 5 - closegraph()
Step 6 - Stop
```

Flow Chart

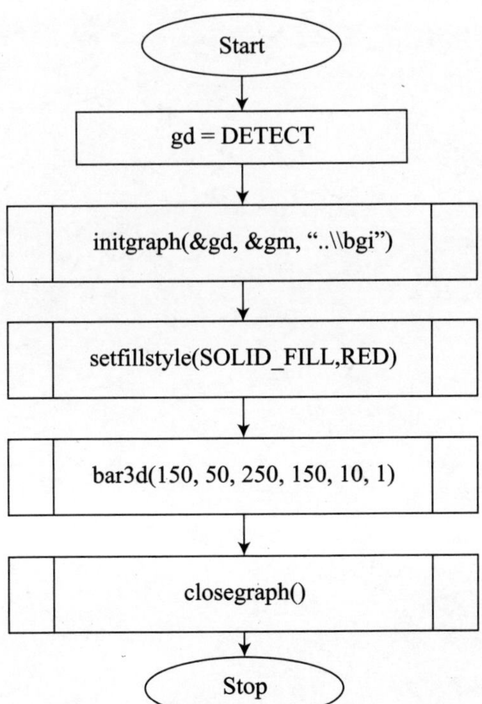

Output

Appendix

B

PROBLEM SOLVING EXERCISES—WITH ALGORITHM AND PSEUDOCODE

SOLUTIONS AVAILABLE ON OLC

Practice Problem 1 Write a program to display the Fibonacci series.

Algorithm

```
Step 1 - Start
Step 2 - Accept the length of the Fibonacci series from the user (len)
Step 3 - Initialise variables num1 = 0, num2 = 1
Step 4 - Display the values of num1 and num2
Step 5 - Initialise looping counter i = 1
Step 6 - Repeat Steps 7-11 while i <= len-2
Step 7 - Set fab = num1 + num2
Step 8 - Display the value of fab
Step 9 - Set num1 = num2
Step 10 - Set num2 = fab
Step 11 - Increment the value of i by 1
Step 12 - Stop
```

Flow Chart

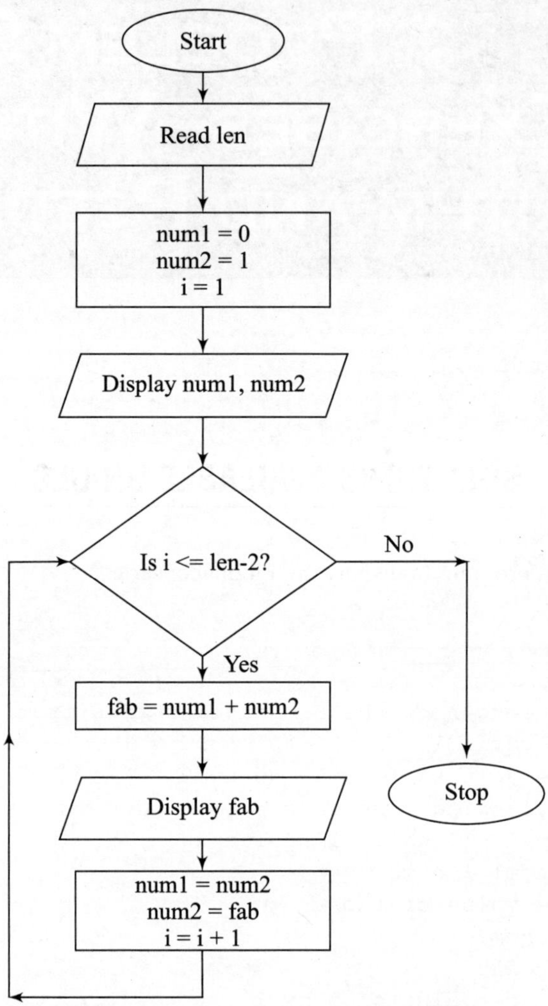

Pseudocode

```
BEGIN
DEFINE: Integer num1, num2, len, i, fab
SET: num1=0, num2=1
DISPLAY: "Enter Length of the Fibonacci Series: "
READ: len
DISPLAY: num1, num2
FOR: i = 1 to len-2
     COMPUTE: fab = num1 + num2
     DISPLAY: fab
```

```
    SET: num1 = num2
    SET: num2 = fab
END FOR
END
```

Practice Problem 2 Write a program to find out whether the given number is even or odd.

Algorithm

```
Step 1 - Start
Step 2 - Accept a number from the user (num)
Step 3 - If remainder of num divided by 2 (num/2) is Zero then goto Step 4
else goto Step 5
Step 4 - Display "num is an even number" and goto Step 6
Step 5 - Display "num is an odd number"
Step 6 - Stop
```

Flow Chart

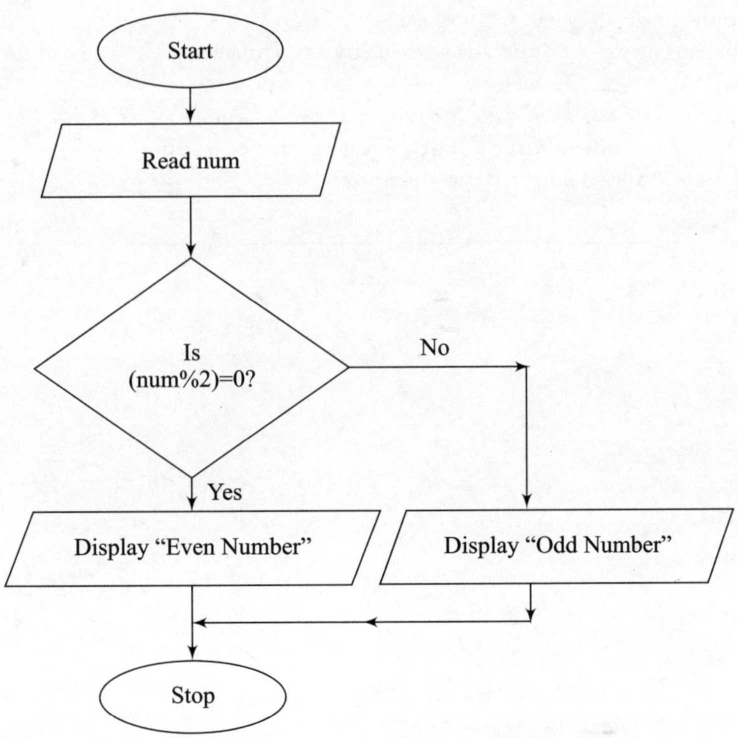

Pseudocode

```
BEGIN
DEFINE: Integer num
DISPLAY: "Enter a number: "
READ: num
IF: num%2=0
     DISPLAY: "'num' is an even number"
ELSE
     DISPLAY: "'num' is an odd number"
END IF
END
```

Practice Problem 3 Write a program to find out whether the given number is a prime number.

Algorithm

```
Step 1 - Start
Step 2 - Accept a number from the user (num)
Step 3 - Initialise looping counter i = 2
Step 4 - Repeat Step 5 while i < num
Step 5 - If remainder of num divided by i (num%i) is Zero then goto Step 6
else goto Step 4
Step 6 - Display "num is not a prime number" and break from the loop
Step 7 - If i = num then goto Step 8 Else goto Step 9
Step 8 - Display "num is a prime number"
Step 9 - Stop
```

Flow Chart

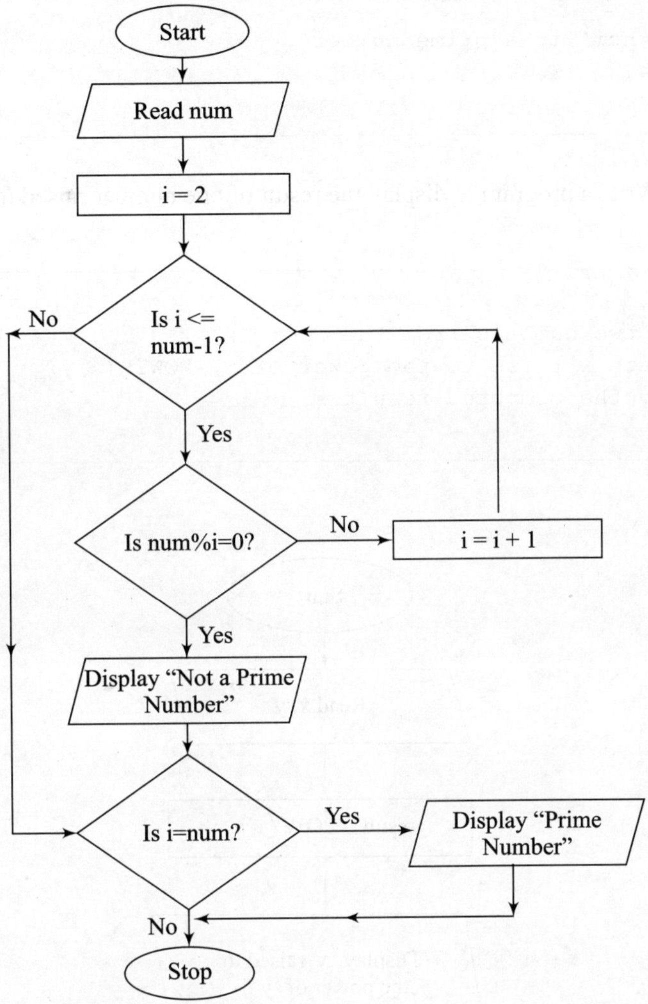

Pseudocode

```
BEGIN
DEFINE: Integer num, i
DISPLAY: "Enter a number: "
READ: num
FOR: i = 2 to num-1
     IF: num%i=0
        DISPLAY: "'num' is not a prime number"
        BREAK
     END IF
```

```
END FOR
IF: i=num
      DISPLAY: "'num' is a prime number"
END IF
END
```

Practice Problem 4 Write a program to display the result of one number raised to the power of another.

Algorithm

```
Step 1 - Start
Step 2 - Accept two numbers from the user (x,y)
Step 3 - Calculate x raise to the power of y, POWER(x,y)
Step 4 - Display the computed result
Step 5 - Stop
```

Flow Chart

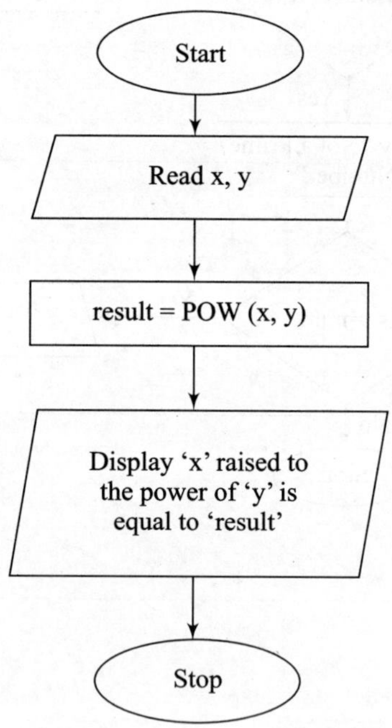

Pseudocode

```
BEGIN
DEFINE: Integer x, y
DEFINE: Long Integer result
DISPLAY: "Enter the values of x and y: "
READ: x, y
COMPUTE: result = POW(x,y)
DISPLAY: "'x' raised to the power of 'y' is equal to 'result'"
END
```

Practice Problem 5 Write a program to display the square root of a number.

Algorithm

```
Step 1 - Start
Step 2 - Accept a number from the user (num)
Step 3 - Calculate square root of num, Sqrt(num)
Step 4 - Display the computed result
Step 5 - Stop
```

Flow Chart

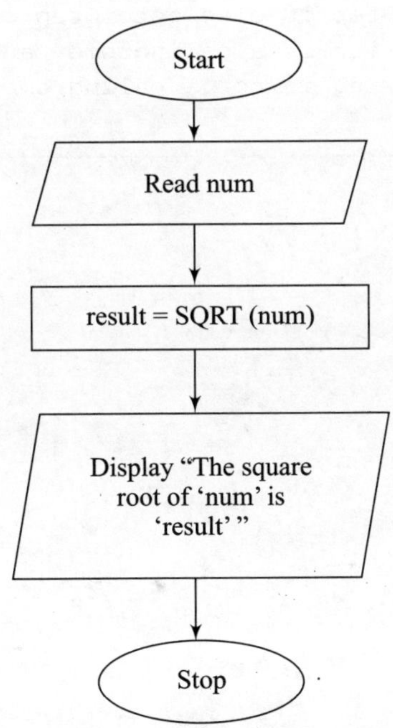

Pseudocode

```
BEGIN
DEFINE: Integer num
DEFINE: Real result
DISPLAY: "Enter the value whose square root is to be computed: "
READ: num
COMPUTE: result = SQRT(num)
DISPLAY: "The square root of 'num' is 'result'"
END
```

Practice Problem 6 Write a program to determine whether a given string is a palindrome or not.

Algorithm

```
Step 1 - Start
Step 2 - Accept a string from the user (str)
Step 3 - Calculate the length of string str (len)
Step 4 - Initialise looping counters left=0, right=len-1 and chk = 't'
Step 5 - Repeat Steps 6-8 while left < right and chk = 't'
Step 6 - If str(left) = str(right) goto Step 8 else goto step 7
Step 7 - Set chk = 'f'
Step 8 - Set left = left + 1 and right = right + 1
Step 9 - If chk='t' goto Step 10 else goto Step 11
Step 10 - Display "The string is a palindrome" and goto Step 12
Step 11 - Display "The string is not a palindrome"
Step 12 - Stop
```

Flow Chart

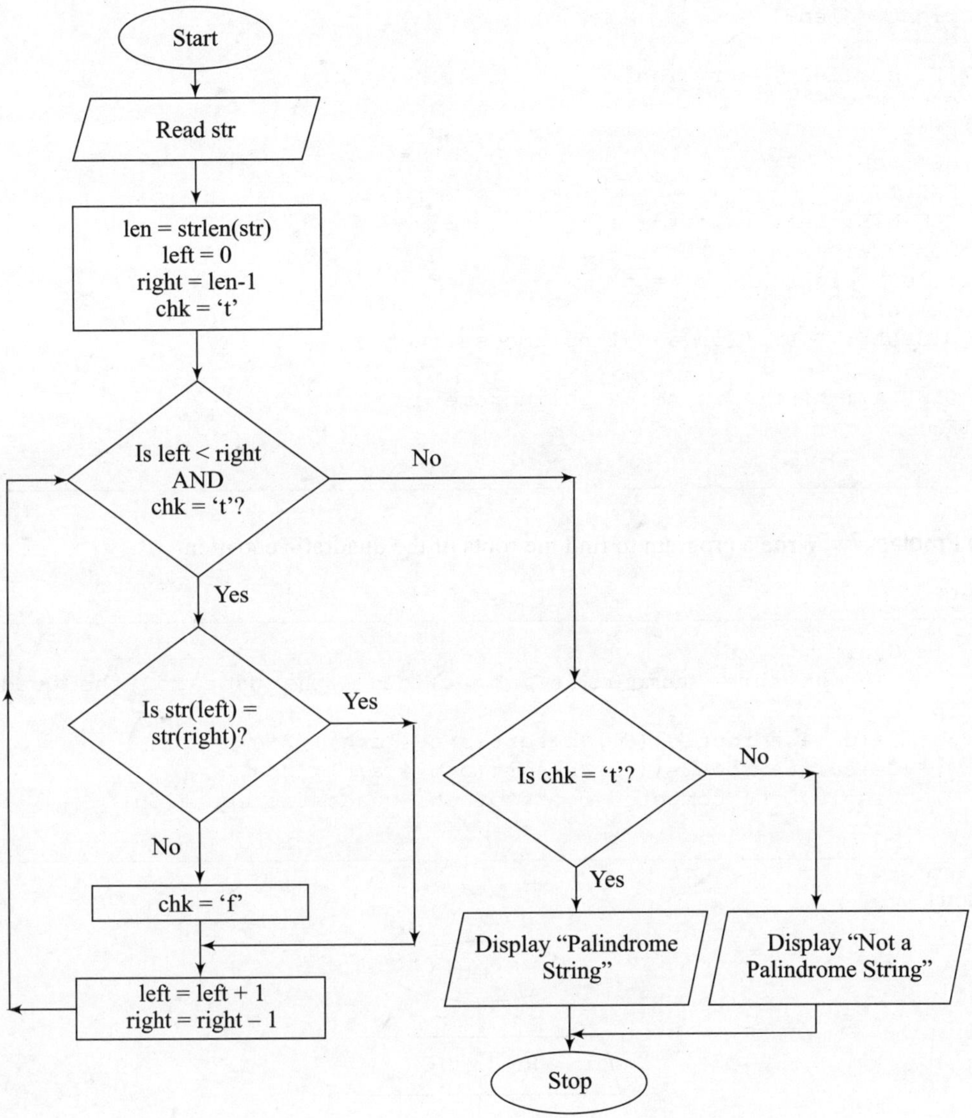

Pseudocode

```
BEGIN
DEFINE: String str
DEFINE: Character chk
DEFINE: Integer left, right, len
SET: chk = 't'
DISPLAY: "Enter a string: "
READ: str
COMPUTE: len = strlen(str)
```

```
SET: left = 0
SET: right = len-1
REPEAT
     IF: str(left)=str(right)
     CONTINUE
     ELSE
     SET: chk = 'f'
     END IF
     COMPUTE: left = left + 1
     COMPUTE: right = right - 1
UNTIL: left<right AND chk='t'
IF: chk='t'
     DISPLAY: "'str' is a palindrome string"
ELSE
     DISPLAY: "'str' is not a palindrome string"
END IF
END
```

Practice Problem 7 Write a program to find the roots of the quadratic equation.

Algorithm

```
Step 1 - Start
Step 2 - Accept three numbers (a, b, c) from the user for the quadratic
equation ax^2 + bx + c
Step 3 - Calculate root1=((-1)*b+sqrt(b*b-4*a*c))/2*a
Step 4 - Calculate root2=((-1)*b-sqrt(b*b-4*a*c))/2*a
Step 5 - Display the computed roots of the quadratic equation
Step 6 - Stop
```

Flow Chart

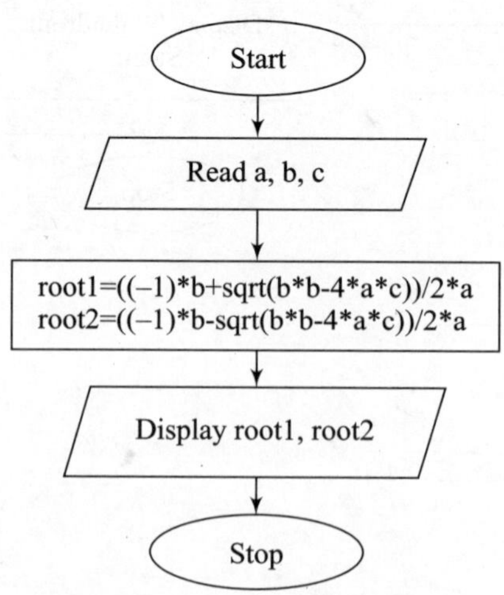

Pseudocode

```
BEGIN
DEFINE: Integer a, b, c
DEFINE: Real root1, root2
DISPLAY: "Enter the values of a, b and c for the quadratic equation ax^2 + bx
+ c: "
READ: a, b, c
COMPUTE: root1=((-1)*b+sqrt(b*b-4*a*c))/2*a
COMPUTE: root2=((-1)*b-sqrt(b*b-4*a*c))/2*a
DISPLAY: "The roots of the quadratic equation are 'root1' and 'root2'
END
```

Practice Problem 8 Write a program to find the area of a circle.

Algorithm

```
Step 1 - Start
Step 2 - Accept the radius of the circle from the user (radius)
Step 3 - Calculate area of the circle using formula area = 3.14 * radius *
radius
Step 4 - Display the computed area of the circle
Step 5 - Stop
```

Flow Chart

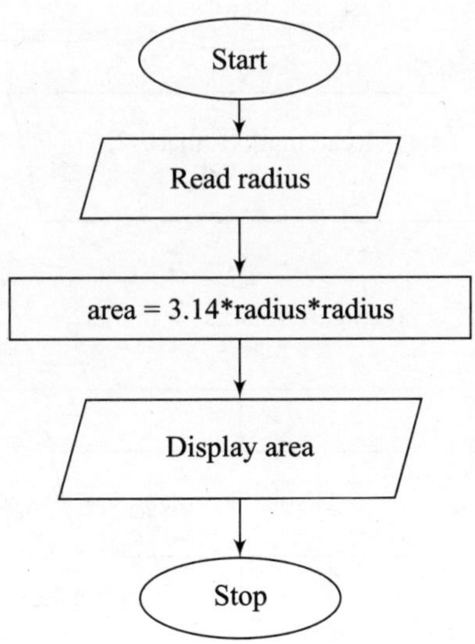

Pseudocode

```
BEGIN
DEFINE: Real radius, area
DISPLAY: "Enter the radius of the circle: "
READ: radius
COMPUTE: area = 3.14*radius*radius
DISPLAY: "The area of the circle is 'area'"
END
```

Practice Problem 9 Write a program to find the average of marks obtained by a student in three subjects.

Algorithm

```
Step 1 - Start
Step 2 - Accept the marks in three subjects from the user (marks1, marks2,
marks3)
Step 3 - Calculate average marks using formula, average = (marks1 + marks2
+ marks3)/3
Step 4 - Display the computed average of three subject marks
Step 5 - Stop
```

Flow Chart

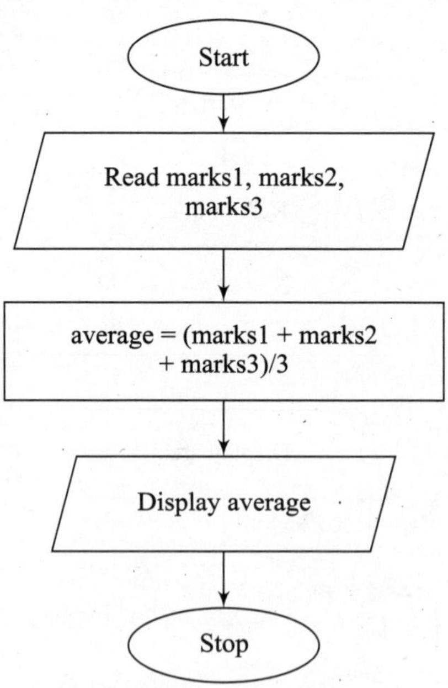

Pseudocode

```
BEGIN
DEFINE: Integer marks1, marks2, marks3
DEFINE: Real average
DISPLAY: "Enter the marks in three subjects: "
READ: marks1, marks2, marks3
COMPUTE: average = (marks1 + marks2 + marks3)/3
DISPLAY: "The average value of marks is 'average'"
END
```

Practice Problem 10 Write a program to determine whether the given year is a leap year or not.

Algorithm

```
Step 1 - Start
Step 2 - Accept an year value from the user (year)
Step 3 - If remainder of year value divided by 4 (year%4) is 0 then goto Step
4 else goto Step 5
Step 4 - Display "'year' is a leap year" and goto Step 6
Step 5 - Display "'year' is not a leap year"
Step 6 - Stop
```

Flow Chart

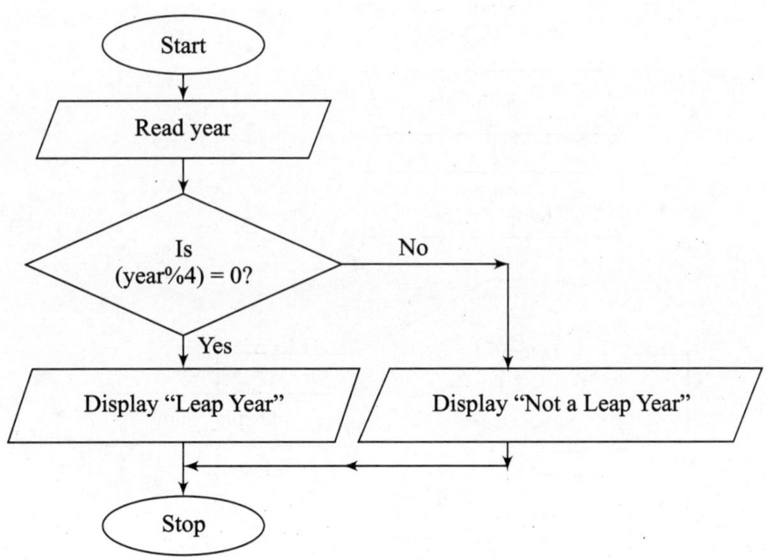

Pseudocode

```
BEGIN
DEFINE: Integer year
DISPLAY: "Enter the year value: "
READ: year
```

```
IF: year%4=0
    DISPLAY: "'year' is a leap year"
ELSE
   DISPLAY: "'year' is not a leap year"
END IF
END
```

Practice Problem 11 Write a program to find the sum of digits of an integer.

Algorithm

```
Step 1 - Start
Step 2 - Accept an integer value from the user (num)
Step 3 - Define a variable Sum to store the sum of digits and initialise it
to 0
Step 4 - Assign the value of num to a temporary variable (temp=num)
Step 5 - Repeat Steps 6-7 while temp is not equal to 0 (temp!=0)
Step 6 - Calculate Sum = Sum+(temp%10)
Step 7 - Calculate temp=temp/10
Step 8 - Display Sum as the result containing sum of digits of num
Step 9 - Stop
```

Flow Chart

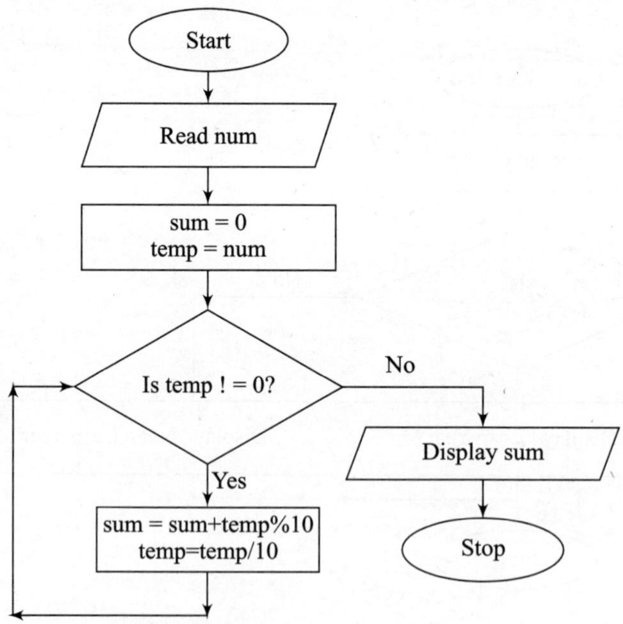

Pseudocode

```
BEGIN
DEFINE: Long Integer num, temp
```

```
DEFINE: Integer sum
SET: sum=0
DISPLAY: "Enter an integer value: "
READ: num
SET: temp=num
REPEAT
     COMPUTE: sum = sum+temp%10
     COMPUTE: temp=temp/10
UNTIL: temp!=0
DISPLAY: "The sum of digits of 'num' is 'sum'"
END
```

Practice Problem 12 Write a program to find the length of a string.

Algorithm

```
Step 1 - Start
Step 2 - Accept a string from the user, str
Step 3 - Calculate the length of the string, strlen(str)
Step 4 - Display the computed result
Step 5 - Stop
```

Flow Chart

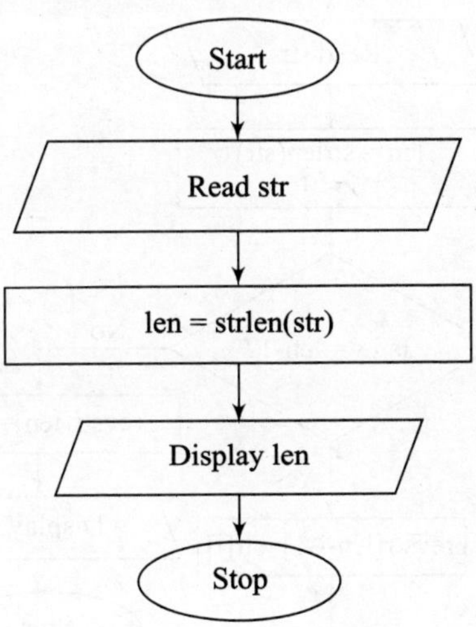

Pseudocode

```
BEGIN
DEFINE: String str
DEFINE: Integer len
DISPLAY: "Enter a string: "
READ: str
```

```
COMPUTE: len = strlen(str)
DISPLAY: "The length of string 'str' is 'len'"
END
```

Practice Problem 13 Write a program to display the reverse of a string.

Algorithm

```
Step 1 - Start
Step 2 - Accept a string from the user (str)
Step 3 - Calculate the length of string str (len)
Step 4 - Initialise looping counter i=0
Step 5 - Repeat Step 6-7 while i < len
Step 6 - Set revstr[len-i-1]=str[i]
Step 7 - Set i = i+ 1
Step 8 - Set revstr[len]='\0'
Step 9 - Display revstr as the reverse of the original string str
Step 10 - Stop
```

Flow Chart

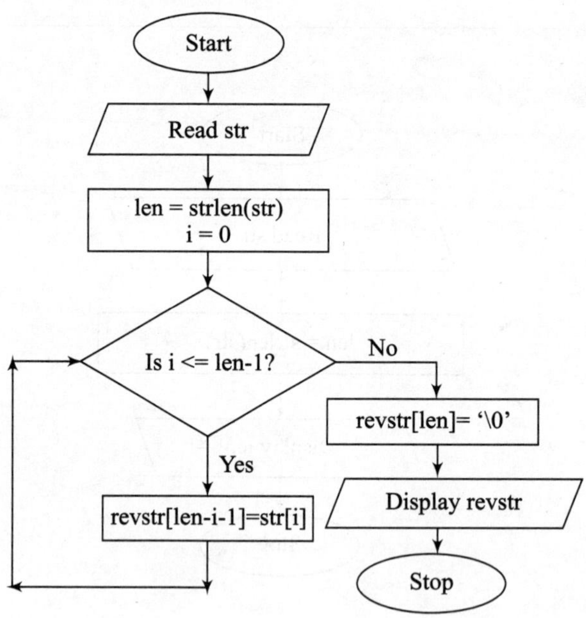

Pseudocode

```
BEGIN
DEFINE: String str, revstr
DEFINE: Integer i, len
DISPLAY: "Enter a string: "
```

```
READ: str
COMPUTE: len = strlen(str)
FOR: i = 0 to len-1
     COMPUTE: revstr[len-i-1]=str[i]
END FOR
SET: revstr[len]='\0'
DISPLAY: "The reverse of string 'str' is 'revstr'"
END
```

Practice Problem 14 Write a program to determine whether there is a profit or a loss during the selling of an item.

Algorithm

```
Step 1 - Start
Step 2 - Accept the cost price and selling price of an item from the user
(cp, sp)
Step 3 - If sp>cp then goto step 4 else goto step 5
Step 4 - Display "There is a profit of (sp-cp)" and goto Step 8
Step 5 - If cp>sp then goto step 6 else goto step 7
Step 6 - Display "There is a loss of (cp-sp)"
Step 7 - Display "No profit no loss!"
Step 8 - Stop
```

Flow Chart

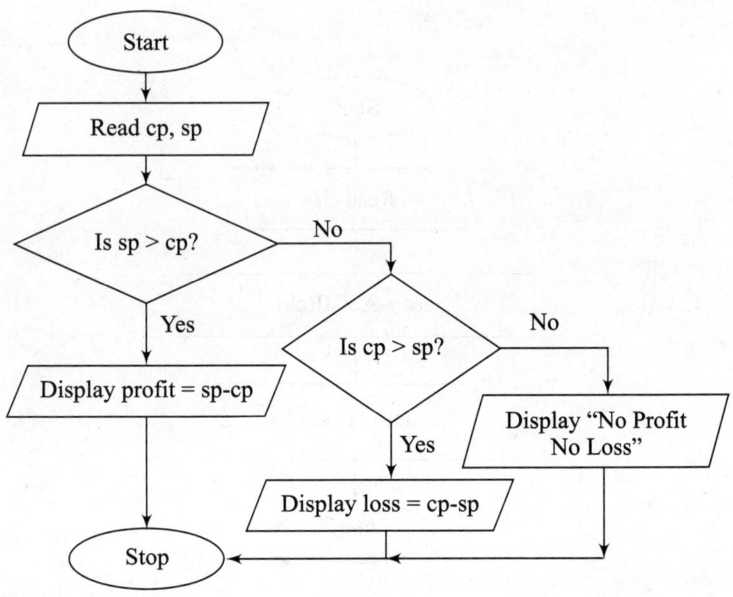

Pseudocode

```
BEGIN
DEFINE: Long Integer cp, sp
DISPLAY: "Enter the cost price and selling price of an item: "
READ: cp, sp
IF: sp>cp
     DISPLAY: "There is a profit of 'sp-cp'"
ELSE
    IF: cp>sp
      DISPLAY: "There is a loss of 'cp-sp'"
    ELSE
      DISPLAY: "No profit no loss!"
    END IF
END IF
END
```

Practice Problem 15 Write a program to print the ASCII value of a given character.

Algorithm

```
Step 1 - Start
Step 2 - Accept a character from the user (ch)
Step 3 - Determine the ASCII value of ch
Step 4 - Display the computed ASCII value
Step 5 - Stop
```

Flow Chart

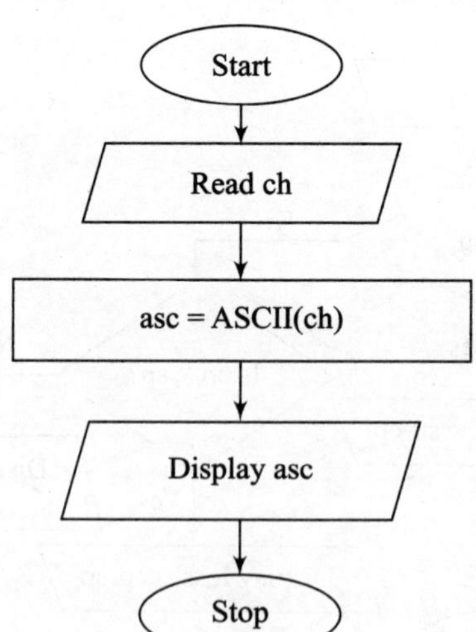

Pseudocode

```
BEGIN
DEFINE: Character ch
DEFINE: Integer asc
DISPLAY: "Enter a character: "
READ: ch
COMPUTE: asc = ASCII(ch)
DISPLAY: "The ASCII value of 'ch' is 'asc'"
END
```

Practice Problem 16 Write a program to find out whether a given number is positive or negative.

Algorithm

```
Step 1 - Start
Step 2 - Accept a number from the user (num)
Step 3 - If num is greater than 0 (num>0) then goto Step 4 else goto Step 5
Step 4 - Display "num is a positive number" and goto Step 6
Step 5 - Display "num is a negative number"
Step 6 - Stop
```

Flow Chart

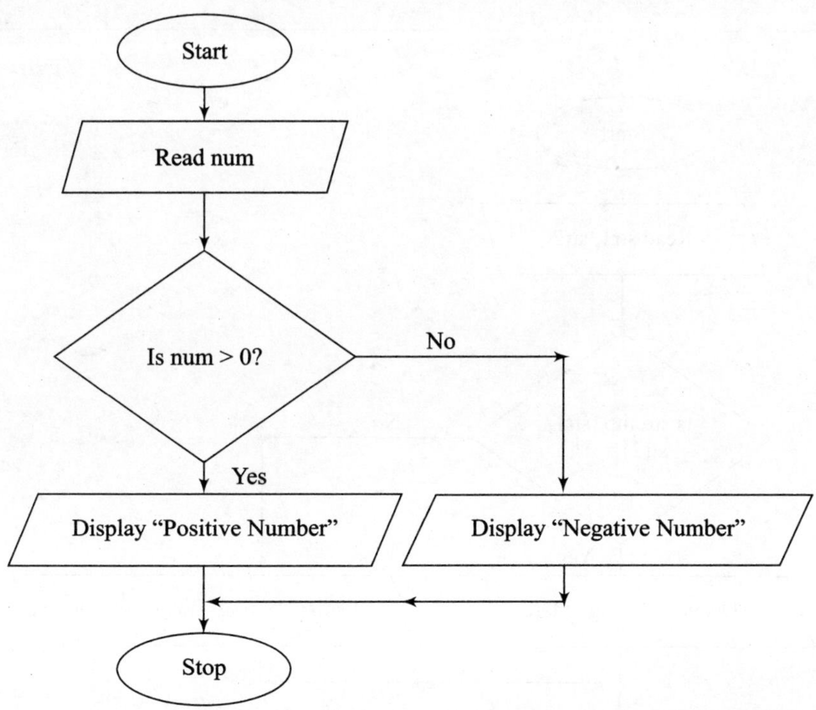

Pseudocode

```
BEGIN
DEFINE: Integer num
DISPLAY: "Enter a number: "
READ: num
IF: num>0
     DISPLAY: "'num' is a positive number"
ELSE
     DISPLAY: "'num' is a negative number"
END IF
END
```

Practice Problem 17 Write a program to compare two strings.

Algorithm

```
Step 1 - Start
Step 2 - Accept two strings from the user (str1, str2)
Step 3 - Compare the two strings str1 and str2 using a string comparison
function. If str1 and str2 are same goto Step 4 else goto Step 5
Step 4 - Display "The two strings are equal" and goto Step 6
Step 5 - Display "The two strings are not equal"
Step 6 - Stop
```

Flow Chart

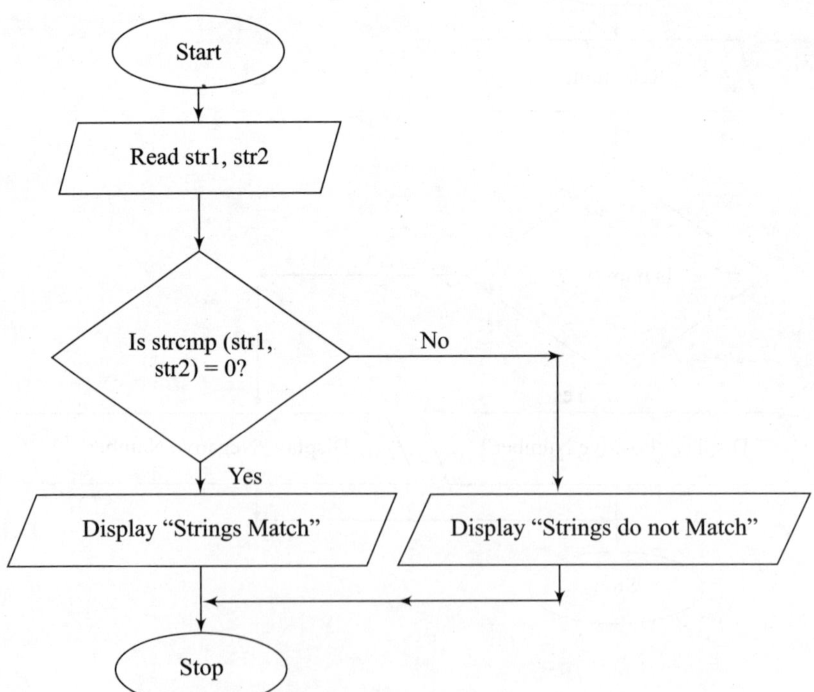

Pseudocode

```
BEGIN
DEFINE: String str1, str2
DISPLAY: "Enter the 1st string: "
READ: str1
DISPLAY: "Enter the 2nd string: "
READ: str2
IF: strcmp(str1, str2)=0
    DISPLAY: "The strings str1 and str2 are equal!"
ELSE
    DISPLAY: "The strings str1 and str2 are not equal!"
END IF
END
```

Practice Problem 18 Write a program to calculate speed.

Algorithm

```
Step 1 - Start
Step 2 - Accept the value of distance traveled in KMs (d)
Step 3 - Accept the value of travel time in hours (t)
Step 4 - Calculate speed using formula, speed = d/t
Step 5 - Display the computed value of speed
Step 6 - Stop
```

Flow Chart

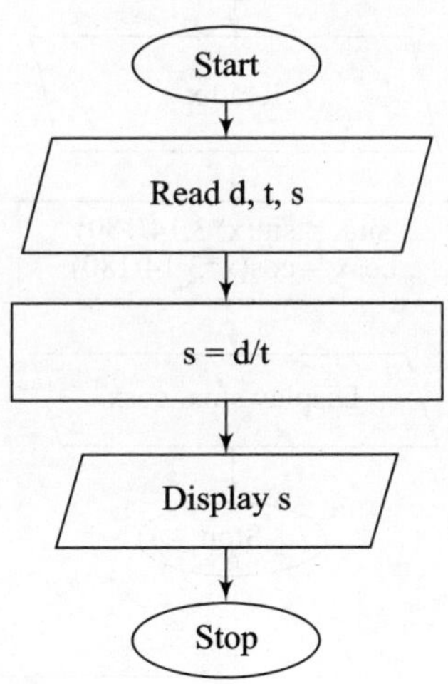

Pseudocode

```
BEGIN
DEFINE: Real d, t, s
DISPLAY: “Enter the distance traveled in Kms: ”
READ: d
DISPLAY: “Enter the travel time in hours: ”
READ: t
COMPUTE: s = d/t
DISPLAY: “Speed = ‘s’ Km/h”
END
```

Practice Problem 19 Write a program to find the sine and cosine of a given value.

Algorithm

```
Step 1 - Start
Step 2 - Accept the degree value, the sine and cosine of which is to be
calculated (x):
Step 3 - Calculate Sin(x) = sin(x*3.14/180)
Step 4 - Calculate Cos(x) = cos(x*3.14/180)
Step 5 - Display the computed Sin(x) and Cos(x) values
Step 6 - Stop
```

Flow Chart

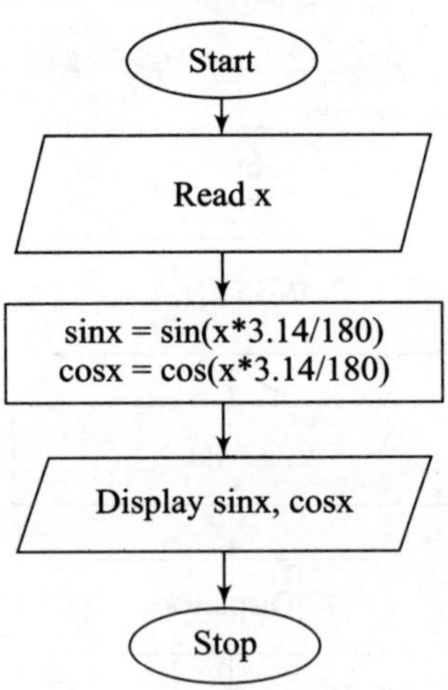

Pseudocode

```
BEGIN
DEFINE: Real x, sinx, cosx
DISPLAY: “Enter the degree value, the sine and cosine of which is to be
calculated: ”
READ: x
```

```
Compute: sinx = sin(x*3.14/180)
Compute: cosx = cos(x*3.14/180)
DISPLAY: "Sin('x')='sinx'"
DISPLAY: "Cos('x')='cosx'"
END
```

Practice Problem 20 Write a program to determine whether a given number is Armstrong or not.

Algorithm

```
Step 1 - Start
Step 2 - Accept a number from the user (num)
Step 3 - Store the value of num in a temporary variable temp, temp=num
Step 4 - Define a variable sum and initialise it to 0
Step 5 - Repeat Steps 6-8 while temp > 0
Step 6 - Calculate i=temp%10;
Step 7 - Calculate sum=sum+i*i*i;
Step 8 - Calculate temp=temp/10;
Step 9 - if num is equal to sum then goto Step 10 else goto Step 11
Step 10 - Display "num is an Armstrong number" and goto Step 12
Step 11 - Display "num is not an Armstrong number"
Step 12 - Stop
```

Flow Chart

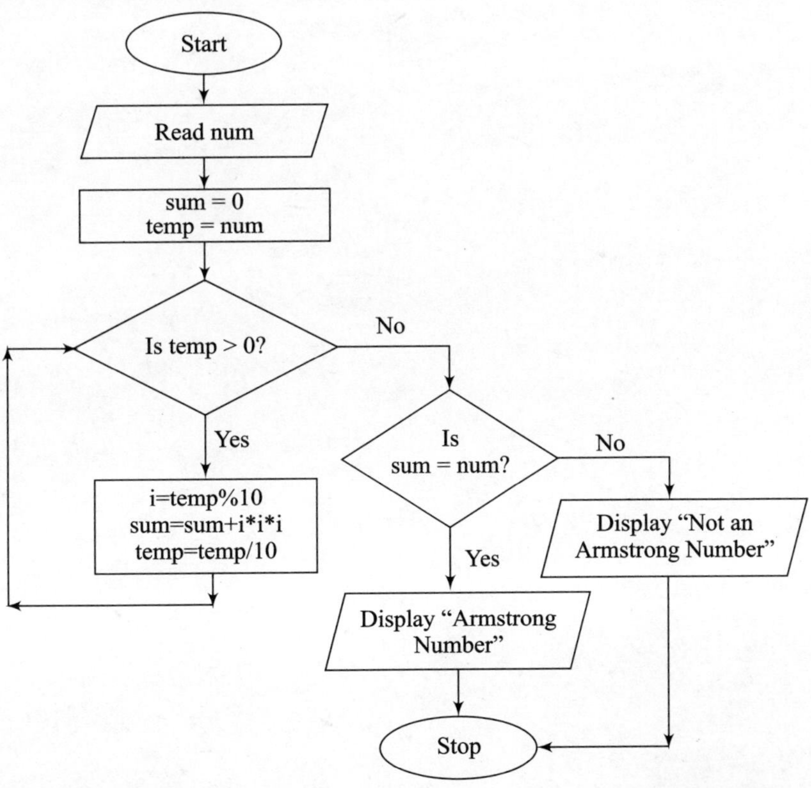

Pseudocode

```
BEGIN
DEFINE: Integer num, temp, sum, i
SET: sum = 0
DISPLAY: "Enter a number: "
READ: num
SET: temp=num
REPEAT
     COMPUTE: i=temp%10
     COMPUTE: sum=sum+i*i*i
     COMPUTE: temp=temp/10
UNTIL: temp>0
IF: sum=num
     DISPLAY: "'num' is an Armstrong number"
ELSE
     DISPLAY: "'num' is not an Armstrong number"
END IF
END
```

Appendix

C

Fundamental Standard Library Modules

There is a wide range of methods in Python's standard library. In this section, some fundamental standard library modules are discussed. Any Python program uses these modules either directly or indirectly.

1. BUILT-IN FUNCTIONS AND EXCEPTIONS

The __built-in__ module comprises built-in functions or methods, such as `len, int, max` and `range`. The Exceptions module comprises all the built-in exceptions. Python automatically imports both the modules at the time of start-up, and makes the content of all these modules available to all the programs.

2. OPERATING SYSTEM INTERFACE MODULES

The modules in this group are imported by `os`. It provides file manipulation and process operations. `os.path` offers a platform-independent way to put file names and time together that allows functions or methods working with date and time.

Some networking and thread support modules also belong to this group.

3. TYPE SUPPORT MODULES

There are many built-in `types` that support modules in the standard library. The `string` module allows the use of string operations and manipulations. The `math` module is responsible for performing many math operations and calculations and the `cmath` module allows the same for complex numbers.

4. REGULAR EXPRESSIONS

The regular expressions support for Python is provided by `re` module. Regular expressions are used to match strings and slice the substrings. They are nothing but the patterns of strings that are written in special syntax.

re Module

`re` module is a built in module in Python programming language which provides support for regular expressions. A regular expression consists of some special sequence of characters that helps us in finding another strings or matching set of strings using some predefined syntax which are kept in a pattern. When any error occurs while handling the regular expressions, python interpreter throws a `re.error` exception.

There are two very important functions in re module which are listed below:

1. `match()` function
2. `search()` function

1. `match()` function

It matches the RE pattern to the string.

Syntax

```
re.match(pattern, string)
```

where,

pattern – pattern stands for the regular expression which is to be matched in the string.

string – it is the string in which the searching will be done to match the pattern at the starting of the string.

On successful match, `match()` function will return a **match** object, **None** otherwise.

2. `search()` function

It searches the first occurrence of the Regular Expression within the given string.

Syntax

```
re.search(pattern, string)
```

where,

pattern – pattern stands for the regular expression which is to be matched.

string – it is the string in which the searching will be done to match the pattern anywhere within the string.

On successful search, `search()` function will return a **match** object, **None** otherwise.

5. LANGUAGE SUPPORT MODULE

There are various modules in this group, such as `sys` that helps in accessing various interpreter variables like module search path and interpreter version. Operator provides many built-in operators. For copying objects, it provides `copy` and `gc` in garbage collection facilities.

`sys` Module

`sys` helps in accessing various interpreter variables, such as module search path and interpreter version.

`argv`	List of command-line options passed to the program
`maxint`	Largest integer supported by `IntType`
`modules`	Dictionary for mapping module names to loaded modules
`platform`	String describing current platform
`ps1`	String containing text for primary prompt, normally >>>
`ps2`	String for second prompt, normally . . .
`stdin`	File object for standard input
`stdout`	File object for standard output
`stderr`	File object for error output
`exit(n)`	Exits function by raising `SystemExit` exception

`random` Module

This module helps in generating random numbers or select a random item from a series or sequence.

`choice(s)`	Randomly select an element from `s`
`randint(a,b)`	Return a random integer number greater than or equal to `a` and less than or equal to `b`
`random()`	Return a random number between 0 and 1
`randrange(a,b)`	Return a random value from a range

`time` Module

This module measures the number of seconds since 'epoch'. The standard value of epoch in Unix and Windows OS is January 1, 1970 and it is January 1, 1900 in Macintosh.

`time()`	Return seconds since the epoch
`gmtime(seconds)`	Converts time into a tuple representing year, month, day, hour, minute, second, weekday, day and dst.
`localtime(seconds)`	Same format as `gmtime()`, but for a local time zone
`mktime(tuple)`	Takes a tuple in the format of `gmtime()` and returns a number representing seconds in the `time()` format
`asctime(tuple)`	Takes a tuple in the format of `gmtime()` and converts to string in 'Mon June 10 10:12:12 2006' form
`clock()`	Returns the current CPU time in seconds as a floating point number
`strftime(format, tuple)`	Produces a string representation of time as a tuple and produces it in `gmtime()` format, which is as per the format described in the first argument.
`strptime(string, format)`	Reads a string representing time in a described format and returns a tuple similar to `gmtime()`

The commands used in `strptime()` and `strftime()` for formatting are as follows:

%a	Abbreviated weekday name
%A	Full weekday name
%b	Abbreviated month name
%B	Full month name
%c	Appropriate date and time representation
%d	Day of the month as a decimal number
%H	Hour (24 hour clock) as a number
%I	Hour (12 hour clock) as a number
%j	Day of the year as a number
%m	Month as a decimal number
%M	Minute as a decimal number
%p	AM or PM
%S	Seconds as a decimal number
%U	Week number (0–53) of a year
%w	Weekday as a decimal number
%x	Appropriate date representation
%X	Locals appropriate time representation
%y	Year without century as a decimal number (0–99)
%Y	Year with century as a decimal number
%Z	Time zone name
%%	The % character

`re` Module

This is a module that is required for regular expressions. Regular expressions are used to match strings and slice substrings. These are patterns of strings that are written in special syntax.

Common patterns that are used for forming regular expression are as follows:

<table>
<tr><td>Text</td><td>Matches literals</td></tr>
<tr><td>&</td><td>Start of the string</td></tr>
<tr><td>$</td><td>End of the string</td></tr>
<tr><td>(...)*</td><td>Zero or more occurrences</td></tr>
<tr><td>(...)+</td><td>One or more occurrences</td></tr>
<tr><td>(...)?</td><td>Optional (0 or 1)</td></tr>
<tr><td>[chars]</td><td>One character from range</td></tr>
<tr><td>[^chars]</td><td>One character not from range</td></tr>
<tr><td>Pat | pat</td><td>Alternative (one or another)</td></tr>
<tr><td>(...)</td><td>Group</td></tr>
<tr><td>.</td><td>Any character except new line</td></tr>
</table>

os Module

This module provides file manipulation and process operations. `Os.path` offers a platform-independent way to put together file names and time that allows functions or methods working with date and time.

`environ`	A mapping object representing the current environment variables
`name`	Name of the current operating system
`mkdir(path)`	Make a directory
`unlike(path)`	Delete a file
`rename(src, dst)`	Rename a file

tempfile Module

This module is used to create temporary files at the time of execution of a program.

`mktemp()`	Returns a temporary distinct file name
`mktemp(suffix)`	Returns a distinct temporary file name with a given suffix
`temporaryFile(mode)`	Creates a temporary file with the given node